The Mobil ILLUSTRATED GUIDE to NEW ZEALAND

By the same authors
Mobil New Zealand Travel Guides: North Island and *South Island*

The Mobil ILLUSTRATED GUIDE to NEW ZEALAND

Diana & Jeremy Pope

Photographed by Martin Barriball

RM

REED METHUEN

First published 1982
Reprinted 1985, 1986

REED METHUEN PUBLISHERS LTD
39 Rawene Road, Auckland 10

ISBN 0 474 00217 9

Printed by Everbest Printing Co Ltd, Hong Kong

Front cover: Mount Taranaki.
Insets, left to right: Southward Car Museum, Paraparaumu; Tuhoe youngster; Westland forest highway, near Ross; native wood pigeon.
Back cover: *Top, left to right:* Coromandel assay house; Abel Tasman National Park; tuatara.
Bottom, left to right: Safari vehicles, Farewell Spit; Mansion House, Kawau Island; the steamer Earnslaw on Lake Wakatipu.

Acknowledgements

This book is the result of the combined labours of many. The authors were aided, in particular, by Sue Upton in Wellington and Jill Tasker in London, and by multifarious departments, national park boards and information offices. Martin Barriball was assisted by numerous people and institutions during the course of his 18-month photographic assignment around the country, and the help and co-operation he received from all of them is both warmly remembered and greatly appreciated.

All three benefited enormously from the energy and enthusiasm of Jane Parkin, Bill Wieben and Graham Wiremu, all of Reeds, whose personal attachment to the project kept all of us going at times when we might well have flagged. Jane and Graham also contributed the text on pp. 120–121 and 62–63 respectively.

The publishers, in turn, would like to thank the following people and institutions for their permission to use material as follows: The Alexander Turnbull Library for historical photographs; Nancy M. Adams for her drawings of alpine flowers; the Dunedin Public Art Gallery for the Hodgkins painting on p. 143; David Fuller for his recipe for crayfish on p. 111; Graeme Hampton for his photograph of motor cycling on p. 49; Fraser Gardyne for his photograph of Putiki Church on p. 89; the Manawatu Art Gallery for the Colin McCahon painting on p. 91; the Ministry of Foreign Affairs for works reproduced on p. 120; John Nankervis for the mountaineering photograph on p. 131; the New Zealand Post Office for use of the postage stamp on p. 127; the New Zealand Co-operative Rennet Company for the photograph of cheese production on p. 85; the New Zealand Wool Board for the photographs of sheep breeds on pp. 136–137; Mr G. E. Smith of the Pukeiti Rhododendron Trust for the photograph on p. 85; Rodney Smith for his photograph of glowworms on p. 56, and Connie Wright for the photograph of the royal albatross chick on p. 140. Thanks are also due to John Ashton, John Drawbridge, Gordon Walters and Downstage Theatre for their assistance with illustrative material.

There were, in addition, a huge number of people who answered queries, checked references and who did what they could to keep the text as free from error as possible. They in no way share the author's responsibility for either the factual content or the opinions expressed.

Diana and Jeremy Pope

Martin Barriball

Publisher's acknowledgement

The publishers acknowledge with thanks the generous assistance received from Mobil Oil New Zealand Ltd in helping to meet the substantial costs incurred in commissioning the photographs which illustrate this book. The Mobil subsidy has, in turn, helped reduce the retail price of the book to bring it within the reach of a wider readership.

Contents

The North Island

The South Island

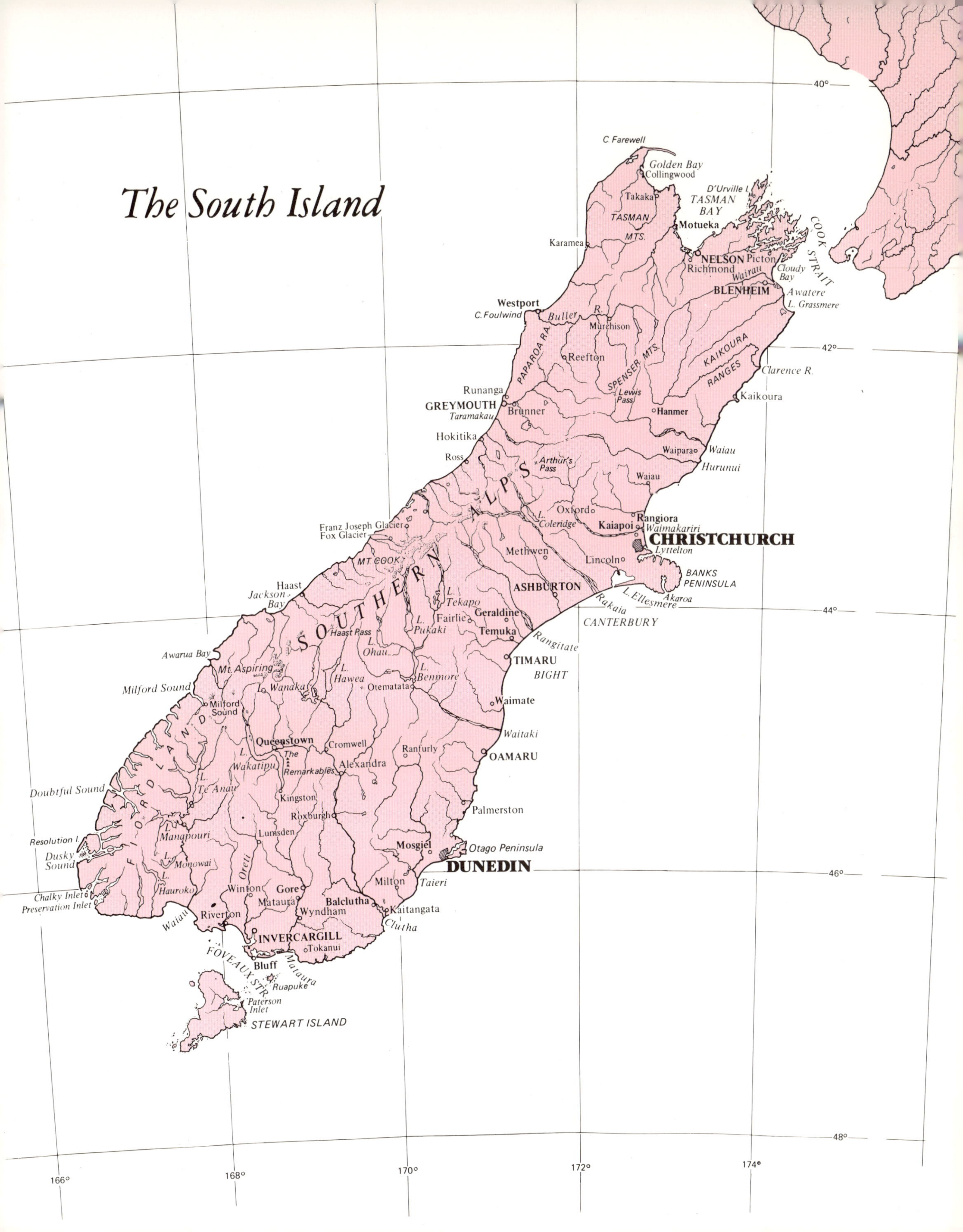

Introduction

When travel writers come to describe New Zealand they exhaust their supplies of superlatives. Piling praise on praise, they catalogue its list of wonders – its mountains, its forests, its thermal wonders; its unspoilt beaches and countryside, and, above all, the unashamed friendliness and openness of its people.

Some may chide the New Zealander's preoccupation with weekend leisure. Visitors like Clement Freud, after writing of a visit to Australia in the late 1960s, concluded: "I also visited New Zealand. But it was closed". Others, with unabashed nostalgia, see in the country glimpses of Britain as it used to be – with lovingly cared-for old cars on the roads, incomparable fish-and-chips, cheerful hotel service and a relaxed attitude to life whatever the economic difficulties of the moment.

Times move on, and Freud's comment is no longer as apposite as it was two decades ago: the "six o'clock swill" has gone from our pubs (though they still close all day Sunday) and Saturday shopping is eroding the great New Zealand weekend, the time when the nation as one person traditionally gives itself over to the beach, to concreting paths, to building boats in backyards, to rugby, racing and beer. However, it remains a truism that the country's productivity cannot be measured in terms of its Gross National Product when so much wealth is generated by spare-time activity. The nation, both by instinct and of necessity, is dedicated to do-it-yourself.

Indeed, much of our mythology revolves around Number-8 fencing wire and the belief that the average Kiwi can fix anything with it. Pre-eminent is the example of Richard Pearse, a South Canterbury farmer who, working entirely alone and without the backing of any commercial organisation, came within a whisker of beating the Wright brothers into the air in a machine largely fashioned from flattened-out sheep-dip tins. More typical is the roadworker whom we met up a blind, gravel road deep in the Southern Alps when our brand-new car jammed in first gear fifty kilometres from anywhere.

"Never seen one of these before," he offered as he crawled underneath. But within five minutes he had put matters to rights with a rusty nail found lying on the road.

Coupled with the pioneer's positive approach to problem-solving is a parallel tendency towards understatement. Athlete Peter Snell, after breaking the world one-mile record in his first-ever race over the distance, almost apologised: he had meant only to break four minutes. Edmund Hillary, returning to camp with Sherpa Tensing after conquering Mt Everest, broke the news with a casual, "Well, we knocked the bastard off."

Together, about 2.7 million people of European descent (Pakeha) share with some 280,000 Maori and 91,000 Polynesian Pacific Islanders a country slightly larger than the United Kingdom or about half the size of France. Its three main islands stretch over about 1,600 kilometres and lie roughly north/south. The climate varies with the latitude, from a warm sub-tropical in the far north to a cool temperate in the deep south. As well, there are a number of outlying islands, including Raoul Island, the most northerly, and the sub-antarctic Campbell Island in the Southern Ocean. The Chatham Islands, lying to the east of Banks Peninsula, are the largest, and all three provide meteorological services to the mainland.

Geographically New Zealand is placed in the southernmost tip of the triangle of islands that comprises Polynesia (literally "many islands"), which extends over the ocean to as far away as Easter Island, 6,400 kilometres to the east, and to the Midway Islands, 8,000 kilometres to the north. Its nearest neighbour, Australia, is some 2,000 kilometres to the north-west, while to the east there is no significant land mass between New Zealand and the South American mainland – across an ocean that could accommodate all of the world's continents.

"Discovery" in 1642 is credited to Abel Tasman, a Dutch explorer, but as the islands were already populated (the aggressive inhabitants caused him to flee without setting foot ashore) we must look to the indigenous Maori to identify the rightful claimant. In their mythology it was Maui, a god who achieved a series of fabulous feats before he died attempting to gain immortality for man, who fished the land from the sea. The same myth recurs throughout much of Polynesia, suggesting the theory that Maui may have been an ancient adventurer who discovered a number of islands which appeared from below the horizon as though drawn up from the deep. Some Maori tradition, however, accords the honour to Kupe, who would have flourished about 950 A.D. He is recorded in the popular histories as having visited the land he named Aotearoa ("land of the long, white cloud"), a land he found quite deserted.

The archaeological record is far from complete and the Maori's oral histories, too, have been distorted by early chroniclers who developed a thesis that they had come in an organised "Great Migration" about 600 years ago, to encounter and overwhelm the Moriori already living here. In fact, the only Moriori were living in the bleak Chatham Islands, some 800 kilometres to the east of Christchurch, but Pakeha folklore has firmly fixed on the notion that there were two – and only two – distinct waves of pre-European settlement from other parts of Polynesia. On the contrary, the evidence suggests that a number of canoes found their way here, more probably by accident than by design, and over a period of some centuries.

It is, however, clear that these remote islands were peopled only during the last millenium, and that hitherto the flora and fauna had been able to evolve uniquely free from rodents and browsing animals. Flightless birds took the place of

browsing animals in the ecology, and later the pre-eminent of these, the moa (a magnificent spectacle of up to four metres in height which was hounded to extinction), formed the basis for the culture of the nomadic hunter-gatherer, the Moa Hunter. Later, with the arrival of the *kumara* (sweet potato) and other plants, agriculture began to be practised and a more stable society developed, the population being drawn to the warmer, more northerly regions of the North Island and away from the plains of Canterbury where the moa had once roamed in great numbers.

When Captain Cook in 1769 became the first European to set foot on these islands, he estimated a Maori population of perhaps 100,000, though as he kept very much to the coast this could only be the most tentative of guesses.

Cook took the tantalising line Tasman had left on European atlases, turned it into three main islands and claimed them for Britian. Sealers and whalers were quick to seize upon Cook's "discovery", but the British Government was less enthusiastic. Not until 1840, after scandals had rocked the British parliament concerning the way in which the Maori was being ill-treated by European traders and adventurers, were steps taken formally to annex the islands.

A "Treaty of Waitangi" was duly drawn up and the signatures of as many chiefs as possible secured. The document offered the Maori the protection of Queen Victoria in return for the Crown's having the sole right to purchase land from them. A bewildered Maori people, decimated by the diseases and the rifles which the traders had brought with them (and which had escalated a sustainable level of inter-tribal conflict into near genocide), grasped both the God of Peace brought by the missionaries and the prospect of protection from rapacious adventurers offered by the British.

Among the pressure groups urging annexation in Britain was the New Zealand Company, a group with the dream of transporting a cross-section of society (excepting only its lowest denominator – ours was never a penal colony), in order to establish a Britain in the South Seas. Soon migrant ships were arriving regularly. If the theorists were proved quite wrong – the land speculators stayed at home rather than emigrate with their money to provide employment for the labourers – the "Wakefield scheme" did succeed in providing land for the landless, and in satisfying many a craving which contemporary Britain effectively denied. Today, New Zealand is essentially a society of house-owners.

Land hunger led to conflict. Maori tribes had never foreseen the Treaty of Waitangi as an open door to unlimited immigration, and they began to refuse to sell the land the administration needed.

While war inflamed the North Island, the south (sparsely populated by the Maori) was preoccupied with gold rushes. The New Zealand Company's Scottish settlement at Dunedin blossomed into the country's commercial centre and thousands flocked into Central Otago from the Victorian and Californian goldfields to take their chance with fortune.

The gold dwindling and the wars over, the settlers' economy slumped, only to be revived in 1881 by the introduction of refrigeration, which brought within reach the meat-starved markets of Europe. Hitherto sheep had been run simply for their wool, and surplus stock were slaughtered or driven over cliffs to destruction. By then, too, the migrant population had surpassed that of the Maori, rendering the indigenous population a minority in its own land.

Lacking the mineral resources of the other colonies, New Zealand turned itself virtually into one large farm. For a century agriculture was to provide over 90 per cent of the country's export earnings, and the economy was to become so interlocked with that of Britain – supplying massive quantities of cheap butter, cheese and lamb – that the latter's entry into the European Economic Community had catastrophic consequences. Europe, with its expensive and artificially created surpluses of dairy products, had no intention of preserving indefinitely New Zealand's traditional access to British markets. No matter that New Zealand dairy farmers could produce butter and cheese, ship it halfway round the world and still market it at a fraction of the Europeans' cost; no matter that they were the world's most efficient and economical producers of dairy products. They were told to find other markets, and when they had built these up, a far from obliging Europe did not hesitate to dump its own surpluses there. Access for lamb was preserved, under special arrangements, but these in turn have come under increasing scrutiny as European farmers covet the British market while knowing that they are quite unable to match the New Zealand farmers' costs of production.

As a consequence, and exacerbated by world depression and the shocks of oil price rises, New Zealand has seen its comparative standard of living slide dramatically. Once rated as among the highest in the world outside North America, today the country ranks well down the list.

The statistics, however, conceal a lifestyle a good deal more affluent than might be supposed. New Zealand is essentially a low-income, low-cost country and one in which the people have developed a knack for making money – and things – go a long way. Indeed, they may be said to have achieved the impossible dream of relative affluence without effluence, and to have built a society whose agricultural base enhances rather than impedes its prosperity.

An increasing concern with the environment expresses a determination by many New Zealanders to keep it this way. In the late 1960s, for example, massive numbers demonstrated their opposition to the raising of Lake Manapouri, forcing abandonment of government plans for hydro-electric development in the area, and more recently there has been increased unease about the management of the remaining areas of native forest. Another manifestation was the emergence in 1972 of the Values Party, a small political grouping which, although not represented in Parliament, has, along with other conservation groups, been instrumental in promoting awareness of the need for a sympathetic, less plunderous approach to the environment.

Although for decades New Zealand boasted of having not only the most beautiful country in the world but also the most successful multi-racial society, only in recent years have people started to face up to what this really means. There is now, more than ever before, an increasing awareness of the duties placed on the majority in a multi-cultural society – duties not simply of tolerance but of positive understanding, appreciation and respect. Nor is this confined to the Pakeha, for the Maori, too, is having to accommodate the fact that significant numbers from other islands in the region have come to share their corner of the South Pacific.

Certainly, the settler society avoided the traps that ensnared their counterparts in South Africa, and equally surely the Maori secured a very much better deal in New Zealand than did the Aborigines in Australia or the Indians in North America. This may have been due more to the adaptability of the Maori than to the liberalism of the Pakeha, although the fact that the country was settled by the British in the 1840s, at a time when English humanitarianism was at its peak and in the immediate aftermath of the abolition of slavery, must also have contributed.

For the tourist, the Maori continues to stand for concert parties at Rotorua and a "plastic *tiki*" trade in souvenirs. But for the Pakeha the Maori represents an accommodation that is still taking place. Maoris are found at every level of society and in all walks of life. Indeed, a male Maori judge was appointed before a woman of either race had attained judicial office. Nevertheless, a greatly disproportionate number of Maoris and Polynesian Islanders swell the crime statistics and the ranks of the unemployed as visible and constant reminders that there is still some distance to be travelled before equality can be regarded as having been achieved. In part, though, this represents the degree to which the once-rural Maori has become urbanised in the last 40 years, for with the move to the cities has come erosion of their social structure.

In some cities multi-cultural *marae* (meeting places) are being established, to fortify the urban groups from all parts of Polynesia. But on particularly symbolic occasions Maoris will journey back to their traditional tribal areas, to the sacred marae where their forebears for generations debated important tribal decisions, there to receive distinguished visitors, to marry or to mourn the passing of loved ones. In the Maori tradition of the extended family – mutually sharing, mutually supporting – the Pakeha is beginning to see as precious some aspects which they themselves have lost. Just as there remains much for the Maori to learn from the Pakeha, there are many ways in which the Maori approach can enrich and strengthen the Pakeha's way of life.

To the urbane visitor from Europe, the Pakeha may be somewhat disarming in his or her openness and frankness; to the Maori, both European and Pakeha can appear lacking in sophistication. As one wrote in a description of what it means to be a Maori: "We welcomed them with the finest poetry our language could command . . . and were rewarded with tea-cup conversation in reply."

Conversation aside, the New Zealander is a voracious reader and a prodigious buyer of books (spending an average of $63 a head each year, a record among English-speaking countries). A strong crafts tradition is reasserting itself; spinning wheels proliferate and figures suggest that more New Zealanders now go to pottery classes than belong to tennis clubs – yet the clubs themselves have waiting lists. Thus the lack of fleshpots which so depressed Clement Freud is perhaps made up for in other, more creative ways. And if artistic pursuits are making inroads into the hitherto supreme passion for playing sports, so too appreciation of art has at times threatened the dominance of rugby as the nation's number one spectator interest. Recent art exhibitions have drawn attendances far greater than those at rugby internationals!

New Zealanders have traditionally tended to entertain at home, and an essential part of the act of friendship is an invitation to join them there – a practice contributed to by the absence of small, neighbourhood pubs and cafés and a set of liquor licensing laws that demands such high standards in licensed restaurants that their prices have driven them out of reach on all but the most special occasions. In recent years, however, the growth of more modest "bring your own" (wine!) restaurants has added a new dimension to the country's nightlife. Nevertheless, restaurant menus almost invariably lack the traditional Kiwi dishes of roast lamb followed by pavlova (meringue cake) topped with kiwifruit: when New Zealanders eat out they eat what they don't have at home.

Socially, New Zealanders have been fiercely egalitarian; politically they are radically conservative. In 1883 theirs became the first nation to extend the vote to women; they created the first Welfare State in the 1930s; medicine is free, and they pioneered no-fault accident compensation for all. Innovative, too, was their espousal of the Ombudsman, the first outside Scandinavia and now a feature in virtually every country of the western world. Their conservatism is, however, far from *laissez-faire*: when anything goes awry they look to the Government (by which is usually meant the Prime Minister) to intervene and sort it out. Closely aligned to their North American sisters is an assertive feminist movement, with a lively Women's Electoral Lobby and other groupings.

The country has a character and a fascination that can only be lightly and incompletely sketched in an introduction, but many of the features we have touched upon are fleshed out in more detail in appropriate sections of the regional coverage. Nor is this fascination widely understood by New Zealanders. We ourselves, after travelling much of the world, became interested in writing about our country as a personal journey of discovery, for our travels had made us realise just how little we knew of the land we called our own. That journey continues, and this book is an essential part of it.

A place in Polynesia

Lovely, lonely, loyal: the description of New Zealand could not be more succinct. Tucked away in the extreme south-western corner of the enormous expanse of Polynesia, more remote than any other land mass of consequence and with close economic and cultural ties with Britain (which have renewed links with Europe across the generations), New Zealand has taken a long time to shed its self-image of being a "Britain in the South Seas" and to orientate itself towards a view of geography that places it even in the correct hemisphere. To the amazement of outsiders, even fourth-generation New Zealanders can still speak of England as "home".

The old certainties were shattered by a series of hammer-blows. Blind dependence on Britain for defence collapsed with the fall of Singapore in 1942; reliance in perpetuity on markets in Britain evaporated with the latter's entry into the EEC; finally, restrictions imposed on New Zealanders' hitherto automatic right of entry into Britain shocked the national consciousness towards adulthood. The Mother Country was rejecting its offspring.

Perhaps inevitably, this has led New Zealand into alliances with the United States and Australia, in the ANZUS and the SEATO pacts, and so into conflict both in Malaysia and Vietnam in pursuit of the doctrine of "forward defence" – an "insurance premium" for remaining beneath the U.S. umbrella.

The loss of British markets has also kindled interest in the Pacific Island states for trade and as outlets for expertise, and with this has come a greater awareness of the country's responsibilities towards its very much smaller and extremely disadvantaged neighbours. The links are now many.

The country is responsible for the external relations of the Cook Islands and Niue (both former dependencies and now able unilaterally to move to full independence at any time). It administers the Tokelaus (most of whose people have resettled in New Zealand), and German Samoa (captured by New Zealand forces on the outbreak of hostilities in Europe in 1914) has been ushered to independence as Western Samoa. All enjoy, or have enjoyed, New Zealand citizenship, so that as well as being the largest and most developed country in Polynesia, New Zealand is also home to most Polynesians.

More broadly, New Zealand, with Australia, plays a major role in both the South Pacific Commission and the South Pacific Economic Council, organisations which foster economic development and co-operation among the islands of the region, many of which are fellow members of the Commonwealth. New Zealand has also developed a reputation for championing the causes of small island states in other international forums.

RAROTONGA *An island of unspoilt beauty which is "home" for thousands of New Zealanders.*

The land

New Zealand's varied landscape has been shaped over millions of years by the universal geological processes of earth movement, erosion, sedimentation, metamorphism and igneous activity. Yielding to enormous pressures, the earth's crust in the general region has been constantly warping and breaking, with some areas being forced downwards and others upwards to jut from the sea and be exposed to attack by the forces of wind, wave, rain and glacier. The consequent erosion has washed mud and rock onto the sea floor to form deposits of sedimentary rock and conglomerate which, in turn, have been thrust once more above the surface.

Although now "young" in terms of its raw and little-weathered landscape, New Zealand has a geological record which reveals "no vestige of a beginning, no prospect of an end". For hundreds of millions of years there have been land masses in the area, with New Zealand being at times very much larger or very much smaller than it is today. Periodically it may even have disappeared completely beneath the waves.

Further evidence of these processes is found on the sea floor. Apart from coral atolls, the Pacific Ocean is broken only by volcanic upthrusts (such as Hawaii and the other islands of the mid-Pacific), but here in its south-western corner the contours of the sea bed are less monotonous, being characterised by deep trenches and broad ridges, brought about by the same phenomena of folding and warping that give rise to the New Zealand land mass.

The process is, of course, a continuing one, and even in the miniscule period of European occupation significant changes have taken place. The shoreline around Wellington rose abruptly by almost two metres in the severe earthquake of 1855; at Murchison in 1929 a sudden fault lifted a section of road by some four metres, and two years later, at Napier, fully eight square kilometres of land was raised from the sea.

Augmenting this land-building has been volcanic activity, with lava outpourings creating such distinctive features as Banks Peninsula, the site of Dunedin, the peninsula on which Auckland stands, Mt Egmont and the Volcanic Plateau where rise the mountains of the Tongariro National Park.

Furthermore, during the various ice ages, vast quantities of water were locked up by the growth of the polar ice caps, only to be released as temperatures rose again. These events caused sea levels around the world to fluctuate, and around the New Zealand coast their effect was sufficient to join temporarily the North and the South Islands across Cook Strait, and tie Stewart Island to the tip of the South Island. Since the last ice age, the sea has risen to flood many river valleys, creating the intricate drowned river systems that now form the harbours of the northern North Island, of Otago and Banks Peninsula, as well as the fiord fingers of Fiordland and the jagged inlets of the Marlborough Sounds.

The sea

New Zealand is essentially an island nation: remote, set apart, a far-flung fragment of land in a corner of the world's largest ocean. No point is more than 110 kilometres from the coast, and with most of the cities and larger towns hugging the shore, the sea looms large in a lifestyle whose essential ingredients include such pursuits as swimming, surfing, boating, yachting, fishing and skin diving. Of the many who harbour the dream of building a boat in their backyard and sailing around the world, a surprising number seem to accomplish it.

While the sea acts as a natural "fence" around the great New Zealand farm, protecting it from the diseases and afflictions that beset agriculture in other lands, it does attract numerous overseas fishing fleets, principally from Japan, to the country's new 320-kilometre Exclusive Economic Zone. Although New Zealand's own fisheries exports to some 40 countries worldwide earned some $162 million in 1980, the local fishing industry has never exploited on a large scale the opportunities which its 1.5 million square kilometres of water afford. Of the 700 or so species of marine fish known in New Zealand waters, only some 70–80 are regarded as commercially significant, and the obstacles of economic harvesting, processing and marketing, together with an awareness of the intrinsically limited nature of the resource itself, have ensured that the nation's economy remains land-based.

The people

The 3.15 million people of New Zealand, drawn from every corner of the globe, have a diversity which tends to be obscured by their overwhelmingly northern-European origin. Members of minority groups are generally small in number, with even the Maori less than ten per cent of the population.

Several areas still retain signs of their beginnings as pioneer ethnic settlements: the "Englishness" of Christchurch, the Scandanavian surnames of southern Hawke's Bay, the Germanic names of the Puhoi and Riwaka areas, the slightly rolled "r" that identifies Otago and Southland's Scottish ancestry. Of the Chinese attracted to the gold diggings in the 1860s, some remained. Their descendants tended towards market gardening and fruit and vegetable retailing until, quite recently, they entered the professions in significant numbers.

Perhaps responding to the pressures from the Anglo-Saxon majority which have likewise repressed the assertion of Maori culture, these and other minority communities have tended to preserve their customs in a quiet and discreet fashion that can leave the community at large almost wholly unaware of their existence – except in particular fields of specialist expertise or, more recently, in ethnic restaurants and cultural events.

The emphasis has always been on encouraging the immigration of people from the British Isles, so that even today about 80 per cent of those citizens who were born outside New Zealand are of British stock. The pattern was set in the first years of British rule, when there were then about 60,000 Maori, chiefly living north of Lake Taupo. Organised by the New Zealand Company, regular shiploads of migrants had started leaving Britain even before the country had been formally annexed in 1840. A dearth of labour and the need to construct railways into the uninhabited hinterland saw the young colonial government invest heavily in encouraging immigration from Britain through the 1870s, with the government meeting most or all of the fares. Economic depression was followed by a further huge influx at the turn of the century and up until the outbreak of war in 1914. Both World War I and World War II were followed by huge waves of migration from Britain, augmented after World War II by large numbers of Dutch who have proved among the most successful of the migrant groups.

In recent years, economic decline has limited the country's ability to absorb large numbers of new settlers, so that only those with needed skills have been permitted permanent entry. There is by law no national or racial impediment to those who wish to migrate, but it is officially conceded that the requirement for applicants to seem reasonably fitted to New Zealand society does, as a matter of practice, create a barrier. This requirement is, however, occasionally waived in times of international crisis, when limited numbers of refugees have been taken in – for example, from Hungary after the Soviet invasion of 1956, from East Africa and from Vietnam and Kampuchea.

The most conspicuous change in the population's generally bland composition in recent years has been in the number (approximately 91,500) of Polynesian Pacific Islanders who have settled here. Migrants from the Cooks and Niue (who enjoy New Zealand citizenship as of right), Western Samoa and Tonga have tended to congregate in Auckland, where many have found unskilled jobs, but in times of unemployment have borne a disproportionate burden.

The nation's origins are firmly embedded in its manner of speech, characterised by elements of "London cockney", a high proportion of slang (some of which preserves Victorian expressions today seldom heard beyond Australia) and a literal pronunciation of transplanted English place-names which can render them incomprehensible to the British ear. A number of expressions derive from Australia – "mob", "creek", "paddock" and "bush" – although the accent is perhaps less pronounced than it is across the Tasman.

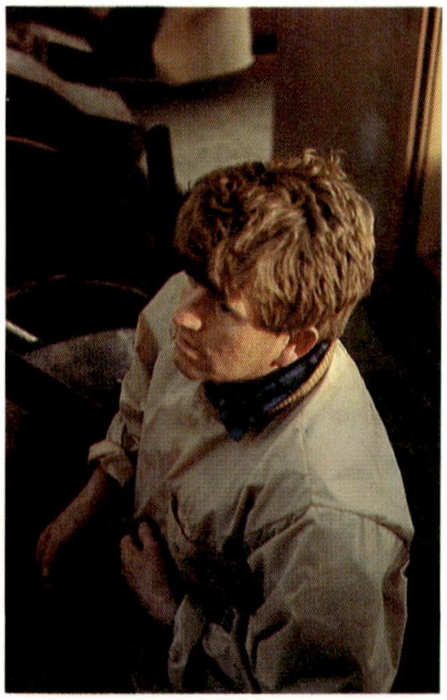

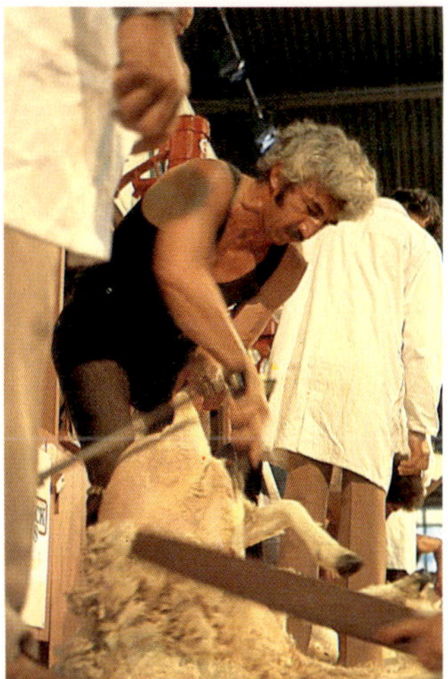

The North Island

The far north

ROAD TO REINGA *Much of the area the road dissects has escaped the encroachment of sand only through the efforts of farmer and forester.*

Fabled in legend and enshrined in the folklore of both Maori and Pakeha, Northland is both a beginning and an end. For the Pakeha it marks the origins of the missionary work that led inexorably to the country's being annexed by Britain; for the Maori it was from Cape Reinga, a point of the peninsula which cleaves the Tasman Sea from the Pacific Ocean, that the spirits of the departed bade farewell to Aotearoa and began a subterranean journey back to their legendary "Hawaiki" homeland.

Yet other compelling claims compete for attention. The climate in the far north is truly sub-tropical, the coastline enticing, the beaches inviting. It is a region in which to linger, in which to move slowly – yet one in which a bumpy bus ride to Cape Reinga along Ninety Mile Beach, complete with racy commentary, can be a highlight. If not completely "winterless", the weather is hospitable at all times of the year and is in summer tempered by the proximity of the sea. Kauri forest once covered much of the region, leaving behind a legacy of precious gum, which was later plundered by hordes of fortune-seeking gum diggers. Many men prospered, but the land, already leached by kauri leaves, suffered grievously. Even today the soil is poor and cultivation sparse; but forestry ventures promise new prosperity and stability for the region.

CAPE REINGA'S LIGHTHOUSE *The end of the road and a view of where sea and ocean meet.*

HOUSE CARVING *In the Wagener Museum.*

A FABLED POHUTUKAWA Down its roots went the departing spirits.

Aupouri Forest A vast area of hitherto drifting sand dunes along a lengthy expanse of Ninety Mile Beach has been anchored successfully by an afforestation programme designed to preserve farmland but yielding unexpectedly good results in timber. The sand is at first checked by the planting of grasses, which then shelter lupin. In turn the lupin nurtures and feeds pine trees through their infancy.

Cape Reinga Popularly regarded as the country's most northerly point (an honour that in fact belongs to the less accessible Surville Cliffs to the east), Cape Reinga affords a dramatic view of the joinder of Pacific Ocean and Tasman Sea, while its quaint lighthouse awaits its obligatory photograph. Here too is the gnarled pohutukawa of Maori legend. Clinging tenaciously to an alien cliff face, the tree is the departing place for spirits.

TWO DISTINCTIVE TOWERS The Ratana church at Te Kao reflects the symbolism of a religious sect founded in the 1920s around charismatic Wiremu Ratana, a successful faith-healer from near Wanganui. The teaching is basically Christian, the following largely Maori. The twin towers represent the founder's sons, both saints of the church, named for the Greek letters Alpha and Omega, the beginning and the end.

MAGNETIC MANGONUI *A township on Doubtless Bay, born of the early kauri timber trade.*

WAGENER MUSEUM *Venerable antique gramophones enliven a varied collection of memorabilia at Houhora Heads.*

NINETY MILE BEACH *The bus to Reinga seems lost in the heat of shimmering sand.*

Doubtless Bay A vast crescent of golden shimmering sand and a series of delightful coves draw throngs of holidaymakers here in summer. Cook did not enter the bay when he sailed past here in 1769, but after pondering whether the northern peninsula was an island he concluded, rightly, "Doubtless, a bay"

Houhora Once crowded with fortune-seeking gum diggers, the settlement is but a shadow of its former self. Claims for attention lie in its tavern (the country's most northerly) and, more cogently, in the museum at Houhora Heads which was founded by descendants of a Pole who came here in the 1850s. The beach is favoured by fishermen, and local tales tell of smugglers. A good place for picnicking and camping.

Te Kao Prominent here are the distinctive towers of the Ratana church (*pictured*).

Kaitaia The main centre of "the north" serves surrounding farmland and prospers visibly from the visitors lured here from the south. Many use the town as a base from which to explore the region. Of special interest is a rumbustious bus ride to Cape Reinga, with one leg following Ninety Mile Beach – a corrosive stretch which most will wish to spare their cars.

Ninety Mile Beach The beach, though lengthy, does not merit its name: it is 90 kilometres rather than 90 miles long. Each summer the scene of a hugely popular and well-rewarded fishing contest, it also witnessed the setting of a world land speed record in 1932 and acted as runway for Kingsford-Smith's epic return crossing of the Tasman a year later. Today the beach's reputation as a prime source of the treasured toheroa is wearing distinctly thin, as dwindling numbers of the sought-after shellfish have led to extremely limited "seasons" and even at times total bans on their being taken. The related tuatua, though, are found in substantial numbers and are a flavoursome substitute.

Parengarenga Harbour The bar here glistens with silica sand used in glassmaking.

Whangaroa Harbour The harbour stands in contrast to the inlets of the Bay of Islands, and is given unique character by its curious pinnacles, all of which bear biblical names. There is excellent boating here, though sailors might pause to recall the fate of the *Boyd*, whose passengers and crew almost all fell victim to a surprise attack here in 1809 by a local tribe. The "Boyd Massacre" was widely publicised and for a time deterred other would-be visitors. Today the harbour is a vision of tranquillity.

CAMPING Camp sites are not as plentiful as might be thought in the extreme north, but appealing sites are at Houhora and at Taputupoto Bay – the country's northernmost camping ground (*above*). Cape Reinga itself, though used to visitors, has no facilities and prospective campers can be taken by surprise.

CAPE MARIA VAN DIEMEN *Of the place-names bestowed by Abel Tasman in 1642, only two have survived: the others were surplanted by Cook or have reverted to their original Maori names. The cape (or more correctly an islet of it) was the last part of the country seen by Tasman, and is named for the wife of his sponsor, the Governor of the Dutch East India Company in Batavia. The other surviving name is that of the Three Kings Islands, offshore from Reinga, where Tasman spent Epiphany.*

WHANGAROA ON HORSEBACK *One way to attain a harbour view.*

PINNACLES *Uneven erosion of hard and soft rock has created a sharply defined landscape near Whangaroa.*

The Bay of Islands

MORNING OVER THE BAY OF ISLANDS *It has long forsaken its bawdy image of 150 years ago, with the bustle of yachts and holidaymakers replacing the hustle of licentious whalers.*

"The cradle of New Zealand's history" holds endless fascination, whatever one's inclination. Here ride the shadows of such giants of the past as Cook, Charles Darwin, the mighty Hongi Hika and his nephew, Hone Heke. Here, too, dawned both Christianity and British rule, tangible reminders of which remain in the mission churches and houses, and the revered Treaty House. A sheltered sea and, especially, big-game fishing are added attractions in a region still largely unspoiled by its popularity.

HIBISCUS FLOWER *Lush vegetation lends a splash of tropical splendour to the north.*

CRUISE SHIP CALLS *Ocean liners mingle with the ever-present yachts and launches.*

RUSSELL'S MUSEUM A working model of Cook's *Endeavour* is one of many exhibits in the Memorial Museum named for the explorer.

AFTER A RECORD-BREAKER *Numerous world-record catches of marlin, tuna, yellowtail, thresher, mako and hammerhead sharks have been taken from local deep-sea fishing launches.*

Bay of Islands There are about 150 islands scattered over the sheltered waters of the Bay, while seaward-probing arms only add to the richness of the seascape. A favourable climate and rich soils lend themselves to intensive farming, and in pre-European times the tribe centred here, the powerful Ngapuhi, came to dominate much of the North Island. The Ngapuhi's affluence attracted traders, whalers and adventurers before New Zealand's first missionary, Samuel Marsden, arrived in 1814 to bring Christianity to a people grown war-weary. A distinctive cross in Rangihoua Bay marks the scene of his first service. Less known, however, is the place on Moturua Island where, in 1772, the French explorer Marion du Fresne buried a bottle containing his claim to the country for France. Along with about 25 of his crew, he was killed shortly afterwards, at Assassination Cove, perhaps for having trespassed on *tapu* (sacred) ground. The Bay is best seen by joining the half-day "cream trip" at Russell or Paihia.

Kaikohe Set on level farmland in the very heart of Northland, the town supports a number of light industries. From the crest of Kaikohe Hill the coastline on both sides of the Island can be seen. Curiously, Kaikohe's memorial to Hone Heke is not to the celebrated chief but to his great-nephew, who died at the age of 40 having still spent almost half his life as a Maori Member of Parliament.

Kawakawa The administrative centre of Bay of Islands County is remarkable principally for the railway line which enables trains to share the main street with motor vehicles. The battle site of Ruapekapeka and the Waiomio Caves are both nearby.

Kerikeri Among the most fertile areas in a country renowned for productivity, Kerikeri engenders more than prolific quantities of citrus and sebtropical fruits. Over the years it has also developed a strong tradition for handicrafts, and cottage industries abound. At Kerikeri Inlet a gracious old mission house stands alongside a quaint stone store, which has been restored to its original design by the Historic Places Trust. There, too, a reconstructed Maori village faces across the water to the wooded site of a pa used by Hongi Hika (*c.* 1780–1828), a Ngapuhi chief who ranged over the North Island and as far south as Cook Strait.

STONE STORE, KERIKERI *One of New Zealand's oldest buildings (1833).*

RELICS OF THE DEEP *Kelly Tarlton's Museum of Shipwrecks is unique for the richness of its collections and its shipboard atmosphere.*

LOCAL CRAFTS *Dolphins and marlin fashioned from kauri are some of the craft items available in the area.*

CITRUS FRUIT *Kerikeri orchards are famous for producing huge quantities.*

CREAM TRIP *A celebrated launch run around the Bay with supplies and visitors.*

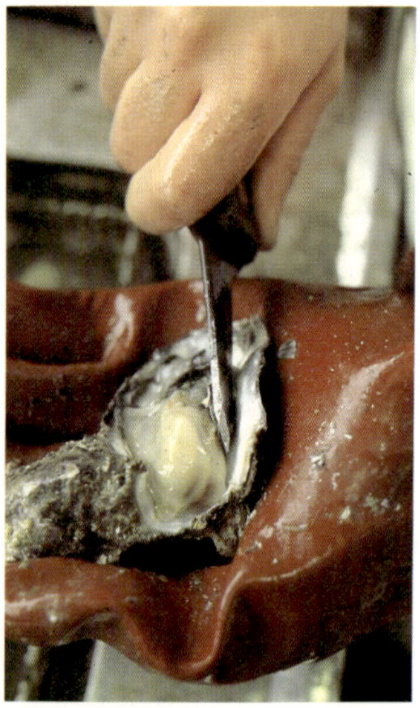

PACIFIC ROCK OYSTERS *Found only in the upper-tidal rocky zone of northernmost New Zealand, the oysters are farmed commercially and with increasing success. All beds are State owned.*

Ngawha Springs If uninviting in colour, the mercury soda springs are said to have curative properties and to have been used by the Maori for treating wounds received in battle.

Ohaeawai and Lake Omapere Major engagements took place here in 1845 after Hone Heke had sacked Russell and forced the British to evacuate what had been planned as the new colony's capital. The Redcoats suffered serious casualties, particularly on the second occasion when Heke's men put the British to flight. Thereafter, the Ngapuhi chief's *mana* knew no bounds, though six months later the war in the north was to end in a decisive engagement at Ruapekapeka. The first encounter was by the shores of Lake Omapere, which is less than three metres deep at its maximum point. The Ohaeawai site is now marked by a church.

Opua Although Paihia and Russell are but a short distance apart, the journey by car would be considerable were it not for the Opua ferry.

Paihia Tradition has it that a pioneer missionary, looking for a site for his mission, saw the bay here and exclaimed to his Maori guide: "Pai (good) here!" Fortunately his knowledge of the language was to improve to the point where he could help compile the first Maori dictionary (still a standard text), but the town's name is, in Maori, meaningless – even if its site on the water's edge could not be bettered.

Paihia's early history is also the country's. Here the first ground was consecrated and the first church erected; from the beach missionaries launched the first boat. Here, too, the first volume printing was undertaken (by the missionary Colenso who, for the first time, produced the New Testament in the Maori language). The missionary settlement has evolved into a substantial holiday and retirement centre, with an inevitable string of motels and restaurants along the foreshore. Neighbouring Waitangi is only a stone's throw away, but accommodation there is limited, so many who come to visit the Treaty House and who stay overnight do so at Paihia.

At Waitangi Bridge is the fascinating shipboard museum wherein are displayed a variety of objects recovered from some of the most famous of the wrecks around the New Zealand coastline. Treasures include gold, silver, bronze and precious stones, the *Elingamite* treasure and Rothschilds' jewellery.

From the wharf a passenger ferry runs across to Russell, and one can join either the round-the-bays "cream trip" or the boat trip to Cape Brett which passes through a remarkable natural rock tunnel in Piercy Island.

RECONSTRUCTED MAORI VILLAGE *A reconstruction of a pre-European Maori* kainga *(unfortified village) at Kerikeri.*

AT ANCHOR *Keelers at Kerikeri Inlet.*

Waitangi Known as the nation's birthplace, it was here in 1840 that a treaty, purporting to vest sovereignty over the country in Queen Victoria, was signed by the British and a number of local chiefs. Intended as a benign, paternalistic gesture – local Maori were frequently the object of scandalous treatment by visiting British seafarers – it soon turned to tragedy. A local chief, Hone Heke, rebelled against the imposition of the customs duties that followed annexation – taxes that deterred whaling ships from calling and so drastically reduced local trade. This forced the abandonment of Kororareka (Russell) and led to the war in the north. The fighting quelled, war later flared farther south, initially in the Taranaki, when the Government rigidly and illegally enforced fraudulent land sales it had negotiated. The treaty that was to have protected the Maori was thus seen as having denuded them of much of their land. Understandably, the national celebrations which take place on the lawn of the Treaty House on 6 February (*left and right*) and traditionally attended by the Governor-General are viewed by a body of Maori opinion as an annual reminder of a treaty both misrepresented to, and misunderstood by, those who signed it.

The Treaty House itself (*above left*) dates from 1833. It was assembled here from timber pre-cut in Sydney, and served as the home for the first British Resident, James Busby, who helped "negotiate" the treaty that was signed in his garden. In the grounds is an unusual Maori meeting house (*above right*). Usually a *whare runanga* reflects the ancestry and history of a particular tribe, but this, as a memorial to the centenary of the treaty, incorporates carvings from tribes throughout the country. The house displays an intriguing collection of historical material but not the treaty – that is in the National Archives in Wellington.

KOROMIKO *A native species of* Hebe.

OPUA FERRY *Between Russell and Paihia.*

WAIMATE MISSION HOUSE *Once a thriving mission farm, later a theological centre.*

Russell Russell's waterfront bestows considerable character: trees and Victorian architecture soften a scene marked by the movement of launches and yachts. Efforts are made to preserve the Victorian atmosphere of the town: the recent reshingling of the police station roof, for example, ensures that the links with a colourful past are maintained. Solid Christ Church (1835) bears the scars of past fighting, while the only other building to have completely survived the sacking of the town is the elegant Catholic mission station, Pompallier House. Like the church, however, it too has been radically refurbished.

The Bay of Islands is one of the world's top big-game fishing areas and Russell is geared to cater for fishermen and fishing vessels alike. The season extends from about November to June, although yellowhead can be caught on light tackle between July and September. Launches are available for charter for deep-sea fishing, line fishing, picnic cruises and skin diving. At the wharf one may also join the "cream trip" or other outings to the open sea and Piercy Island.

Waimate North The handsome mission house here was built in 1831 and was the scene of the country's first major farming experiment. The building, the sole survivor of three similar houses built by the missionaries in the 1830s, is open to the public. Set in magnificent grounds, it has been furnished and restored as closely as possible to its original style, thanks largely to records left by its original inhabitants. Many of the early missionaries' possessions are also on display. Built largely of kauri, it has an attractive symmetrical appearance; unusual, however, was the inclusion of the kitchen inside the house rather than in an outhouse as was customary. In the churchyard, noted for some high carved Maori headboards, lie soldiers killed in the war of 1845. Nearby is Bedgood smithy and wheelwright's shop, one of the country's first "industrial complexes".

Whangarei and environs

THE COLOURS OF THE NORTH *Typical of the coves that beckon along the coast to the north-east is this pohutukawa-fringed bay.*

WHANGAREI FALLS *A pleasant picnic spot.*

ORUAITI CHAPEL *A pioneer memorial.*

Whangarei, the "capital" of Northland, the "winterless north", rests on the lip of the country's finest deep-water port – a feature which attracted the oil refinery to nearby Marsden Point and with it a new prosperity. The city was fortunate, too, that the decision to site the installations here was taken before the discovery of vast quantities of gas and oil condensate off the Taranaki coast, for the claims of New Plymouth might later have proved irresistible.

The rugged, jagged hills which nurse the sheltered harbour are crowned by the magnificence of Mt Manaia (403 metres), whose five peaks, silhouetted against an eastern sky, are rich in the suggestion that is the lifeblood of mythology.

Its climate and proximity to the more proclaimed enticements further north render Whangarei an exceptionally pleasant place to live, but to the visitor the lure of the north tends to obscure the generous endowments close to hand. These include deep-sea fishing at Tutukaka, bathing along an intriguing coastline, and bush walks through small stands of kauri.

SYMBOLS OF PROSPERITY *The yachts of Aucklanders mix with locally owned craft.*

TOWNSCAPE *A segment of the panorama afforded from atop Mt Parahaki.*

WHANGAREI HEADS *In the distance are the figures on Mt Manaia. In mythology a jealous husband was about to slay his eloping wife when all were turned to stone.*

Waipu A portrait of the austere leader of the Scottish Highlanders who founded the town is displayed in the museum, the "Hall of Memories". The bay, looking out to the Hen and Chicken Islands, affords excellent surfing and fishing.

Whangarei From a backwater town whose past development had been hampered by transport problems, Whangarei blossomed into a burgeoning city after it was chosen as the site for the country's oil refinery, whose flare stack at Marsden Point may be seen from afar as it burns off waste gases. An oil-fired power station followed and industries mushroomed. This sudden growth and prosperity stems from and is maintained by Whangarei's deep-water harbour, capable of handling some of the world's largest tankers. Crude oil shipped in bulk has, since 1964, been broken down here: previously, refined products had to be shipped from the Middle East – a more costly undertaking. In addition to imported crude, the refinery processes New Zealand's own condensate shipped from Taranaki.

But despite today's industrial base, with sheet glass-making, fertilizers and cement looming large, Whangarei wears a gentle air, as towering hills to east and west and a lush surrounding countryside combine to provide both a rural "feel" and a reminder of the city's recent role as little more than a farming centre. Too many travellers simply pass through in their eagerness to reach the Bay of Islands. Yet to pause is to be able to enjoy a scenic run out to Whangarei Heads, to contemplate the past in the Glorat Museum and the passage of time among the Clapham clocks exhibits. Though for safety reasons the refinery cannot be visited, impressions of the magnitude of the undertaking may be gained from nearby car parks. Whangarei Falls are only five kilometres away, and there are a number of pretty parks, some with stands of kauri. The lookout on Parahaki, with its panoramic view, is easily reached, either by car or on foot through Mair Park.

CLAPHAM CLOCK MUSEUM The display of over 400 antique clocks generates a cacophony of ticks and chimes.

MARSDEN POINT *The nation's oil refinery.*

FACES OF THE NORTH *The north is home for many of New Zealand's Maoris.*

NATURE'S STATUES *Weathered limestone at the Waro reserve near Kamo.*

Hokianga Harbour

A VIEW FROM OMAPERE *Approached from the south, the Hokianga Harbour opens out with a dramatic suddenness.*

OPO AND FRIENDS The dolphin "Opo" brought world fame to tiny Opononi when, for only the second time in history and the first in nearly 2,000 years, a wild dolphin chose to befriend children in the water, cavorting with them and giving them rides.

NGAWHA SPRINGS *Warm relaxing pools on the road to the Bay of Islands.*

Hokianga Harbour The harbour, a drowned river system with a hazardous bar, is one of very few natural harbours on the country's west coast. It was of considerable significance in pioneer days, when its bar claimed many vessels during the height of the kauri timber trade, and ships plied its arms as far as Horeke.

Horeke A tiny settlement on the inner reaches of the harbour, notable for the Mangungu Mission House. Originally built here in 1838, it was subsequently dismantled and removed to Onehunga to serve as a parsonage. More recently it has been returned to its original site by the Historic Places Trust.

Kohukohu A town which once dominated the harbour in size and importance has what is reputed to be the oldest bridge in the country – though certainly not the largest!

Omanaia Missionaries emphasised that "good Christian" converts not only renounced old spiritual ways, but also their material culture. Understandably, this rigidity spawned resistance, and buried in the churchyard here is Papahurihia, who led local Maori opposition. Both church (long ceased to be used as such) and burial ground are closed to visitors.

Omapere Attractive views encompass harbour, heads and the golden sand dunes that encroach on farmland. Across the water is where Kupe is reputed to have farewelled the land he had discovered.

Onoke Still standing here is the modest house of the self-styled "Pakeha-Maori", Judge Maning, an Irishman who moved here in 1833 and later helped establish the Maori Land Court.

CLENDON HOUSE Situated at Rawene, overlooking the Hokianga Harbour, this house is little changed from when it was first built in about 1860. James Clendon was a ship's master who visited the area in 1829, then traded in the Bay of Islands, where he was the United States Consul. When the country became a British colony, he sold his home at Okiato for it to become New Zealand's first Government House. It was as a Resident Magistrate that he finally came to live here, but in retirement his commercial ventures failed, and this house soon passed into his father-in-law's ownership. It is now owned by the Historic Places Trust and is open to visitors.

STANDING ON STILTS *Clusters of buildings standing on stilts over the water lend charm to both Rawene (pictured) and Horeke.*

KING OF THE KAURI *Te Matua Ngahere, the "Father of the Forest", may be as many as 2,000 years old and is one of the largest of the trees in the Waipoua Kauri Forest.*

The broad and serene sweep of Hokianga Harbour contrasts starkly with the bustle of the Bay of Islands. There, history, land and sea are the stuff of commerce: here, not so very far distant, the land seems to live as much in the past as in the present and any hunger for tourist traffic seems half-hearted. Here was to be the kingdom of Baron de Thierry, "Sovereign Chief of New Zealand", but the Frenchman's grandiose schemes collapsed and he ended his days not holding court, but teaching piano in Auckland.

To the south rise the massive kauri trees of the Waipoua Forest, some venerable to the point of antiquidy and easily the giants of the New Zealand forest. Here they grow more or less in their primitive environment, dwarfing the trees beneath. Their saplings, straight and lacking knots, show at a glance why it was that the British Navy was prepared to come so far to plunder them for use as masts and as spars. Indeed, the sapling's name, "ricker", is a corruption of "rigger". The main road carves through the forest for nearly 16 kilometres, with tracks to the major trees well signposted.

MAXWELL'S HUT *An early bushman's hut turned museum in Waipoua Forest.*

Opononi Popular with holidaymakers for its safe bathing, good boating and plentiful fish, Opononi can be translated as meaning "place of bountiful hospitality". A monument to the dolphin "Opo" is on the seafront. Another, to Kupe, is nearby at Pakanae.

Rawene A waterside township brimful with personality (*see picture*). A ferry from here links with Kohukohu on the northern shore.

Trounson Kauri Park A stand smaller and quite different in character from Waipoua.

Waipoua Kauri Forest Over 2,500 hectares of mature kauri forest comprise the last significant stand of the tree that contributed much to the country's development. Cook had recognised its value, and before long the British Navy was here, plundering the forests for timber for shipbuilding. Early settlers, too, used it for their homes, and an export trade quickly developed. Timber was being cut very much faster than the trees could regenerate, but as the trade dwindled another took its place – gum. The kauri exudes a resin that hardens on contact with the air, and was found to have a high value in the manufacture of varnishes.

A rush followed, with many migrants, principally from Yugoslavia, pouring in to search for gum from kauri forests long departed, poking deep into the soil with long rods then digging down when the omens seemed good. In so doing they ravaged large areas of land, and desolate tracts pitted with gum holes are still to be seen in the north.

NORTHLAND PASTORAL *A century ago this was dense forest like the hills in the background.*

Maori myth

Maori culture is rich in myths and legends. They tell of the creation of the universe, of gods descending into humans. They describe the emergence from the sea of the land they called Aotearoa and rehearse the coming of canoes from a "Hawaiki" homeland to populate its shores.

These tales embody, in the absence of a written language, many aspects of Maori culture – customs, beliefs, knowledge, skills, religion, superstition – but above all they represent the accumulated store of experience. All that had been learnt and practised was woven into Maori oral literature, etched into carvings and mirrored in song and dance to be re-created, renewed and adapted by each generation. Inevitably, as is the nature of folklore, sources disagree, for there can never be one, single, "authentic" version.

These stories are moving and beautiful in their own right, for the Maori traditionally had a highly sophisticated command of poetic language, and a colourful rendition was itself an aid to memory. Not infrequently behind their elaborate texture lay a practical and vital purpose which formed the very cement of the Maori's culture. For example, some legends tell of Kupe, the Polynesian explorer credited with being among the first to visit the country's shores, chasing a *wheke* (octopus) all the way from Hawaiki after it had stripped bait from his fishing line. They tell of a furious encounter, in the course of which Kupe chased the octopus along the Wairarapa coast and into Cook Strait, detailing the account so minutely as to provide an oral map to the Marlborough Sounds, an important and tricky area for navigation. Another account tells of a canoe's being wrecked on the North Otago coast. Curious boulders on the beaches are described as petrified kumara and gourd seeds washed ashore; a particular reef is described as the canoe's hull, and the peaks of the ranges to the north are given the names of passengers. Even Mt Cook is given the name of a boy who was carried on his grandfather's shoulders and was thus the tallest of the survivors. The account is of an overland journey so detailed that none who knew it could be lost.

Not surprisingly (for the people share a common origin), many aspects of Maori mythology are echoed in other islands of Polynesia. Even Maui, the great fisher of land from the sea, must be shared with other island groups.

Unfortunately, if inevitably, the oral tradition was an early casualty of European settlement. New questions were asked to which new answers had to be found, and although a number of early settlers (including Sir George Grey) played a major part in preserving what they could understand of the myths and legends, they fed their own interpretations back, giving rise to such phantoms as the "Great Migration". The Europeans had migrated here *en masse*, so thought the Maori would have done likewise. Such distortions continue to this day to mar the popular understanding of historical fact.

Kaipara Harbour

MINUTE MINNIESDALE CHAPEL *In a solitary setting above Kaipara Harbour stands a tiny chapel (1867), not far from Port Albert.*

The dairylands north-west of Auckland are probed by the long fingers of a tranquil harbour to present a scene of serenity – a happy blend of land and water.

The prospect today masks the bustle of yesteryear, when small boats hustled to and fro, ferrying kauri timber, gum and agricultural produce to the infant and fast-growing Auckland. Occasionally, too, there is the reminder of unfulfilled promise – such as at Port Albert, where a determined settlement of over 3,000 turned their hands to everything they could imagine before yielding to the dictates of an uncertain tidal harbour and a plague of crop diseases.

The area demands a lingering appreciation, a savouring at leisure of an endlessly changing relationship of sea and farmland. Perhaps its most outstanding single feature is to be found at the tiny town of Matakohe, with its unequalled collection of kauri gum and a memorial church to the country's first native-born Prime Minister.

PARAKAI HOT POOLS *Helensville's mineral springs open all day and into the evenings.*

KERERU *The native pigeon ranks as one of the most magnificent of the species, both in size and brilliance of plumage. Its numbers have dwindled with the forests.*

OTAMATEA KAURI AND PIONEER MUSEUM *Matakohe's museum is a celebration of the kauri. Colonial furniture* (below) *and the largest kauri gum collection in the world* (above) *testify to the beauty and richness of a once great natural resource. The gum, seen here in every size, shape and colour, was much sought-after about the turn of the century. Long rods known as "gum spears" were used to prod the swamps where mighty forests had once stood; other gum was taken by climbing trees.*

PASTURELAND, MATAKOHE *Cabbage trees on the upper reaches of the harbour.*

Dargaville A dairying centre on the banks of the Wairoa River about 60 kilometres north of the entrance to Kaipara Harbour, Dargaville perpetuates the name of its Australian founder and serves as a jumping-off point for visits to the Waipoua and Trounson Kauri Forests to the north. The wharf recalls the town's role as a port in the heyday of the kauri timber and later gum trades. The area's history is captured by the local museum, housed in what began as the Dargaville family's stables. Large areas of land in the locality, for generations unproductive as a result of the gum digging, have been rehabilitated in recent years.

Helensville At the opposite end of the harbour from Dargaville lies Helensville, also a dairying centre but one named not for its founder but for a pioneer's wife. Set on a hillside above the Kaipara River, the town once had a shipping role: indeed, its principal access to Auckland (today only 50 kilometres by road) was a hazardous voyage around North Cape to the Waitemata. Hot springs at Parakai draw visitors from far afield, and a number of motels have their own thermal pools.

COATES MEMORIAL CHURCH Twice decorated for bravery in World War I, locally born Gordon Coates is depicted in Matakohe's church as a knight in armour. As the country's first native-born Prime Minister (1925–28), he could not live up to the expectations of the electorate, but his political career continued and he made outstanding contributions both during the Depression and in the War Cabinet.

A RURAL SETTING *The main highway near Matakohe passes through rolling dairy country typical of the north.*

PAHI DOMAIN *A colossal fig tree dominates the seaside recreation ground.*

Kaipara Harbour The harbour's many arms penetrate deep into the shoreline but are little seen from the main highway. Its dangerous bar has claimed many ships, some of whose skeletons still rest on North Spit, near Pouto. The harbour's importance ended with the era of coastal shipping.

Matakohe A tiny settlement on the northern reaches, renowned for its museum and church.

Pahi A short detour from Highway 12 leads to a pleasant picnic spot, with good boating, swimming, camping – and shade from a Moreton Bay fig tree of truly gargantuan proportions.

Port Albert Now simply a cluster of houses, this was where in the 1860s a special settlement of about 3,000 Nonconformists struggled against all odds in a battle to wrest a living from the land. Their enterprise and their failure are recorded in the Albertland Museum.

Wellsford A farming centre on the neck of land which bridges Northland to Auckland.

KAURI FOREST, WAIROA RIVER, KAIPARA (1839) *Early timber-felling techniques are faithfully observed in a watercolour by the New Zealand Company surveyor-artist Charles Heaphy. Heaphy's works, noted for their draughtsmanship, command high prices more for historical than for artistic reasons. The early travellers sketched as today's take photographs.*

DISUSED LIFTING BRIDGE *A relic of Dargaville's days as a coastal shipping port.*

The Hibiscus Coast, Islands of the Hauraki Gulf

A YACHTING PARADISE *A well-laden yacht cruises on the Hauraki Gulf, whose waters are nursed by the mainland to the west and the long, northward-reaching arm of the Coromandel Peninsula to the east. Sheltered from all winds save the northerly (Hauraki means "north wind"), it is a perfect haven for boats. Many of its islands have been incorporated into the Hauraki Gulf Maritime Park.*

Paving the way north along the eastern coastline from Auckland lies a golden chain of beautiful beaches, shelving into the island-freckled reaches of the Hauraki Gulf. Such gems so close to the country's metropolis ensure the presence of numerous commuter and retirement settlements as well as, in summer, hosts of good-humoured holidaymakers.

Yet solitude, too, is near at hand. For a little inland lies tranquil, tiny Puhoi, unusual for its wayside shrine and unique for its Bohemian origins. It was to the solitude, too, of Wenderholm that the former British Prime Minister, Sir Anthony Eden, retreated for a time to recuperate from the double blows of surgery and the Suez crisis which marked both a turning point in world history and his own political demise.

The Gulf itself, almost landlocked by Great and Little Barrier Islands, is a fabled fishing ground and a paradise for boats large and small. Across its waters, passenger ferries and swift launches whisk commuters and visitors to a scattering of homes and remote picnic and camping places.

Hauraki Gulf Maritime Park The park takes in dozens of islands which, by purchase, gift or transfer from local bodies, have been amalgamated with areas already owned by the Crown to establish a maritime park. The islands and their uses vary. Some are so remote and inaccessible that they are unsuited for recreation but ideal for the study of wildlife and the preservation both of bird species and of the small relic populations of the reptile tuatara. Others are reached more easily and are picturesque settings for holiday outings. Their histories, too, are varied. Rangitoto, youngest of the islands, is enshrined in Maori legend; Browns Island was farmed by the partners Campbell and Brown who foresaw the birth of Auckland; Motuihe has served both as a quarantine station and prisoner-of-war camp, and North Head, the only part of the mainland included in the park, preserves a long-time military fort with emplacements dating from every time of crisis, real or imaginary, since 1885.

VOLCANIC ORIGINS *An aerial view reveals the crater on Browns Island. Rangitoto, in the background, is yet another of many volcanoes which pepper the region. According to legend, it was still erupting when the Maori arrived.*

CLEMATIS *One of about nine endemic species.*

BOHEMIAN ORIGINS Puhoi's history reflected in stained glass.

KAWAU ISLAND *Mansion House (c. 1862) was created by an early Governor, Sir George Grey, who later became Prime Minister, and has been restored inside and out by the Historic Places Trust. Much visited by private boats, the island is also accessible by ferry from Sandspit, near Warkworth.*

East Coast Bays Auckland's northern suburbs string out along a series of close, east-facing bays.

Great and Little Barrier Islands The two islands that guard the entrance to the Gulf could not be more different: geologically Great Barrier is a detached piece of the Coromandel Peninsula while Little Barrier is a volcanic cone of comparatively recent origin. Great Barrier supports a small permanent population and is visited by holidaymakers; Little Barrier, virtually untouched by humans or by browsing animals, is a protected wildlife sanctuary.

Kawau Island A delightful corner of the Gulf, with Grey's gracious Mansion House and imposing gardens. Wallabies he introduced are now widespread and the occasional kookaburra may also be heard.

Orewa A tranquil seaside town with a fascinating aquarium. In summer it assumes a more hectic pace as holidaymakers descend to swell the town to the size of a small, bustling city.

Waiheke Island The largest and most settled of the Gulf's islands, it has a variety of sheltered bays and offers excellent fishing.

Waiwera Aside from the beach, which is akin to Orewa, attractions are enhanced by hot springs and the extensive Wenderholm Reserve.

Warkworth A farming centre distinguished by the country's satellite station. Close by is Mahurangi Peninsula, less populated than Whangaparaoa and with fine beaches. Diving is a popular sport here, and access to Kawau Island is from Sandspit.

Whangaparaoa Peninsula Very closely settled and within commuting distance of Auckland, the peninsula compensates with a myriad of inlets which ensure that, whatever the breeze, a sheltered swimming spot can be found.

SANDSPIT *A launching place for runabouts on the Mahurangi Peninsula.*

PUHOI'S PUB *Relics and photographs of Puhoi's colourful past lend the hotel an atmosphere all its own.*

SPACE LINK *The antenna of Warkworth's satellite station.*

STITCHBIRD The stitchbird belongs to the "honey-eater" family which also includes the tui and bellbird. Unlike the others, found throughout the country, this native bird is now found only on Little Barrier Island. The name refers not to nest-building but to its high-pitched call. The Maori once hunted the birds for food and used its yellow feathers in the manufacture of cloaks.

PALM BEACH *A sheltered resort on the northern side of Waiheke Island.*

Auckland

A CITY OF THE SEA *Spanning the waters of the Waitemata to link the suburbs of the North Shore with the heart of Auckland city is the Harbour Bridge, recently widened to accommodate increasing traffic.*

In the country's metropolis a population of a million sprawls over an area larger than that of Greater London. Washed by twin seas, flanked by twin harbours, the city is characterised by many volcanic cones, the thousands of yachts that speckle its bays and a vigorous outdoor lifestyle. Its ethos, too, is more assertive than is found elsewhere.

QUEEN STREET BUSTLE *Pedestrians criss-cross the main street's intersection with Wellesley Street.*

As well as being the uncrowned capital of New Zealand (a title it officially enjoyed from 1840–65 and whose removal may now be seen as an unintended act of decentralisation), the city is acknowledged as being the "capital" of Polynesia, as it is now the home of more Polynesian Islanders than any other centre. This has brought with it problems of integration for Islander and New Zealander alike, but also adds the cosmopolitan riches of ethnic variety which the country's other cities largely lack.

Auckland's growth, and the "drift to the north" generally, have posed major economic problems for more southerly regions. Two-thirds of the country's population now lives north of Lake Taupo, conferring on Auckland a degree of economic domination that imperils more distant industries. Those to the south may mock the bustle, describing the city as "Little Sydney" (which in many ways it resembles), but they also acknowledge that those transferred here quickly succumb to its special charm.

OFF TO THE ISLANDS *The Waiheke ferry departs for the islands of the Hauraki Gulf*

OUTDOOR LIVING *A restaurant in High Street exemplifies Aucklanders' addiction to sun and fresh air.*

A city of volcanoes Auckland rests on the narrow isthmus of Tamaki Peninsula. On either side spread the generous harbours of Waitemata and Manukau, which all but sever the North Island in two. Both are river valleys formed during the last ice age and drowned when the sea's waters rose. The character of the shoreline along the open sea contrasts starkly. The wild coast to the west, characterised by titanium-rich black sand which becomes uncomfortably hot on a sunny summer's day, is pounded by the rollers of the Tasman Sea while that to the east enjoys the shelter of the Coromandel Peninsula. Though this has led to Auckland being characterised as a "city of the seas", it is pre-eminently one of volcanoes. Among the more than sixty craters that pockmark the terrain, several are prominent landmarks: One Tree Hill, with its lonely tree and obelisk; Lake Pupuke at Takapuna; Mount Eden; Mount Albert; the Waitakeres, and the graceful island cone of Rangitoto that seems to sweep into every eastwards seascape. Each evidences the fury with which the isthmus was formed. The thermal springs at Helensville and elsewhere not far distant hint that the process may not yet have ended.

"The spouse of a hundred lovers" The isthmus takes its name from the Maori name, Tamaki-makau-rau, "the spouse contested by a hundred lovers", not for reasons of promiscuity but to reflect the keen way in which its possession was contested among tribes in the region. Maori legend tells of battle after battle, giving the isthmus as frenzied a history under human habitation as it had had during its formation. Almost every volcanic cone was fortified, pre-eminent being the pa on One Tree Hill, but even these massive fortifications were, on occasion, successfully attacked and laid waste. Today, traces of the various pa may be seen on Mount Eden and Mount Albert as well as on the steep slopes of One Tree Hill.

The isthmus gradually became untenable with the emergence of Ngapuhi as the country's strongest tribe early in the nineteenth century. Based in the Bay of Islands, Ngapuhi roamed south with increasing frequency and daring as they gained guns from visiting whaling ships. The local population dwindled further in the face of epidemics, and by the time the isthmus was chosen to be the first substantive capital, in 1840, it was virtually deserted.

Once upon a capital . . . Unlike the other "main" centres of Wellington, Christchurch and Dunedin, Auckland was not a "planned" settlement, fed with migrants arriving regularly from Britain. Rather it was the arbitrary creation of the first governor, Hobson, shortly after he had concluded the Treaty of Waitangi. Hobson's choice infuriated the New Zealand Company, who had anticipated that its settlement at Wellington would be preferred, and it bombarded the British Government with objections and complaints. But the Governor's choice was well made. Anxious to prevent strife between Maori and Pakeha, he had selected a site which was easily defended and which effectively severed the two major areas of Maori population, of which about three-quarters was living north of Lake Taupo. He had noted the ease of communication by water, ready access to essential stands of forest and the agricultural potential of the red volcanic soil. Important, too, in the choice was the initial absence of Europeans, Auckland being declared capital at a time when its Pakeha population numbered just two. One of the pair, Sir John Logan Campbell, lived to greet as Mayor the Duke and Duchess of Cornwall on their royal tour of 1901.

LANDMARK *One Tree Hill and monument.*

A VARIED ARCHITECTURE *The construction of the new is matched by the energetic refurbishment of the old. From left: part of the university; a hair salon off Queen Street; Vulcan Lane; modern high-rise.*

AUCKLAND WAR MEMORIAL MUSEUM In the parkland setting of the Domain, the Museum covers the general disciplines of zoology, botany and ethnology. A large display is devoted to the two world wars. Particularly strong sections concern the Maori and the Pacific. *Below from left*: Kawe, a Caroline Islands goddess; a carved wooden Buddha (c. 1450A.D.); a pre-European Maori carving.

CELEBRATING THE HARVEST *Dancers in traditional Dalmatian costume mingle with more conventionally attired visitors at Auckland's annual Wine Festival. A number of major vineyards are near the city.*

GREER TWISS SCULPTURE *In Karangahape Road.*

Volcanic viewpoints Some of the smaller volcanic cones have been quarried out of existence for their scoria. The three largest, however, have been preserved as scenic reserves, and each offers a magnificent and somewhat different panorama. One Tree Hill is topped with a towering column to celebrate Sir John Logan Campbell's admiration for the Maori people, while at the base of the obelisk the Founder Citizen of Auckland lies buried. Somewhat higher is Mount Eden (196 metres), with a view which encompasses the whole of the Auckland isthmus. Mount Albert, marginally less spectacular, like the others is plainly marked with the earthworks of fortified pa. Its green slopes contrast sharply with surrounding suburbia.

Varied museums and art galleries The Auckland War Memorial Museum, in a parkland setting, ranks with the country's best and has a particularly splendid display of early Maori material. "Journey's End" Cottage and Museum, built as a Fencible cottage, recalls Onehunga's origins as a fencible settlement, one of a chain of settlements established to secure the infant Auckland from attack by surrounding it with military settlers (*Jellicoe Park*). The roomy kauri cottage of an early cleric, Ewelme Cottage (1863-64) contains much original furniture (*Ayr Street, Parnell*) and contrasts with the grandeur of the colonial mansion of Alberton (*Mt Albert Road*). The ingenuity of Kelly Tarlton's Underwater World (*Tamaki Drive*) fascinates all. In totally different vein is the Museum of Transport and Technology (*Great North Road, Western Springs*) but even this augments computers, steam engines and a fine array of aircraft with a pioneer village to preserve interesting colonial buildings that might otherwise have been demolished. The museum is of special interest on "Live Weekends", when everything that can move does.

The city is a major centre for artists, and their work is to be found for sale in the many private galleries that abound, as well as in the Auckland City Art Gallery (*cnr Kitchener and Wellesley Streets*), which also has a good collection of Gothic art.

CRAFT MARKET *Potters, weavers, silversmiths, woodworkers and leatherworkers ply their trade in Brown's Mill, off Darby Street.*

MISSION BAY BEACH *The scene of early missionary endeavour is now given over to summertime leisure.*

WAITAKERE RANGES *Native bush softens the volcanic origins of the hills.*

Interesting buildings Auckland's beginnings are remembered in the 120 hectares of Cornwall Park, where Acacia cottage (1841), built as John Logan Campbell's early home, has been moved onto the land he once farmed. St Stephen's Chapel (1856–57) was where the constitution for the Church of the Province of New Zealand was signed in 1857 (*off St Stephens Avenue, Parnell*). Also in Parnell is a pleasing cluster of ecclesiastical buildings which includes Selwyn Court (1863), the Cathedral Church of St Mary (1888) and the modern Holy Trinity Cathedral (*cnr St Stephens Avenue and Parnell Road*), as well as the Victorian cottage shopping complex of Parnell Village (*259 Parnell Road*).

Choice beaches The choice lies between the wild, ocean-swept beaches of the west coast (personified as male by the Maori) and those of the sheltered east coast (personified as female). To the west, Piha (the most popular) (*40 km*), Muriwai (*43 km*) and Whatipu (*44 km*) each has its devotees, with Whatipu offering the safest bathing. The inner-harbour beaches are, of course, more affected by the tide, but Mission Bay is of special appeal. To the north, along the east coast, lies a chain of beaches from North Head to the much-indented shoreline of the Whangaparaoa Peninsula (*37 km*). Farther north are the seaside resorts of Orewa (*40 km*) and Waiwera (*48 km*), the latter's beach being augmented with thermal pools.

Around and about Henderson (*18 km NW*) is the centre of a flourishing wine-making district, with a number of establishments welcoming passers-by both to sample and to buy. The early winemakers were Dalmatians, originally drawn by the pickings of the kauri gum-digging era, some of whose descendants continue what has become a family tradition. From Henderson, too, a pleasant drive leads through the well-bushed Waitakere Ranges, with walks to waterfalls and through stands of kauri. To the east lie the beaches at Howick (*22 km*), a village-flavoured commuter town redolent of its origins as a military settlement.

PIONEER AVIATOR *With empty tins and a collection of farmyard bits and pieces, Richard Pearse (1877–1953) almost succeeded in racing the Wright brothers into the air. The inventive genius of this South Canterbury eccentric is displayed at the Museum of Transport and Technology, Western Springs.*

A "SELWYN" CHAPEL The tiny St Stephen's Chapel in Parnell, in whose churchyard many Auckland pioneers lie buried.

A SURFER'S PARADISE *North of Piha.*

SUNRISE *Day breaks over the city and the Westhaven marina.*

RUN FOR FUN *The annual "round the bays" run draws well over 60,000 entries. Joggers and serious athletes alike are encountered at every turn.*

THE FACE OF JUSTICE? *Gargoyles embellish the High Court in Waterloo Quadrant.*

A capital denied Auckland was to enjoy just 25 years as the country's capital. During that time the city grew and prospered, partly at the expense of the Maori tribes to the south, whose land was acquired after bloodshed followed their refusal to sell voluntarily, and partly as a consequence of the presence of British troops. When these departed the economy sagged, and the settlement's plight was aggravated by the unbridled opulence of Dunedin, booming as a result of gold strikes. By then Dunedin was the commercial and entrepreneurial heart of the country, and it threatened secession if the capital was not moved south. Dunedin's apparent intransigence is the more understandable when one appreciates that at the time the most speedy line of communication with the then capital was by way of Sydney. Before long, in 1865, the capital was moved to Wellington, and Auckhand's fortunes ebbed lower still. Too late, the gold that had robbed Auckland of her crown restored her fortunes – fabulous finds were made on the Coromandel Peninsula, just across the Hauraki Gulf, and these revived the commercial instincts in the Aucklanders which have never since flagged.

Today Auckland's domination over the country is near total. This continues to grow as the magnet of its large population (and so its workforce and its markets) attracts ever-increasing industry at the expense of less well-populated regions to the south. Major industrial activities include the manufacture of clothing, footwear, foodstuffs, domestic appliances, textiles, furnishings and building materials. As well as having more heavy industry than any other centre, it is also home to engineering and allied trades.

SHEEP IN THE CITY'S HEART *A view of Cornwall Park.*

STRAND ARCADE *One of several shopping arcades adjoining Queen Street.*

PARNELL VILLAGE *A cluster of boutiques in a Victorian setting in Parnell Road.*

OMINOUS REMINDER The rifle slits of Albert Barracks (1846–52), near Albert Park, mark the tempestuous beginnings of the colony.

RESTAURANTS PROLIFERATE *A typical "new" restaurant at Herne Bay.*

A FASCINATION FOR THE SEA *Thousands of boats are owned by Aucklanders; others are for hire. Still more are taking shape in garages and back gardens. The Anniversary Day Regatta (January) is billed as the world's largest.*

The city's heart The city's principal street, Queen Street, flanked by some of the country's largest departmental stores, dips gently downhill to meet the harbour. From the waterfront is seen Auckland's Harbour Bridge – over 1,000 metres of steel spanning the Waitemata Harbour to link the increasingly popular North Shore directly to the downtown area. Inevitably its design earns the nickname, "the coat-hanger", while the Japanese-built extensions adding additional lanes on either side are known as the "Nippon clip-ons". Cutting across the upper reaches of Queen Street is Karangahape Road, Auckland's counterpart to Sydney's Kings Cross, where the varied ethnic origins of the city's multi-cultural population are best appreciated. Only two blocks from Queen Street and adjoining the oldest buildings of the University of Auckland, is Albert Park, popular with lunchtime office workers. The park marks the site of the Albert Barracks, built in 1846 in Auckland's early uncertainty. Only the rifle-slit walls behind the university's administration building have survived. From the foot of Queen Street numerous launches leave to cruise the island-scattered waters of the Hauraki Gulf on what is, for some, a commuter run. For those with less time, or who would also see the city from the air, amphibious flights leave from Mechanics Bay.

ANIMALS FROM THE WORLD OVER Auckland's Zoological Gardens, the country's most comprehensive, also house native animals and boast a nocturnal kiwi house. The animals are fed in the afternoons.

A POLYNESIAN BANQUET *. . . but held indoors.*

PONSONBY GRAFFITI *Murals add colour to inner-city architecture.*

HOBSON'S GRAVE *The country's first Governor lies in the old Symonds Street cemetery.*

ALBERTON This romantic 18-roomed colonial mansion dates from 1862 and is furnished in the period *(100 Mount Albert Road; open daily)*.

South Auckland

IRON HORSE *At Glenbrook a vintage railway recalls technology before the steel mills.*

South of the metropolis of Auckland the land fans out wide and prosperous, with essential dairylands and market gardens. The "threat" to the area (if such it can be called) today lies in the expanding city to the north, but much of the fascination in its past derives from a threat to the south – from dispossessed Maori tribes and the establishment more than a century ago of "pensioner" or "Fencible" settlements as an outer defensive screen for the then-capital. Granted land in return for light military duties, former Imperial soldiers, specially recruited and brought here, divided their time between guarding the burgeoning town of Auckland and growing food to feed it. Howick, Onehunga, Panmure and Otahuhu were all born in this fashion.

To the south, beyond the Bombay Hills, lies the abundance of the Waikato.

FOOD FOR A CITY *Pukekohe's prodigious market gardens and farmlands have fed Auckland for over a century.*

Bombay A farming hamlet on Highway 1, Bombay is as far removed from its Indian namesake in character as it is in distance. Its name derives from that of an early immigrant ship and lends itself to that of the Pukewau Range, now more familiarly the Bombay Hills, which mark the boundary between the Auckland and Waikato regions. Here market gardening is pre-eminent. Roadside stalls tempt the passing motorist while fields of seasonal vegetables, fruit and horticultural produce spread out in an ever-changing chequerboard of brown and green.

Drury A rapidly growing industrial and commercial centre, Drury is typical of several South Auckland townships whose sturdy rural heritage has changed dramatically in the last few decades. Strategically placed at the head of an inlet on the Manukau Harbour and also on the Great South Road (now designated Highway 1), its former role as a vital supply depot for troops fighting in the Waikato has a modern equivalent in the supply of industrial goods for the national and export markets.

Glenbrook From quiet obscurity the locality was plunged into national focus by the decision to site the country's sole steel mill here. The mill exploits some of the potential of the vast quantities of ironsand found on a number of west coast beaches.

NEW ZEALAND'S GATEWAY *For most overseas visitors, their first contact with the country is at Mangere International Airport.*

PAKURANGA *An aerial view of residential development in an expanding Auckland.*

GLENBROOK STEEL *From scrap and iron-sand the material for industrial processing.*

Howick A seaside commuter suburb of Auckland, Howick still retains something of a village atmosphere. This dates from its founding in 1847 by Fencibles who began the work of taming the landscape while guarding Auckland against the possibility of attack. Fragments surviving from these times are Shamrock Cottage (*Selwyn Road*), The Garden of Memories (*Uxbridge Street*) and All Saints' Church (*Selwyn Road*).

Manukau city One of the country's newer cities, Manukau is the product of the population explosion experienced by Auckland in the aftermath of World War II and later.

PUKEKOHE GRAND PRIX The country's premier motor race is held here annually.

Pakuranga Until quite recently a farming and fruit-growing area, the town has mushroomed to accommodate a growing Auckland. The Lloyd Elesmore Park (*Bell Road*) preserves a number of elegant and historic old buildings, including one of only two two-storeyed Fencible cottages (moved here in 1895).

Papakura Another of the early frontier towns, Papakura preserves a military link in its large Army camp. The picturesque Hunua Falls are only about 16 kilometres away, and at Pukekiwiriki pa site (*Red Hill Road*) there is a magnificent panorama as well as a fine example of a pre-European pa.

Pokeno Here there is an old military cemetery and a stone memorial to those who died near here in 1863. Queen's Redoubt, a major establishment, was sited about 400 metres away.

Pukekohe Extensive market gardens take full advantage of the rich volcanic soil, but dairying and sheep farming also loom large. A particularly appealing view over the town and countryside is gained from Pukekohe Hill. Curiosities include two once-fortified and battle-scarred churches, Pukekohe East Presbyterian Church and St Brides, Mauku. Each January the town experiences the excitement of the New Zealand Grand Prix.

FENCIBLE COTTAGE *History at Howick.*

ALL SAINTS', HOWICK (1847) *One of several distinctive churches built around Auckland by Bishop Selwyn, Anglican primate of New Zealand from 1842–68.*

Sport

A passion for sport runs deep in the nation's psyche, drawing on the colonists' competitive nature and their genius for co-operation. Perhaps no other country of comparable size sets for itself such high standards, or has produced as many champions. At the Olympic Games, middle-distance runners – Lovelock, Halberg, Snell, Walker – have passed into legend; rowing-eights and yachtsmen have defeated the world's best, and even a lowly ranked hockey team has returned with gold medals. Denis Hulme has won the world motor-racing drivers' championship; Edmund Hillary was the first to scale Everest; Timaru-reared Bob Fitzsimmons held the world heavy-weight boxing crown; Clark McConachy defeated all comers at billiards; Anthony Wilding won ten Wimbledon tennis titles, and even the country's seldom-fancied cricketers have scored wins over all the major cricket-playing nations.

Despite the variety of these successes ,and the determined and dedicated followings that a plethora of sports enjoy, rugby union continues to dominate the public consciousness, though today not as totally as once was the case. Only in the valleys of Wales is a similar religious fervour encountered. There, rivalry was sparked from the outset when, in their first encounter in 1905, the All Blacks were robbed of victory by an inept referee – a contentious defeat which still rankles whenever the sides clash, but one which has been more than avenged by a lengthy, unbroken string of All Black victories. The passion for rugby is challenged only by a fondness for horse-racing, and government-owned betting shops (TABs) ensure that this is a profitable pastime for the taxpayer as well as for the jockey clubs.

Away from the sports fields, countless numbers of New Zealanders jog endlessly along city streets and country roads, many in training for particular sports, but most simply for the joy of running. In such an atmosphere "new" sports have emerged. The country can lay claim to having originated the sports of girls' marching, wood chopping and competitive sheep-shearing. At this last, New Zealand shearers have swept the boards, while in the country's woolsheds, upwards of 500 sheep have on occasions been shorn in a single day by just one man.

Apart from competitive sports and as befits a people come to escape the gamekeeper and his laird and to deny any property in wild game, there is excellent trout fishing throughout the country, good salmon in some rivers, and wild pigs and goats to shoot. Deer, once plentiful, now prove elusive as their numbers in the ranges have been run down with the boom in deer farming. Big-game fish can be taken from boats off the east coast of Northland and the Bay of Plenty, where several world records have been set. The *Guinness Book of Records* also attributed to a Mayor Island boat the longest individual fight, when a huge broadbill was played for over 32 hours and the boat towed fully 50 kilometres before the line eventually snapped – the "one that got away" that still made the record book!

The many mountains offer superb skiing, especially for those who relish skiing off-piste in the powder snow of the Southern Alps. Helicopters and ski-planes can whisk them to virgin snow for some of the finest skiing to be found anywhere.

KZ 10

CLUB
5-3-77
S/MARLIN
24 KG B/S

Coromandel Peninsula

A BEACH IN MERCURY BAY *North of Whitianga the Coromandel landscape offers something for everyone: shining sand, brilliant sea, steep cliffs and both pasturelands and native bush competing for the hills.*

WHITIANGA'S FISHING BOATS *Trevally, snapper and tarakihi are caught along the coast.*

The Coromandel Peninsula juts like a giant claw from the South Auckland coastline to cleave the Hauraki Gulf from the Pacific Ocean. To the east, the Pacific provides a series of splendid surf beaches, while to the west lie the sheltered waters of the Gulf. Between, the peninsula rises wild, rugged and high – remarkably so for its comparatively narrow width – reflecting starkly its volcanic origins. Extensive bush reserves cover the mountainous ranges forming the peninsula's backbone. Forest tracks are popular with the walker, many studded with relics of early kauri-felling and gold-mining days. Kauri timber, gum and gold drew men to the Coromandel in the last century. Today the peninsula serves a dual farming and recreational role.

It is the beauty of the scenery, with its sandy beachcs and overhanging pohutukawa trees, that attracts holidaymakers every year to Coromandel. Swimming, boating, fishing and waterskiing are popular on both coasts. Areas like Pauanui, virtually uninhabited a few years ago, are now blossoming resorts with a growing holiday population.

EARLY GOLD-MINING MACHINERY *Relics on the Karangahake field, Ohinemuri River.*

SEASIDE SPRINGS Hot water is where your toes find it – on Hot Water Beach. The springs seep through the sand, which can be scooped out at low tide to provide an open-air bath tub.

Coromandel The township is redolent with nostalgia: today's quiet, pretty farming and holiday settlement once seethed with gold miners and echoed to the perpetual thump of gold batteries as the white quartz was pounded to surrender its metal. Not that all the gold has gone, for on Tokatea Hill above the township, and from where there is a stunning view out over the peninsula and the Hauraki Gulf, pockets of gold-flecked quartz may still be seen. Indeed, the problem of extraction disillusioned the get-rich-quick miners, who soon moved on and denied to the field's finder the Government's reward for the country's first "payable" goldfield. The essentially Victorian architecture and public buildings dating from mining days are testimony to the township's sudden birth and comparative lack of renewal. There is good camping, picnicking and safe (if tidal) bathing at nearby Long Beach.

FORMER ASSAY HOUSE *One of several historic sites in the township.*

VICTORIAN PUB *Thames has a number of classic wooden colonial buildings.*

Cooks Beach It was on this hospitable stretch of shoreline in Mercury Bay, across from Whitianga, that Captain Cook observed the transit of Mercury (he had previously observed the transit of Venus in Tahiti). While he was ashore making his observations, a strange group of Maori rowed out to the ship to trade. When one refused to return a piece of cloth, he was shot and killed – an event which troubled Cook "because I thought the punishment a little too severe for the Crime". Six days later he formally displayed "English Colours" and took possession of the North Island.

Coromandel Forest Park The park spreads over nearly 70,000 hectares of the peninsula, affording excellent tramping. Hidden in the hills are a number of dams, originally built to trap water which was released suddenly to sweep kauri logs down towards the coast. Some areas of kauri forest still survive, and in others the forest giant, now protected, is slowly regenerating.

Hahei An attractive, unusually coloured beach with walks to blowholes, pa sites and majestic Cathedral Cave.

Mount Moehau A strenuous seven-hour climb to the highest point on the Moehau Range, near the peninsula's tip, leads to the most spectacular of panoramas.

Ohinemuri River Gold workings between Paeroa and Waihi are attracting increasingly large numbers of visitors.

HAHEI BEACH One of the two once-fortified Maori pa sites at the south-eastern end of Hahei Beach. The beach below is tinted pink by millions of fragments of shell. Walks lead to blow-holes, an awesome spectacle when a heavy sea is running, and to the vast cavern, carved out by the sea and named Cathedral Cave.

Paeroa On the edge of the Hauraki Plain and technically in the Waikato, Paeroa is a household name for the drink made from local mineral water and marketed nationally as "Lemon and Paeroa". Towards Waihi lies a series of old gold-mining areas, and the Ohinemuri River, where there is good fishing.

SHAGS *A very elegant species.*

THE COROMANDEL COASTLINE *A view of the peninsula's softer face, turned towards the gentle shelf of the Hauraki Gulf.*

WHITIANGA FERRY *It runs regularly across the Narrows to Ferry Landing.*

STRIKING GOLD *A steady hand and a little concentration can be rewarded with colours at Karangahake.*

KIWI INGENUITY A local example, suggesting that the New Zealander may be refining, rather than losing, the knack for improvisation. Farming communities throughout the world have traditions of resourcefulness, but in few countries has this been transported so firmly into the towns.

Tairua A recently developed beach resort backed by the Tairua Forest, stretching up into the peninsula's jagged spine.

Thames The town literally mushroomed when amazing finds of gold were made in 1867. Today the peninsula's principal centre, Thames is hard to picture as a prospering and feverish settlement almost twice the size of Auckland and completely landlocked by belligerent tribes. For over a decade its only access was by sea, with ships trading across the Gulf from a depressed Auckland whose fortunes received a much-needed boost from the gold. Much of the metal was embedded in quartz, and in the early 1870s there were almost 700 stamper batteries thumping day and night, their constant hammering providing a continuous background to daily life. The winnings were considerable, one claim in a single year returning almost $2 million. The town quickly assumed a look of substance that has long survived the gold, which had virtually dried up by 1924. Its late Victorian architecture is highly regarded, most noticeably in a number of hotels – the Lady Bowen, Brian Boru and Cornwall Arms. Gold-mining relics abound, including the School of Mines complex (which includes a major mineralogical museum), the Queen of Beauty pump (a massive device, once the largest in the Southern Hemisphere, which provided common drainage to underground workings), a gold battery (still in working order, used by local enthusiasts who continue to work their claims more as a hobby than out of hope) and the local historical museum. The hills behind the town are still, as described in 1868, "pierced with innumerable tunnels that very much resemble an immense rabbit warren".

Thames (taking its name from the nearby river which Captain Cook compared to London's) today has a solid heavy-engineering base which stems directly from the need for heavy equipment to extract the gold, a need which saw Thames, together with neighbouring Waihi, become the first of the country's industrialised towns. Although interest in gold persists, greater numbers do better by fossicking for gemstones on a richly endowed peninsula.

MINER'S HUT *An Ohinemuri curio shop.*

WHANGAMATA BEACH *The beach is highly regarded for its surf, attracting surfboard riders from all over the country.*

WHITE-FRONTED TERNS *The species is common around the New Zealand coast.*

TAIRUA WHARF *A local fishing spot.*

COROMANDEL POTTERY *Local handicrafts, especially pottery made from nearby clay deposits, flourish in a region renowned for its uniquely "alternative" lifestyle.*

AN OLD HOMESTEAD *On the peninsula, perhaps more than elsewhere, an old-fashioned life-style lingers. Many former city-dwellers now live here permanently.*

Waihi Beach Planned for retiring gold miners, Waihi is a major resort with an excellent beach.

Waihi Like Thames, the town was born of gold fever and its present-day activities have an engineering base, but here it is lightweight electronics. On the hill above the town are relics of the Martha Mine, which closed only in 1953: pundits had thought that the town might die with the mine, but farming development and the introduction of television assured survival. Martha, one of the world's richest mines, produced 225 million grams of gold and 1,680 million grams of silver. In one of those twists of fate for which the goldfields were notorious, the discoverers of the lode in 1878 were unable to finance its exploitation and had to abandon their venture, yet in all its 66 years of production, Martha was never to fail to return a profit. The mine is featured in the town's museum, while on Martha Hill lies Martha Lake, formed when the open-cast section of the diggings were abandoned.

Whitianga In an attractive setting which offers safe and easy anchorage, the summer resort looks out on island-flecked Mercury Bay. Kupe is reputed to have called here, and Cook did, describing in detail the magnificent fortified pa that stood on Whitianga Rock, across the Narrows at Ferry Landing. Big-game fishing charters may be arranged.

TAIRUA *A holiday town in a superb setting beside the Pacific Ocean, enhanced by Paku – a twin-coned, pa-sculptured hillside that was once an island.*

Waikato

A STUD FARM NEAR CAMBRIDGE *The Waikato's consistent ability to produce champion racehorses is a source of both wonder and envy.*

The lush, fertile Waikato wears a mantle of wealth unsurpassed elsewhere. Here graze some of the finest dairy herds; here bloodstock with revered names foal the next generation of Pacific horse-racing champions; here the country's longest river provides much of the North Island's electricity as well as some superb freshwater lakes for water-skiing, rowing and trout fishing.

The prospect, however, has changed markedly over the years. If envious settlers succeeded in what some historians would see as a straightforward war of conquest to wrest by force the fertile river flats that Waikato Maoris would not sell, the settlers' success brought hardship with it. Much of the region was swampy and the Government, impoverished by wars, had little capital to finance essential drainage. Only in the 1900s did the countryside assume its soft, tamed countenance, with scarcely a vestige of unworked land.

LEAFY CAMBRIDGE *Exotic rather than native trees give Cambridge a special character.*

THE *RANGIRIRI* The hulk of the hardy gunboat as it lay for decades before being raised to stand in Hamilton's Memorial Park. Built in 1864 for war service on the Waikato, she was a paddle-steamer with a mounted gun and loopholes for riflemen. Her name derives from a battle which took place the previous year near Huntly, in which the Imperial forces were rebuffed.

TEMPLE VIEW *The Mormon temple.*

Cambridge A town of trees with a village green, Cambridge comes close to the Englishness its founders sought. Nearby is Lake Karapiro, venue for the 1978 World Rowing Championships and the farthest downstream of the Waikato hydro lakes.

Hamilton Girt by some of the richest farmland and intersected by the broad, limpid Waikato River, Hamilton has blossomed in recent decades from a modest market town to the country's largest inland city. Its destiny lies with the land, and its role as an agricultural research centre is formidable: the quality of research undertaken here has brought breakthroughs in a variety of fields. The University of Waikato, too, enjoys a high reputation. The city's parks and gardens have considerable charm.

LAKE KARAPIRO *The internationally acclaimed site of several major rowing championships, 12 kilometres from Hamilton.*

TE RAPA MILK POWDER FACTORY *Among the world's most modern factories, the result of farmer co-operation.*

GREENHOOD ORCHID *A wild orchid of the genus* Pterostylis.

Huntly The country's largest coal-mining centre is also the scene of a massive power station. Fired both by coal and natural gas, the station at present under construction will have a generating capacity of 1,000 megawatts.

Matamata For many visitors the wealth of the surrounding area is eclipsed by its relaxing thermal pools.

Mercer A small riverside settlement dwarfed by the giant, belching chimneys of the coal-fired generators of Meremere power station. Close to the station are the earthworks of a pa which saw a major encounter in 1863. The base of Mercer's war memorial, once a gaol, began as a gun turret on a Waikato riverboat.

Morrinsville Centre of an area of prodigious productivity, its present prosperity conceals a lengthy struggle to drain the swamps that defeated many Waikato settlers. Close by is the Rukumoana pa, where for a time the Kingmakers of the Maori King Movement would meet.

Ngaruawahia Ngaruawahia hosts the much venerated marae of the Maori Queen with its elaborately carved buildings. The Waikato tribes sought to unify disparate Maori tribes into a single people in order to resist the advances of land-hungry and well-armed settlers, but a number of key tribes opted instead to side with the Europeans and thus settle old and outstanding scores. The Waikato and Waipapa Rivers merge here, the setting for an annual regatta each March, at which are featured canoe races and hilarious canoe-hurdling.

Raglan The Waikato's beach resort has sheltered, safe waters in its harbour and sand dunes whose iron content renders them both black and blisteringly hot in the summer sun.

Te Aroha Until recently, lead and zinc were won from Te Aroha Mountain, which looms large above the town. Te Aroha, charmingly named "the loved one", was once a fashionable Victorian spa, and its quaint Tourist Gardens seem to belong in the pages of a Victorian scrapbook. The waters (and the hot pools) may still be taken.

Te Awamutu A pleasant farming town which presides over the southern Waikato. In its small but well-presented museum is Uenuku, an ancient wood carving said to have accompanied a migratory canoe to New Zealand some six centuries ago.

Te Kauwhata State-owned vineyards here conduct research to increase further the quality of the country's expanding wine industry.

YEARLING SALE *Hamilton's annual sales see keen competition for some of New Zealand's most promising foals.*

MERCER *Gun turret turned memorial.*

HUNTLY COAL Huntly's coal mines feed the Meremere power station and produce about 90 per cent of the nation's coal – in 1979, nearly 1.1 million tonnes of the 1.2 millions produced nationally. The coal is mined largely by open-cast methods from the drained portions of the bed of Lake Kimihia, but underground mining techniques are also used.

FITZGERALD GLADE *Stands of native bush near Tirau enrich an often exotic landscape.*

The King Country

FROM FOREST TO FARM *The familiar aspect of the region's rolling hill-country farms belies their former status as forest.*

GLOW-WORM *A pinhead light with a tiny thread.*

NATIVE DUCK *Scaup* (below) *and shoveller.*

WAITOMO CAVES The fantasy of limestone formations found in the series of caves at Waitomo provides a unique experience. The walks in the caves, which are cleverly lit to highlight special features, are enhanced by the gloom and enlivened by the occasional and unexpected drip of water on the nape of one's neck. Crowning all is the journey on a subterranean river to view in silence a cathedral-like dome studded with the tiny lights of thousands of glow-worms striving to attract minute insects to their sticky, prey-snaring "fishing lines".

The King Country was baptised by history. It was in the wilds of the region that the Maori King Tawhiao and his Kingite forces sought refuge after their attempts to block enforced European settlement had failed. To the Pakeha it was, for a generation, forbidden territory where the Maori King ruled as an independent monarch and strangers ventured at their peril. When an accommodation with the Government was finally achieved, the land was surveyed and formally granted to the tribes in possession of it. However, folklore persists of "secret understandings" with a succession of governments which preserved a degree of autonomy for several decades.

Since those stirring times much of the region has been opened for settlement, much land has been sold or leased and the Maori villages of Te Kuiti, Otorohanga and Taumarunui have grown into substantial towns. Yet a feeling of isolation persists, contributed to by some of the North Island's wildest country. A heavily dissected terrain is shrouded by virgin forest which conceals the true extent of its forbidding nature. After traversing the region the impression remains of a land disrupted but never mastered by human intrusion.

ISOLATION *The upper reaches of Kawhia Harbour harmonise with inland Waikato. The Kawhia area was the original homeland of the Ngati Toa warrior-chief, Te Rauparaha.*

TAHAROA IRONSANDS *The unusually pure sands are shipped to Japan for steel-making.*

Kawhia The long, languid reaches of an isolated harbour witnessed events that changed the pattern of the country's history. In 1821 Waikato tribes combined to attack Te Rauparaha and drive from the region the chief who was later to dominate much of the country. By the township is a vast and ageless pohutukawa tree to which the revered *Tainui* canoe, from which many tribes claim descent, is said to have been moored some 600 years ago. The canoe itself is said to be buried behind the Anaukiterangi meeting house close by where, according to tradition, stone slabs mark its bow and stern. To the south lie the pure ironsands of Taharoa, vast quantities of which are exported to Japan.

Ohakune Well patronised ski fields on the southern slopes of Mt Ruapehu, about 17 kilometres from the township, have accentuated the winter sports role of what had previously been a timber and market-gardening town spawned by the construction of the main-trunk railway. Après ski and hotel facilities are plentiful, but it is essential to book in advance.

Otorohanga On a bend on the Waipa River, the town is mainly a dairying centre. The Waitomo Caves are nearby.

Taumarunui Sited where the Ongarue River meets the Wanganui, the town serves an extensive farming and timber-producing district. It began as a Maori settlement on the junction of two important canoe routes. In summer, canoe parties leave here to paddle to the sea.

Te Kuiti The town combines farming, mining and milling, but is best known as a point from which to visit Waitomo. The splendid meeting house, built by Te Kooti's followers, was presented to the town in thanks for the sanctuary it afforded him at the end of the Land Wars.

Waitomo These world-famous limestone caves have long excited international admiration. Three caves have been developed for easy access and guided tours run regularly. The area has a vast labyrinth of systems, mostly uncharted, and one can only guess at what further wonders await discovery.

MT MESSENGER *Dense native bush and tree ferns characterise an area of unspoilt beauty.*

NATIVE FLAX *Flowering stems stand tall.*

UMBRELLA FERN *One of six tree-fern species.*

MOKAU RIVER ESTUARY *Limpid blue waters wind their way to the sea, with Egmont faint in the distance.*

The Bay of Plenty

MOUNT MAUNGANUI VIEWED FROM THE MOUNT *Seen from the summit of the volcanic cone is the low sand bar that built up gradually until finally tying the cone to the mainland and the busy port it now houses. The sands of Ocean Beach stretch away into the distance.*

"Tickle the soil with a hoe, and it will laugh a harvest" – if propagandists often oversold the attractions of new lands to would-be migrants, this area is one which has fully met the most extravagant claims. Indeed, its first European visitor, Captain Cook, extolled the region's "plenty" after experiencing apparent "poverty" on the neighbouring East Cape.

Here much of the country's prized kiwifruit and tamarillos are harvested. Here the logs of sprawling forests of *radiata* pine are converted into pulp and paper, or shipped out from Mount Maunganui as logs. Here tens of thousands flock each Christmas-time, to double the population and savour long, sun-drenched beaches and the thrill of big-game fishing. Here, too, many choose a warm and friendly place to which to retire.

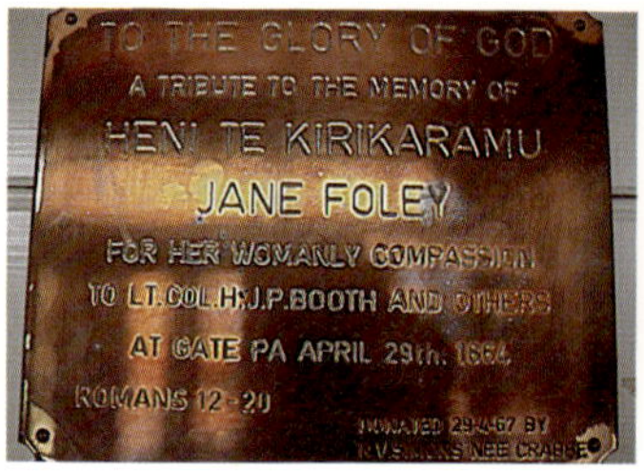

GATE PA *St George's Church at Gate Pa, on the approach to Tauranga, records the events of 29 April 1864 when British troops endeavoured unsuccessfully to dislodge followers of the Maori King from a fortified pa. It had been constructed as a challenge to troops stationed at Tauranga attempting to block communication between Kingite followers on the East Cape with those fighting in the Waikato. Two earlier pa had been built farther away, and the Kingites had even formed a road in from the coast to one of them "so that the soldiers will not be too tired to fight" when the British launched their assault. Twice their chief had written to the British general, informing him of the pa and of the road built for his use, but silence had followed these knightly challenges as the British were waiting for reinforcements. In the meantime the Kingites moved here, building their third pa by a gate in a post-and-rail fence dividing Maori from European-owned land (on the site of today's memorial church). When the attack came, some 1,650 troops were pitted against barely 250 defenders, and were supported in the assault by a variety of heavy artillery, which pounded the pa. The defenders attempted to withdraw, but fire from the rear forced them back into the pa where they inflicted heavy casualties on soldiers bewildered by the maze of fortifications. One third of the storming party fell, including a colonel and most of the officers, for only about 25 Kingite casualties. The chivalry displayed by the Kingites throughout the day was remarkable. After a subsequent clash at Te Ranga, in which the Kingites were soundly defeated, an unusual "Order for the Day" was discovered in which the Kingite warriors were enjoined to exercise the highest level of gallantry.*

INTO THE SURF *The Ocean Beach at Mount Maunganui is a favourite with surfers. In the distance lies Mayor Island, popular as a base for the big-game fishermen who come to the Bay of Plenty each year.*

East Cape Road The stretch of coastline that lies between Opotiki and Gisborne provides some of the finest seascapes in the country. A seemingly endless series of nooks and crannies is spiced with an eventful past which reflects several of the key phases in the country's development, from the coming of the Polynesian to Captain Cook and the whalers who followed him.

It was at Whangaparaoa (the Bay of Whales) that two of the revered ancestral canoes are said to have first landed, the *Tainui* and the *Arawa*. They arrived so close to each other in time and place as to dispute the ownership of a whale beached here. This gives rise to the possibility that the two canoes may have travelled from "Hawaiki" (the Maori's legendary homeland) as a double-hulled canoe, dividing to make a safe landfall. Here, too, the wife of the captain of the *Tainui* is said to have made the first plantings of kumara, the sweet potato whose introduction led to a remarkable change in the Maori way of life. It is regarded as marking the division between the Archaic and the Classic Maori cultures, though it is now considered that the impact of the kumara has been somewhat exaggerated.

Cape Runaway, the eastern extremity of the Bay of Plenty, was named by Captain Cook in 1769 as he journeyed from Poverty Bay after his initial unhappy landing at Gisborne, en route to the Coromandel Peninsula where he was to claim the land for the British Crown. A group of intrepid Maori had put out from the shore to investigate the interloper, but Cook "at this time being very busy" could not afford the time to watch them. Grapeshot was fired towards but not at them, and the warriors, who could never in their lives have experienced anything like it before, prudently paddled furiously away.

Te Kaha, a delightful cove, has the earthworks of a pa which witnessed many

HOLIDAY MAKERS SAVOUR THE SUN *Large numbers of visitors come to enjoy the region's long, hot summers and its welcoming beaches.*

IN MEMORIAM Otemataha Pa Military Cemetery, in Tauranga, holds many of the dead from the engagements at Gate Pa and Te Ranga. Among those buried was Col. H. J. P. Booth, who won the unenviable distinction of being the most senior officer to be killed in the Land Wars. Here, on the headstone of a chief who fell at Te Ranga, a Kingite is portrayed carrying water to British wounded in one of a series of acts of high chivalry witnessed in action at Gate Pa.

THE MONMOUTH REDOUBT *Trenches were dug by British troops in 1864 to guard Tauranga from tribes who were resisting enforced land sales. Several of the redoubt's guns are still here.*

battles in pre-European times, including a sustained seige in 1834. Relics of the bay whalers who operated around the Cape are also to be seen, both at Te Kaha and at Raukokore, where the Catholic Church has a venerable whalebone arch.

Katikati The small rural community in the lee of the rugged Kaimai Ranges enjoys the warmth of both the climate and the hot mineral springs close by. The settlement began in the aftermath of the Land Wars, when the Government was fostering European immigration in the belief that only a strong European population in the North Island could secure the peace. Free passages were offered, with larger grants of land for those who contributed to their own fares. Between 1871 and 1880 more than 100,000 assisted immigrants arrived. Against this background, the Orangeman George Veysey Stewart organised the largest single migration of Irish, 4,000 of whom came to Katikati under the promise of a living easily won from the most fertile of soils. Hitherto, comparatively few Irish had migrated to New Zealand.

Kawerau Situated on level land in the Tarawera River's central valley is one of the country's most industrialised towns, developed as a centre for the processing of forest products. The pulp-and-paper mill site was chosen because of the presence of geothermal steam, which is used in the processes. Tours over the mill are given each afternoon. The town's name, taken from the locality, commemorates a grandson of Toi, the legendary figure who inhabited Whakatane.

Maketu A coastal settlement with two interesting carved meeting houses. Maketu (named for a place in Hawaiki, the Maori's legendary homeland) was where the much revered *Arawa* canoe, from which Rotorua's Arawa people trace their descent, made its final landfall.

Mayor Island Named (with the Alderman Islands to the north-west) by Captain Cook in a moment of frivolity almost wholly lacking in his choice of placenames. The island, resting invitingly some 30 kilometres offshore, is set in waters that teem with such big-game fish as marlin, tuna, kingfish and shark. A number of world records have been set here. The season for the larger fish extends from mid-December to May, but its popularity is such as to make advance booking essential. For those who prefer land to water, tracks lead through delightful bush to pa sites and to the lakes in the twin volcanic craters. Trips can be arranged from Tauranga, Mount Maunganui, Whakatane and Whangamata. There is also good skin-diving to be had around the pohutukawa-fringed coastline.

Mount Maunganui Dominated by the cone of "the Mount", Mount Maunganui was for many years little more than a restful seaside settlement before the maturing of the vast pine forests nearby compelled its development as a deepwater port. The Mount affords a magnificent panorama to those who make the climb ($1\frac{1}{2}$ hrs return). Inevitably, once the site of a huge fortified pa, the Mount was the scene of an epic battle about 200 years ago. At its foot is a naturally heated salt-water swimming pool, while on the famous sweep of Ocean Beach is an intriguing Marineland.

"THE ELMS" *Tauranga grew up around this elegant mission house (1838–47), built by Archdeacon A. N. Brown. The mission was not a success and closed when military settlers took over the district.*

MIDDEN AT THE MOUNT *A pile of shells, the legacy of an ancient feast, at the base of the Mount. Middens such as these assist archaeologists in their study of occupation sites. Fortunately Prehistoric Man was as untidy as his modern counterpart and many "picnic" sites have been identified.*

RIDING THE RAPIDS *Finding adventure on the Wairoa River.*

POHATUROA ROCK *Once a tohunga's cave, now Whakatane's war memorial. The canoe is the* Mataatua.

Ohope A good beach renders Ohope a deservedly popular summer holiday spot. Augmenting the appeal of the open sea are the sheltered waters of Ohiwa Harbour, severed from the ocean by a slim peninsula and affording excellent fishing and water-skiing. Wainui, at the head of the harbour, was where the redoubtable Te Kooti was granted an area of land for himself and his relatives following his pardon in 1883 for his leadership of the last of the armed uprisings against European settlement in the country. No one knows where the old warrior was finally laid to rest, but it is believed to be in this vicinity.

Opotiki The tranquil dairying and fruit-growing town, now the commercial centre of the south-eastern Bay of Plenty, witnessed extraordinary scenes a century ago. Starting as a mission station, European settlement dates from 1865 when a military garrison was established in the aftermath of the gruesome murder of the Rev. Carl Volkner. The nearby 4.4-hectare Hikutaia Domain contains a remarkable range of native flora.

Te Puke A quarter of the country's citrus fruit comes from the "fruit bowl" of which Te Puke is the centre. The town was first settled by Ulstermen, towards the end of the nineteenth century.

Te Ranga Pa A short distance from Tauranga, in Pyes Pa Road, are the remnants of the pa where the British troops exacted a terrible vengeance for their defeat at Gate Pa.

1.

1. *The Kawerau Mill and Mt Edgecumbe. The model town of Kawerau was built in 1953 when a giant pulp-and-paper mill was erected to process neighbouring stands of pine. Here some of the world's fastest newsprint machines produce hundreds of thousands of tonnes of newsprint each year, much for export to Australia and beyond.* 2. *Cut logs are also shipped out through the port at Mount Maunganui.*

2.

A MISSIONARY "MARTYR" The Church of St Stephen the Martyr, Opotiki, records a tragedy unique in New Zealand, for here a missionary, the Rev. Carl Volkner, was martyred in 1865, and his blood served in the chalice in a macabre parody of the Last Supper. Volkner died at the hands of the Hauhau, a movement that saw the Maori as betrayed by the missionaries who had once seemed to support them (Bishop Selwyn had unwisely chosen to serve as chaplain to the British troops). Many Maori had readily embraced Christianity as a religion of peace after inter-tribal wars with newly gained guns had inflicted enormous casualties. Now seemingly denied by the God they had worshipped, the Hauhau developed a creed which equated the Maori with the Israelites in Egypt and in less sanguinary ceremonies intoned chants to induce the Pakeha to leave the country. Volkner's headstone is in the east wall.

Whakatane Characterising the town is the sheer rock of Pohaturoa, which rises oddly from its commercial heart. In tradition, the rock provided a tohunga with a cave. In its shadow, local chiefs signed the Treaty of Waitangi. The town is the centre of a rich dairying and fat-lamb producing region, rich also in timber from the nearby expanses of the Kaingaroa Forest. Inland lies the native bush of the Urewera National Park (*q.v.*), reached only on foot from this aspect. By the rock is a model of the fabled *Mataatua* canoe, to whose crew local tribes trace their ancestry. The canoe's arrival gave the locality its name (literally, to act as a man). A woman, Wairaka, prevented the newly arrived canoe from drifting out to sea by seizing a paddle and, with a cry of "Kia whakatane au i ahau!", averted a tragedy. Her statue stands on a rock at Whakatane Heads.

White Island Some 50 kilometres offshore from Whakatane billows the country's only marine volcano, whose links with the activity in the Rotorua and Taupo areas can be seen from the air on a clear day. The island has occasionally been mined for sulphur. Twelve people are known to have died as the result of its unpredictable activity and today it is given over to birds and derelict mining buildings.

WAIOEKA SCENIC HIGHWAY *The landscape on the direct route between Gisborne and Opotiki, dramatic though it is, is surpassed by that of the slower East Cape road, especially at Christmas, when flowering pohutukawa spike the seascapes. The two routes make a most satisfying round trip.*

CARAVANS AND CANVAS *Summer at the Mount Maunganui motor camp.*

Tauranga The city of Tauranga spreads pleasantly round the southernmost tip of a large natural harbour, facing across the water to Mount Maunganui and the Pacific Ocean. "The Mount" boasts a magnificent deep-water harbour, thanks to extensive dredging, and commercial life divides between the two centres. Surrounding the city are prolific orcharding areas, thick with the lush growth of subtropical fruits which reflect the warmth of the climate and the mildness of the winters. The burgeoning of both the city and the port is comparatively recent, dating from the post-war maturing of vast pine forests and the development of both a pulp-and-paper industry and an export trade in sawn logs. Even more recent has been the completion of the Kaimai Tunnel, which now diverts to Mount Maunganui produce from the Waikato that would otherwise have passed through Auckland, and has confirmed Tauranga's shipping role as the country's largest.

Within the city's limits are picturesque reminders of its beginnings. A pretty but substantial mission house marks the spot where European settlement began with the labours of a single diligent missionary; ominous earthworks remain from the redoubt built by the British troops who followed to displace the gospel with the gun; nearby, the dead from Gate Pa and Te Ranga lie in the tiny Otemataha Pa Military Cemetery, slaughtered in battle and buried by the grief-stricken cleric. In no other New Zealand city are the origins of settlement as well preserved, perhaps because growth came late and only after public attitudes to relics of the past had changed from indifference to dedication.

Within easy reach of Tauranga are numerous sheltered harbour bays and the ocean beach of Mount Maunganui (accessible by ferry as well as road); an Historic Village which reconstructs an early settlement (*in the city, 17th Avenue off Cameron Road*); the Kaiate Falls (*Waitoa Road*) and the Omanawa Falls (*23 km: Omanawa Road*), and the bush of the Whakamarama Scenic Reserve (*22.5 km*).

Maori arts and crafts

Over centuries of isolation, a vigorous and highly distinctive style of art was evolved by the New Zealand Maori.

The complex geometric patterns of woven work – traditionally undertaken by women – contrast with the sweeping curvilinear forms of carving, the work of men. While the women plaited mats and baskets from flax, or wove cloaks decorated with feathers or dogskin and brightly coloured, geometric *taniko* borders, the men carved. They carved anything that was carvable – even themselves, etching into their flesh the deep blue-black tattoo lines of the *moko*.

But it was in woodcarving that Maori art reached its most fantastic accomplishments. The Maori constructed houses, fortifications and war canoes, and wrought weapons, ornaments, utensils and musical instruments. They decorated them with a profusion of figures and designs. On treasure boxes, house carvings and canoes, stylised figures with protruding tongues and glaring eyes of iridescent paua shell writhe between *manaia*, birdlike monsters whose forms are entangled with interlocking spirals of almost filigree delicacy. By contrast, the inside walls of tribal meeting houses are lined with ancestor figures which are carved with massive boldness and solidity to support the roof rafters painted in rhythmic, colourful patterns called *kowhaiwhai*.

Greenstone ornaments were necessarily less intricate. Working only with water, sandstone and sometimes generations of patience, the Maori produced weapons and ornaments such as the well-known *hei-tiki* from translucent nephrite and bowenite. Their clean, simple lines belie the care of their manufacture and the value attached to them.

New Zealand's museums are well stocked with examples of Maori art, but they are not echoes of a dead culture. Only a few elderly women still bear the *moko*, but the other arts and crafts of the Maori are thriving. At the Maori Arts and Crafts Institute, Whakarewarewa (see p. 75), one can watch artists at work and apprentices in training, and purchase examples of their skill. The government sponsors other training programmes, while many individual exponents of carving and weaving continue to work and teach in the traditional manner. New carvings are made not only for marae and meeting houses, but also for universities, government buildings and churches. Flax baskets are a common sight, though today they are likely to carry groceries or school books.

Unique in itself, Maori art highlights New Zealand's uniqueness in the world. It is no coincidence that the huge jets of the national airline, as far removed from classical Maori technology as stone tools are from our own, carry as their logo the traditional symbol of the *koru*.

MAORI CENTENNIAL MEMORIAL MEETING HOUSE, WAITANGI (1940) *This uniquely carved* whare runanga *contains superb examples of carving from throughout the North Island.*

The East Cape and Gisborne

TE ARAROA BEACH *Exhilarating, deserted sweeps of golden sand are a feature of the Cape. In such a setting it is hard to conjure images of the past, when wool was ferried out to ships in surfboats, and sheep, cattle and horses brought in. Timber was simply thrown overboard to be swept ashore by the tide.*

The East Cape's attractions are more real than simply "the world's most easterly hotel" and a mountain, Hikurangi, whose summit first sees a new day's sun. For the Cape was a beginning. Tradition holds that several of the migratory canoes from Hawaiki first touched here, and it was at Gisborne that members of Captain Cook's expedition became the first Europeans to land in New Zealand.

The atmosphere of origins still lingers. Inland, the brooding primeval forest of the Ureweras; venerable, venerated carved meeting houses, and land still suffering from misuse by early European leaseholders (much still Maori-owned), contribute to an overall sense of remoteness. Yet for many this is merely background to a sun-drenched cape studded with inviting beaches, for which the Maori "Christmas tree", the flame-flowered pohutukawa whose gnarled roots seem impervious to salt water, are a common backdrop.

Anaura Bay A classic, lonely beach, this was where Cook made a second landing in search of supplies after his bloody encounter at Gisborne.

Gisborne Fertile market gardens set in verdant valleys surround the city and today mock Cook's name for the area, Poverty Bay. Despite its remoteness, events here changed the course of history: Cook's first landing-place was Kaiti Beach, and it was a local Maori, Te Kooti, who led a brilliant campaign of Maori resistance in the Land Wars with the settlers. Both are remembered in a variety of ways. The beaches here, and some of the country's warmest weather, assure an annual invasion of summertime sunseekers. The museum and art gallery,

TE ARAROA'S CHRISTMAS TREE *New Zealand's most massive pohutukawa.*

YOUNG NICK *Cook promised the immortality of a place-name and, more importantly, a sizeable quantity of rum to the crew member who first sighted land. Twelve-year-old surgeon's boy, Nicholas Young, won the immortality, but we may assume that his mates shared in the balance of his good fortune. His statue stands in Gisborne's Churchill Park.*

Kaiti Hill lookout and Poho-o-rawiri meeting house deserve a visit.

Hicks Bay Points of interest include a splendid carved meeting house, picturesque Horseshoe Bay, good sea fishing, a bush walk to glow-worms, and a derelict freezing works – one of several that closed when roads came to the Cape. It is a popular camping place.

Manutuke A finely carved meeting house incorporates two major Maori legends – the tearing apart of the Sky Father from the Earth Mother, and the fishing up by Maui of the North Island from the sea.

Matawhero The Presbyterian Church, the oldest in Poverty Bay, dates from 1862, and was the only building in the area to be spared by Te Kooti in his campaign against the local settlers.

Patutahi Close by is Rongopai meeting house, built for Te Kooti and decorated with exuberant wall paintings.

Ruatoria Principal centre of the Ngati Porou, where on occasions important tribal ceremonies take place at the Mangahanea marae. Mt Hikurangi (1,839 m) stands due west and is reputed to be the first point on earth to be touched by the new day's sun.

Te Araroa On the foreshore, near "the world's most easterly hotel", stands a massive and venerable pohutukawa (*pictured*). From here a road leads to the lighthouse on the tip of East Cape.

Te Puia The small settlement of Te Puia, with its trees and tiny lake, is a welcome contrast to the rather barren countryside. There is evidence of thermal activity, with a warm, open mineral pool and hot mineral baths at the motel.

Tikitiki The elaborate interior of St Mary's Maori Church (*pictured*) contrasts sharply with its simple exterior.

Tokomaru Bay The locality reflects the vital role that shipping once enjoyed around the Cape, then its only lifeline to the outside world.

CAPTAIN JAMES COOK Dour Yorkshireman and navigator extraordinary, Captain James Cook (1728–79) sailed under secret sealed instructions to seek the land Tasman had seen in 1642. Cook first made landfall on 9 October 1769, but, as with Tasman before him, the local tribe felt threatened and, after bloodshed on Gisborne's Kaiti Beach, a sorrowing Cook departed, naming the area "Poverty Bay", for it afforded him nothing he wanted. Sailing north, he first landed at Anaura Bay and was then directed to Cooks Cove, near Tolaga Bay, where he replenished his supplies and marvelled at the natural archway.

A MAORI MEMORIAL *St Mary's Church, Tikitiki, was built as a memorial to Ngati Porou servicemen killed in the 1914–1918 war, two of whom are depicted in the east window.*

MORERE HOT SPRINGS Nestled enticingly in a bush reserve studded with groves of statuesque nikau are the inviting Morere hot thermal springs, their waters tinged with iodine and lent added curative properties by calcium and sodium chloride. The springs are isolated, being well east of the volcanic belt. Morere, whose name means "a swing" or "a giant's stride", is an ideal stopping place for a picnic and a swim.

Tolaga Bay A sheep-farming centre by the Uawa river mouth, the settlement has a good beach and is close by Cooks Cove, where a relieved Cook found an hospitable welcome.

Waioeka scenic highway Attractive though this slick, direct route between Gisborne and Opotiki may be, the traveller with time to spare should opt for the longer, more leisurely coastal road.

Waihau (Loisels) Beach A typical crescent of golden sand.

Waipiro Bay Once the largest settlement on the East Cape, the township all but died with the demise of coastal shipping and the bypassing of the main road.

Whangaparaoa Famed in tradition, it was here that the *Arawa* and the *Tainui*, two of the fabled canoes of the so-called "Great Migration", landed – so close in time as to argue over ownership of a stranded whale. Folklore also has it that this area saw the introduction of the kumara, which was eventually to transform the Maori economy from that of roving hunter-gatherer to settled agriculturalist.

EAST CAPE LIGHTHOUSE *The light marks the mainland's most easterly point, perceptively identified as such by Cook though he had scarcely begun to circumnavigate the island. East Island, just offshore, was originally home to the light but proved too inhospitable, four men drowning whilst landing supplies.*

Hawke's Bay

"THE SPIRIT OF NAPIER" *A landmark on Napier's Marine Parade.*

THE GREEN GRASS OF THE BAY *Hawke's Bay's pastures, here pictured in the flush of growth, can in the height of summer be bleached grey-white by weeks of unremitting sunshine.*

BLOODSTAINED PATU *A gruesome whalebone museum exhibit from the 1860s.*

"TOILERS OF THE SEA" *Alan Strathern's sculpture at Napier's aquarium.*

TOWERING PALMS *Napier's Kennedy Road imparts an unusually tropical air.*

NAPIER'S AQUARIUM *A multitude of smaller fish to offset the more dynamic display at nearby Marineland.*

WOOL FOR WEAVING *Lambs are reared especially to provide weavers and spinners with a variety of wools.*

A broad sweep of coastline embraces some of the country's finest areas for sheep rearing, orcharding and market gardening as well as the world's only known mainland colony of gannets.

The region pivots on the twin cities of Napier and Hastings, of nearly identical population but radically different in topography and purpose. Napier spills down a sheer bluff to her port and a tree-lined Marine Parade crammed with every form of entertainment. Hastings, as level as a city can be, is ringed with orchards and houses huge food-processing factories, but has less obvious claims for the visitor's attention. For a time Hastings seemed destined to dominate her sister, but the massive earthquake which in 1931 all but destroyed both centres, was creative as well as destructive – large areas of land beside Napier were raised from below sea level to provide it with critically needed space for growth. Despite some intensely fertile alluvial coastal areas, the coastline is in the main both rocky and precipitous. Inland the hills build into rugged ranges which produce a "rain shadow" effect, giving Hawke's Bay both a low rainfall and high sunshine.

FOOD PROCESSING *Hastings produces much of the country's canned and frozen food. Plantings are staggered so that in the harvest season both the food-processing factories and the gangs in the fields can work round the clock to pick the crop at its peak. There is a high demand for seasonal labour.*

Dannevirke and Norsewood Both towns were originally settled by Scandinavians who came to cut a road through the dense forests that once cloaked southern Hawke's Bay. Dannevirke has blossomed into a bustling farming centre, while Norsewood maintains a quieter pace, its origins reflected in a nostalgic museum.

Hastings The city lies long and low on the lengthy Heretaunga Plains, a flatness broken only by the hills of nearby Havelock North, its most desirable "suburb". The plains produce vast quantities of fruit and vegetables to feed the city's huge food-processing factories for canning and quick-freezing. Especially rich and intensively farmed are areas around the Ngaruroro, Tutaekuri and Tukituki Rivers. Highland Games each Easter draw visitors from far and wide, although its high temperatures and relative proximity to East Coast beaches make Hastings a popular summer resort as well. Fantasyland excites children the year round.

HAWKE BAY *The bay itself, with the hump of Napier's Bluff Hill in the distance.*

PANIA OF THE REEF *Napier's love-forlorn maiden.*

CAPE KIDNAPPERS Looking towards Cape Kidnappers (*above*), and two of the thousands of gannets which congregate there from about July to April each year (*below*). The Cape, best visited on foot from Clifton (eight kilometres return), was named by Captain Cook in 1769 after local Maoris attempted to make off with a Polynesian servant boy. The *Endeavour*'s cannons fired, confusion reigned, and the boy dived from his kidnappers' canoe and swam back to the ship. In the excitement, no one seemed to notice the world's only known mainland gannetry.

SHOW JUMPING *Equestrian sports, including polo, have a strong following in the Hawke's Bay district.*

Napier Curious Bluff Hill, originally an island but now tied to the land by a sand bar, gives Napier an unusual identity, accentuated by a Marine Parade which deliberately and unselfconsciously claims the role of a seaside holiday centre. There among lines of Norfolk pines await a remarkable Marineland, an excellent aquarium, a kiwi display house and a wide variety of games and amusements. So, too, does the statue of Pania, a mermaid who in legend came ashore and fell in love with a local warrior but who, when she swam back to see her people, was dragged down to an underwater reef where she may still be seen, her hair flowing like seaweed from the rock.

The city is not only the region's port but is also the country's largest wool centre, with millions of dollars of wool changing hands – mostly to foreign buyers – at regular auctions. In 1931 the city was flattened in the greatest natural disaster the country has known. The trail of destruction stretched the length of Hawke's Bay: huge sections of coastline slumped into the sea, rivers changed course, bridges buckled and vast cracks opened all over the countryside. The city was left in ruins. In all, some 256 were killed; the material loss was incalculable.

Lake Tutira The pretty bird sanctuary recalls the author-naturalist who described breaking in the land here as "a compromise between murdering the sheep and 'making' the country".

"SCANDY" WHEELS *One of several exhibits in Norsewood's museum which recall the area's links with its Scandinavian pioneers.*

Waipawa and Waipukurau Significant farming centres in central Hawke's Bay. Above Waipukurau's main street are the remains of the pa beside which the town grew up.

Wairoa Northern Hawke's Bay's only substantial centre, Wairoa is set in dairying and sheep- and cattle-raising country. Nearby is the beautiful Mahia Peninsula which marks the region's northern boundary.

NAPIER'S MARINELAND Here, dolphins, seals and other mammals delight with breathtaking displays of speed, intelligence and ingenuity.

1.

WINE

3.

2.

The New Zealand wine industry, after suffering from decades of official neglect and little public demand, has blossomed in recent years. After the budget in 1958 slashed wine imports, the country's winemakers expanded their vineyards and increased their plantings of classic varieties. Since then, too, the public palate has been sharpened. Consumption has also been boosted by New Zealanders' propensity to travel to Europe (where a taste for wine is an almost obligatory requirement), as well as by the success of local wines (particularly whites) in international wine fairs. As a result, New Zealanders are now drinking more wine per head than ever before, with local wines claiming most of the market. The major commercial vineyards are to be found in Hawke's Bay and around Henderson (near Auckland) and Blenheim.

The origins of New Zealand's wine industry are obscure. The grape was introduced by the first missionary, Samuel Marsden, in 1819, and the British Resident at Waitangi was producing wine in the 1830s. The first act on the part of the French settlers at Akaroa, too, was to establish small vineyards. However, the oldest winery in the country, dating from 1865, is in Hawke's Bay, at Greenmeadows, where a Catholic Mission still produces sacramental wine but has broadened as well into the secular market. All the wineries welcome visitors, both to taste and to buy, and some arrange conducted tours of their establishments. Among those worth visiting in Hawke's Bay are the Mission, Vidals, Glenvale and Te Mata estates.

4.

5.

ASPECTS OF THE REGION'S WINE INDUSTRY *Grapes being harvested in Havelock North vineyards* (1 & 2)*; wine ageing in oak casks* (3)*; grapes ripening in the Mission Vineyard at Greenmeadows* (4)*; the monastery at Greenmeadows which began winemaking to supply the needs of those performing Mass* (5).

BLUE PENGUINS *Common around the Hawke's Bay coast, the penguin is evenly feathered, with wings reduced to flippers.*

MAIN STREET LIGHT *Wairoa's lighthouse, moved to its present site near the river from an offshore island, is lit each evening.*

Urewera National Park

A GRAND WILDERNESS *The Urewera National Park offers the most spectacular and remote tramping in the North Island.*

TE WHAI-A-TE-MOTU(1870–88) *The meeting house of Mataatua, near Ruatahuna.*

CASCADING WATER *The park boasts many small but spectacular falls.*

The vast brooding forest of the Urewera evokes powerful imagery. Here in mythology a taniwha gouged the lake from the ranges in a frantic attempt to reach the sea; here since antiquity have lived the Tuhoe, the "children of the mist"; here more recently the colonial government stalked Te Kooti in the closing stages of the Land Wars. Despite the coming of the road, one can still feel in this majestic setting the apartness that at the turn of the century saw local Tuhoe deny the Governor entry and permit the Premier to visit their revered meeting house at Mataatua only after he had surrendered his knife, pipe and tobacco.

The national park, with headquarters at Aniwaniwa, centres on the 55 square kilometres of Lake Waikaremoana, a lake whose fabled fishing is rivalled by the tramping and hunting to be had in the surrounding forest.

THE CATCH *Lake Waikaremoana yields one of its plentiful rainbow trout.*

1.

2.

3.

IMAGES OF UREWERA 1. *Camping area, Mokau* 2. *Old timber wagon* 3. Dracophyllum, *a distinctive bush feature.*

WAIKAREITI *Surrounded by primeval bush and reached only by walking track, the lake contains six small islands. One, Rahui, contains its own lakelet. Inaccessibility renders the area a botanists' paradise.*

Surrounding Lake Waikaremoana is a belt of northern rata, rimu and tawa forest, with some miro, hinau and tawhero. Above the level of the lake, red and silver beech gradually assume dominance until at about 1,200 metres the red beech disappears and stands of pure silver beech continue to the timberline. Kiwi, kaka and most other native birds are found throughout.

The ancient Maori had little impact on the environment here; tracks and small eel weirs caused little disturbance. They were also careful to avoid polluting water.

With the Pakeha came problems at Waikaremoana and a decision to end hotel accommodation at Lake House, thus moving habitation away from the lake to reduce enrichment of its waters. Today, however, an excellent camping ground, with cabins and first-class chalet accommodation, allows visitors the luxury of an extended stay at Waikaremoana – "sea of rippling waters".

RUA KENANA (1867–1935) He set up a community at Maungapohatu and to his followers he was a prophet. To others, including the government, he was a subversive and a charlatan. Colourful, enigmatic, he is still revered by some, despite prosecution and jail.

"CHILD OF THE MIST" *A Tuhoe youngster.*

TRAMPERS *One of the gentler walks.*

KAKABEAK *Distinctive bush blossoms.*

Thermal activity

Hot springs are found in many parts of the world, generally in regions of faulted and folded rocks and particularly in areas of recent or continuing volcanic activity. Just occasionally, hot springs contain boiling water, either from cold water which has struck hot rocks or from water which has been trapped temporarily under thick mud.

Geysers form near rivers or lakes, where water seeps down deep channels far into the earth. When it strikes hot rock, steam begins to form, forcing progressively more water up and out of the column, and creating more and more steam. The column gradually becomes lighter and suddenly, as the last of the water is forced upwards, a steam explosion occurs, spouting water high into the air. Where more hot water can then flow into the column, eruptions can continue for some time, as with Whakarewarewa's Pohutu geyser. After an eruption the water settles, the channel gradually fills once more and the process is repeated. The channel itself is generally broken into sharp bends, which effectively prevent convection and so stop the water from mixing to a uniform temperature. Where convection can occur, instead of the water becoming superheated and exploding, thermal pools are formed. The boiling waters also contain dissolved minerals, which slowly build into curious and often colourful silica formations as water evaporates on the surface. No one can predict when a particular geyser will erupt: some do several times an hour; some not for days, or even weeks. They are, however, most active when barometric pressures are low, as this reduces the downward pressure of the column and can precipitate activity.

There are only three noted groups of geysers in the world – in New Zealand, at Rotorua; in Iceland ("the land of frost and fire") and in the United States' Yellowstone Park.

New Zealand's active volcanoes are confined to the Taupo Volcanic Belt, a chain which reaches from the peaks of the Tongariro National Park to where White Island belches steam into the Bay of Plenty sky. Similarly, the largest and hottest of the country's thermal springs are found in this zone. Activity is seen at its most spectacular in a number of valleys near Rotorua and Taupo, and is tapped for the generation of electricity at Wairakei.

To win steam for power generation, bores are sunk and cased with tubes. The escaping steam is then "dried" and led to low-pressure turbines. Water taken from the Waikato River is used to condense the steam as it leaves the turbines, causing it to contract and create a vacuum. This helps double the turbines' output from what it would have been had the steam simply been released into the atmosphere. So far drilling here has only begun to tap the area's potential, and there are plans to increace greatly the amount of electricity generated in this way.

The thermal region

LORD OF THE GEYSERS *Whakarewarewa's massive Pohutu regularly plays to heights in excess of 30 metres.*

TUDOR TOWERS *Rotorua's old bath house.*

BELLBIRD *A honey-eater best heard at dawn.*

For over a century Rotorua has held irresistible fascination, with geysers, boiling mud, furious fumeroles and warm mineral bathing pools as well as myriad lakes, well-rewarded trout fishing and a substratum of Maori culture. This last is commercialised as nowhere else, assuring a wide range of Maori arts and crafts and rousing Maori concerts.

The city skirts the southern shore of Lake Rotorua, serving both as the region's principal commercial centre and the North Island's premier tourist resort. Much of the surrounding land is given over to extensive forestry and sheep farming, introduced to resettle servicemen returning from the 1939–45 war. Despite these substantial preoccupations, for the visitor the lingering impressions are of warm earth, of steam percolating through the most unlikely crevices – from under gravestones and out of street drains – and of an ever-present, pungent odour of hydrogen sulphide.

In mythology, thermal activity came in answer to the prayers of a chief as he lay freezing on a mountaintop; in legend, this was the setting for the romance between Hinemoa and Tutanekai; and in history it was here that Hongi Hika brought his canoes to attack Mokoia Island.

TARAWERA LAKE AND MOUNTAIN *A phantom canoe seen on the lake in 1886 was regarded as a premonition of the mountain's eruption only eleven days later.*

"THE WHITE TERRACES, ROTOMAHANA" *A painting by Charles Blomfield before the 1886 eruption.* Auckland City Art Gallery

RAINBOW SPRINGS Unique trout springs offer bush walks and the opportunity to feed brown and rainbow trout.

COLONIAL VILLAGE *A place to browse.*

VINTAGE "INDIAN" *A lovingly maintained motorcycle ready to rally.*

1.

2.

3.

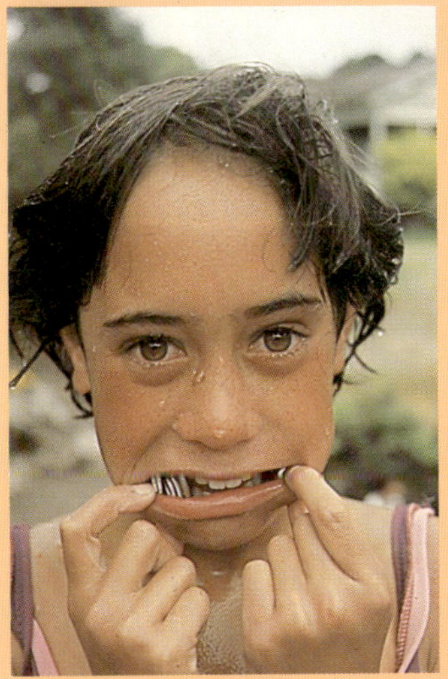

MONEY FOR JAM *A young "pennydiver" at Whakarewarewa.*

A sample of the scenes that await at Whakarewarewa, on the outskirts of Rotorua. 1. *Apprentice carvers at work at the Maori Arts and Craft Institute, where master carvers pass on their ever more appreciated skills to the next generation. Straight-grained kauri and totara are favoured woods. Traditionally carving was amongst the most venerated of callings: women were not permitted even to be present, and waste chips were carefully collected to prevent them being used in cooking fires.* 2. *Bizarre pools of boiling mud.* 3. *A concert party performs an action song. Maori "traditional dress" is less revealing than in pre-missionary times, when men often went naked and women, when not wearing a cloak, covered only their waists.* 4. *A carved gatepost at the entrance of the Model Village, depicting the lovers Hinemoa and Tutanekai.* 5. *A flax weaver at the Institute introduces visitors to her craft. Flax was put to a wide variety of uses, providing fibre for making garments, mats, fishing lines and ropes. Green leaves were used to weave baskets, eel-pots and nets. The fibre is obtained by soaking the leaves in water and then scraping off the unwanted tissue.* 6. *Cooking in thermal steam. The Maori's main way of cooking was by steaming food in earth ovens. A hole was dug and lined with red-hot stones. These were covered with green vegetation, the food was placed on top and the whole oven splashed with water and sealed with more vegetation and earth. Here at Whakarewarewa natural steam made cooking much simpler!*

4.

5.

6.

WHAKAREWAREWA *A general view of the eerie scene which draws visitors from all parts of the world.*

A BROODING, AWESOME VALLEY *Waimangu lacks Whaka's fury but more than compensates in atmosphere.*

NEAR WAIOTAPU *There are many hot streams in the region, where locals go to bathe.*

Blue and Green Lakes In favourable light there is an astonishing difference in the appearance of the two lakes, despite their being the closest of neighbours. Although well able to be appreciated from the roadside, the lakes are perhaps best seen from the track that runs along the shoulder that separates them. The lakes lie by the road to Te Wairoa Buried Village and Lake Tarawera.

Lake Okataina Of the many lakes in the region, Okataina is arguably the most enchanting, completely encircled by native bush and with a magical approach along a road canopied by native fuchsia. Sandy beaches, bush walks and good trout fishing in an unspoilt setting await the visitor, with launch trips, boats and fishing gear available from the lodge.

Lake Rotoiti Although there is a sprinkling of carved Maori meeting houses along its southern shoreline, activity on this elegant lake concentrates at Okere Falls township, where Lake Rotorua drains into Rotoiti by way of an impressive waterfall. Its name, "little lake", refers to its larger neighbour, Rotorua, whose name in turn may be translated as "second lake". Roto itself means "lake".

Lake Rotorua The principal of the "hot lakes" group (so called for their surroundings rather than their temperatures), Lake Rotorua is roughly circular in shape, with alluring Mokoia Island almost in its centre. The city of Rotorua spreads along its southern perimeter. The lake has long been highly regarded by trout fishermen, and a number of trout springs around its edges display free-run trout of gargantuan proportions. In recent times the run-off of fertilisers from farmland that ultimately drains into the lake has brought a prolific growth of weed. This at one time threatened to "kill" the lake and its containment has taxed local and national ingenuity. Boats are for hire, and scenic trips run both on the lake (by boat) and over it (by float plane), all from the wharf on The Parade in Rotorua.

Mokoia Island Lake Rotorua's solitary island beckons with an almost irresistible call. Certainly so it proved to the maiden Hinemoa, whose home was near Rotorua at Hinemoa Point and who fell in love with Tutanekai, a warrior who lived on Mokoia. Hinemoa's family would not agree to the match, but eventually she swam to her lover through the night, guided by the sound of his plaintive flute.

TE WAIROA BURIED VILLAGE *Inundated in an eruption, it is still being uncovered.*

RONGO *A kumara god on Mokoia Island, placed with crops to assure a good harvest.*

KAINGAROA *Deep in the vast pine forest planted on the once-barren pumicelands.*

Ohinemutu A Maori village of considerable character by the lake and within Rotorua's city limits, Ohinemutu was the Maori settlement from which today's city was born. Uniquely it survives, with its splendid meeting house (some of whose carvings are reputed to be almost 200 years old), its quaint Tudor-styled church and, between the two, an odd ceramic bust of Queen Victoria. This was presented to the local Arawa tribe by her son, the Prince of Wales, in gratitude for the support given by the tribe to the colonial government during the Land Wars.

SWAN AND CYGNETS *A typical lake scene.*

In fact, the support sprang simply and purely from traditional hostility felt towards some of the tribes committed to the wars, and siding with the government afforded the Arawa an excellent opportunity to settle some old scores.

Rotorua The city had its beginnings beside the Maori village of Ohinemutu at the end of the Land Wars, as tourists came to marvel at the thermal activity in the area. Soon, with the building of the grandiose Tudoresque bath house in the Government Gardens, the infant settlement took on the character of a spa town. For generations it remained very much a tourist town, until the 1960s saw it develop as the country's fastest-growing centre – in 1950 there were about 120 manufacturing and trade factories within eight kilometres of the city centre; 20 years later there were over 1,000. Today the massive earnings from tourism are icing on a more substantial industrial cake, and industry is taking a greater interest than hitherto in the potential afforded by thermal water, putting it to use in timber kilns, market-garden hothouses, mushroom farms and plant nurseries. For the visitor, a plethora of sights claim attention and too many allow too short a time in which to tackle them.

Te Wairoa Buried Village Foretold by the appearance of a phantom canoe on the waters of Lake Tarawera, a colossal eruption of Mt Tarawera in 1886 (heard as far away as Christchurch) split the mountain in two and overwhelmed the village used by visitors to the fabled Pink and White Terraces nearby. These silica terraces drew admirers from all parts of the world, but they fell victim to the holocaust, as did the tohunga who warned of the impending tragedy. The village ruins have been excavated in part, and are open to the public.

LAKE OKAREKA *One of the smallest of the lakes in the "hot lakes" district.*

Thermal areas Each of the various thermal areas has a character uniquely its own: "Whaka", with its geysers and its Maori village; Tikitere, whose fury is unsurpassed; Waimangu, sullen and brooding and with the crater of what was the world's largest geyser; Waiotapu, with its colours and its curious Lady Knox Geyser, first brought to life by prisoners washing clothes with soap in a hot pool; Orakei Korako, with huge silica terraces hinting of what the volcano destroyed.

HONGI'S TRACK *Cutting a swathe through the bush on the Whakatane highway, the road follows a track used by Hongi Hika in 1823 as he brought men and canoes from Northland with which to lay siege to the Arawa tribe's stronghold on Mokoia Island.*

KIWI AT RAINBOW SPRINGS *The timid and nocturnal kiwi is very rarely seen in the wild.*

Taupo

POWERFUL STEAM *Experience in power generation at Wairakei renders local engineers world leaders in geothermal technology.*

1.

2.

3.

4.

FABULOUS FISHING *The rivers and streams that feed Lake Taupo offer unsurpassed trout fishing.*

The vast waters of Lake Taupo extend over 650 square kilometres in the very heart of the North Island. Taupo township faces south, down the length of the lake to the distant, mauve tableau formed by the smoke and the snow of the peaks of Tongariro National Park. The lake bed, the depth of which remains unknown, was until comparatively recently the scene of frenzied activity: pumice flung in eruptions from its basin only 2,000 years ago deluged much of the central North Island and reached as far as Gisborne. Today the lake assumes a quiescent air, ruffled only by fishermen, boat owners and the occasional squall that necessitates constant vigilance on the water. The surrounding landscape is plainly mantled with pumice as witness to the past.

Thermal activity is much in evidence: at Wairakei, where steam feeds electric turbine generators and wafts high and wide across the countryside; at Tokaanu, and at Taupo itself, where there are public thermal baths and a number of fortunate private dwellings with their own hot pools.

1. *Celmisia, the mountain daisy, is after grass the most common plant on the New Zealand mountainside.* 2. *New-born lambs herald the arrival of spring. Until recently much of the area's potential pastureland would not, in the absence of cobalt, carry stock.* 3. *Tutu* (Coriaria), *one of the few poisonous species of native plant.* 4. *Trolling on Lake Taupo: the purist will always prefer casting a fly.*

"THE PICKET FENCE" *Patient anglers line the mouth of the Waitahanui River.*

SCOURGE OF THE FISHERMAN *Energetic holidaymakers prepare to water-ski on the lake.*

FORESTRY *Above*: Vast areas of pine forest are a feature of the countryside to the north, and huge timber trucks are commonplace. *Below*: The gigantic Kinleith pulp-and-paper mill rises from the farmland.

Kaingaroa State Forest What is reputed to be the world's largest man-made forest owes its existence to a depression (which gave rise to cheap labour) and the discovery of a cobalt deficiency in the pumicelands (which had rendered the plain "unavailable" for farming). Sprawling over some 150,000 hectares, it supplies vast quantities of logs to feed pulp-and-paper mills. Sawn logs are also shipped to Japan from Mount Maunganui.

Murupara The town developed after the 1939–45 war to capitalise on the maturing radiata pine of the Kaingaroa State Forest. The timber town rails logs to Kawerau's mill. There are some obscure Maori cave drawings in the forest nearby.

Opepe The site of a long-abandoned Maori village, this spot on the Napier Road about 17 kilometres from Taupo was where, in 1869, a detachment of troopers was ambushed. Five escaped, but the graves of the nine who died may be seen near the road (*follow the signposted track*). A short walk away is the old water-trough where the troopers had watered their horses while Te Kooti's scout watched, unobserved, from the bush.

Orakei Korako A spectacular series of multi-coloured silica terraces is the focal point of this thermal valley on the lip of the Waikato River north of Taupo. The steaming formations are reached by jet boat across the river. Just downstream is the Ohakuri hydro-electric dam.

Taupo Fishing, thermal pools, geothermal power, a vast lake, a fearsome waterfall and sensational rapids – Taupo has widespread appeal. Sited on the northern shores of the lake, where the mighty Waikato River is born, the town has a highly individual character, marked by rising steam and scrub-covered pumicelands. European settlement began in 1869 with the arrival of the Armed Constabulary, come to hound the enterprising Te Kooti. Their name survives at the thermal A.C. Baths, and the remains of their redoubt are, appropriately enough, near the police station. In addition to its service role, Taupo is a popular place to which to retire (and fish), and its population is in summer swollen with holidaymakers from all over the North Island. It is also favoured by travellers as a restful midway point on the trip between Auckland and Wellington on Highway 1.

Baked trout with cream
Truite Taupo

For those who are caught with a trout but are without a recipe book, and who wish to do more than simply fry it or poach it in rosé.

Butter, shallots, herbs, white wine, cream, lemon juice

Place trout to feed two persons on a buttered, shallow baking dish that has been sprinkled with 2 chopped shallots. Season with salt, pepper, a pinch of thyme and a bay leaf. Pour 4 tablespoons of melted butter over the trout and bake at 190°C for 25–35 mins, basting it several times with butter from the dish. Remove the trout carefully to a hot platter. Deglaze the pan with 3 tablespoons of white wine and ¼ cup of thick cream and strain the resulting sauce into a small saucepan. Boil it briefly to reduce the sauce a little and add salt and pepper (if needed) and a few drops of lemon juice. Pour sauce over the fish and serve at once.

HIGHWAY VIEW *Countryside north of Taupo, near Wairakei.*

TIMELESS TOKAANU *On the southern shore of the lake, at the foot of Pihanga, this settlement has much old-world charm and a lively history.*

LAKE VIEWS 1. *The lake's outlet, birthplace of New Zealand's longest river, the Waikato.* 2. *Acacia Bay, on the lake's northern shore.*

KAINGAROA FOREST *Highway 5 passes through radiata pine in the world's largest man-made forest.*

THE SCENE TO THE SOUTH *The summer view across the Desert Road (which runs south from Turangi to Waiouru) westwards to snowcapped Mt Ruapehu, a major winter ski resort.*

Lake Taupo The bed of the country's largest lake is technically a "caldera" – an enlarged volcanic crater formed by the collapse of the cone. The last eruption took place about 2,000 years ago, when vast areas were literally showered with pumice, and there are hot springs at various points around the lake shore – including some in the lake bed itself – relished by swimmers at Taupo township. With the land thought to be unsuited for farming, it was thermal activity which first attracted interest in the area. The trout for which the lake and its feeder streams and rivers are renowned were first introduced in 1890. Boats, rods and tackle may all be hired: there is no closed season for trout here, although fishing licences are required.

Tokaanu An endearing, enduring village, contrasting with the newness of neighbouring Turangi, Tokaanu rests at the southern end of the lake. Behind the settlement is one of the power stations for the Tongariro hydro-electric project. Although Tokaanu means "cold stone", there is a thermal area here, with open-air swimming baths, a small geyser and much belching mud. St Paul's Anglican Church, a memorial to the area's first missionary, displays a bell shattered by enthusiastic converts as they summoned local Maori to prayer.

Tokoroa By the edge of the Volcanic Plateau in the Upper Waikato basin is one of the country's fastest-growing centres. Tokoroa exploded from hamlet to city in only two decades as the huge pulp-and-paper complex at Kinleith became established.

Turangi Built as a hydro town for the Tongariro power scheme (whose information office is here), the town was designed to become the service centre for southern Taupo. Nearby, in the Tongariro River, is some of the world's finest trout fishing, and beside it a trout hatchery where rainbow trout are reared to stock the country's streams. Trout ova are also sent overseas.

Waihi A minute settlement charmingly sited by the water's edge not far from Tokaanu. The quaint church, decorated in Maori style, has stained-glass windows depicting both Christ and the Virgin as Maori. Near the church is the Te Heuheu mausoleum in which a number of the paramount chiefs of the Tuwharetoa tribe lie buried. Also close by is a comparatively recently carved meeting house which, in customary fashion, incorporates many venerable carvings previously housed in the succession of meeting houses that have stood on the same site over many generations.

1. 2.

1. Christ depicted as a Maori in the Catholic Church of St Werendfried at Waihi. 2. The interior of St Werendfried's, decorated in Maori style. The church dates from 1889. 3. Detail from the east window, with the Virgin Mary shown as Maori. 4. The bell at St Paul's, Tokaanu, shattered by over-enthusiastic bellringers and preserved as a testimonial to missionary endeavour.

3 4.

KOWHAI *Honey-rich flowers of spring.*

HUKA FALLS *The Waikato River plunges.*

Wairakei Billowing steam and a deafening, though muffled, roar mark the scene of an imaginative scheme to tap thermal resources close to the surface and convert them into electricity. Innovations made here have passed into standard practice for this type of engineering, one increasingly resorted to in an energy-conscious era. Visitors are welcome at an information centre, where the technicalities are explained, and on conducted tours around the two power-houses. A palatial hotel incorporates comfortable conference facilities and an excellent golf course. Nearby are the Huka Falls (where the full force of the Waikato bounds over an 11-metre ledge), Huka Village (an historical recreation) and the Aratiatia Rapids (almost a kilometre of foaming, lashing river which has been preserved, despite the Waikato's being diverted for power generation, and which is "turned on" from 2.30 p.m.–4 p.m. when circumstances permit).

PIHANGA SCENIC RESERVE *A segment of the bush skirts of soft, gentle Pihanga as she rises south of Lake Taupo. Her silhouette and mood lend themselves readily to the myth that tells of a battle between the neighbouring volcanoes for her favours. Her outline, however, disguises the fact that she, too, is of volcanic origin and so must be ranked as "male" as the rest of the group.*

LAKE ROTOAIRA *A bush-girt lake, 20 kilometres from Turangi, whose precincts are a special reserve of the Maori people.*

Tongariro National Park

TONGARIRO AND NGAURUHOE *An early Polynesian, Ngatoroirangi, is said to have climbed Ngauruhoe* (centre) *to claim the area for his followers. There, in the perishing cold, he prayed for warmth – and was rewarded with volcanic fire.*

RUAPEHU AND THE CHATEAU Less flamboyant than Ngauruhoe but an active volcano nonetheless, Ruapehu is the most popular peak in the North Island with winter sports enthusiasts. From time to time the waters of its crater lake have rewarded both skiers and climbers with the luxury of a warm swim on the very roof of the North Island, but renewed activity in recent years has seen the temperatures soar.

In a land of contrast and spectacle, none is more vivid than the snow-clad peaks of Tongariro National Park as they soar above the Rangipo Desert. No mountain could be more spectacular than the generally quiescent, lava-lined volcano of Ngauruhoe when in full-throated eruption.

The moods, the mists and the awesomeness of an area still witnessing creation conspire to lend magic to mythology. The peaks in eruption were portrayed as giants feuding for the love of Pihanga, a demure, bush-clad mound at the southern extremity of Lake Taupo. Yet another rival, Taranaki (now Mt Egmont), was driven out, leaving the great gash of the Wanganui River as it flows westward to the sea and ensuring its perpetual isolation.

The park, given by the tribe upon trust for the purpose, preserves in perpetuity a region sacred to the Tuwharetoa.

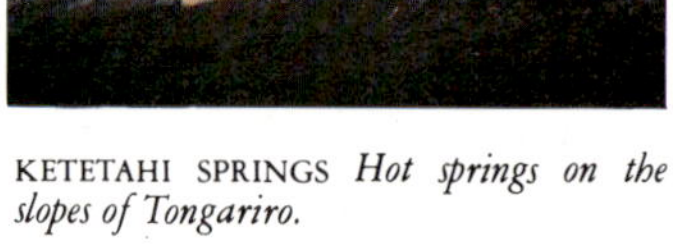

KETETAHI SPRINGS *Hot springs on the slopes of Tongariro.*

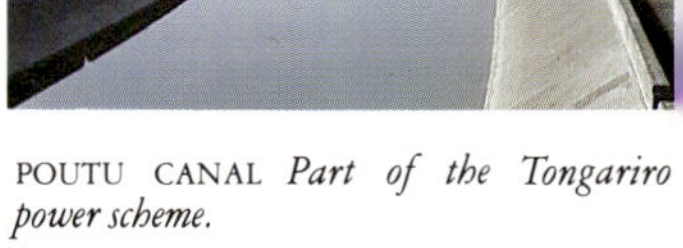

POUTU CANAL *Part of the Tongariro power scheme.*

CREEPING *Myrsine nummularia.*

MOUNTAIN HEATH *Sub-alpine flora tints the plateau in late summer.*

WAIOURU ARMY MUSEUM *A nation's military history is commemorated.*

Whakapapa Activity centres in the main on Whakapapa village, where are found the Chateau (a government-owned hotel complete with golf course), the park headquarters and a well-equipped camping ground with cabins. Beyond lie the Whakapapa ski fields, the first on the mountain to be developed. In summer the headquarters organise conducted tramps and climbs of Ruapehu and Tongariro (there are also numerous marked tracks for independent walkers); in winter chairlifts from the top of the Bruce Road make for an easier ascent. From here, too, it is possible within one day to ski down a mountain, enjoy a thermal swim and catch a trout from either Lake Taupo or the Tongariro River – a more leisurely pace is recommended.

The weather on the mountain can change rapidly, and visitors are warned of the mountain's unpredictable character. Seismic activity is closely monitored, but Ruapehu has been known suddenly to eject vast quantities of hot water, mud and boulders.

TAWHAI FALLS *Talk of a haunted whare here lends the falls a supernatural air.*

Desert Road The name given to the bleak and barren road between Waiouru and Turangi. On a clear day the mountains' presence dominates, but in winter snow and ice force the motorist to eschew scenery and concentrate on the road.

Ohakune The development of the Turoa ski fields has turned a market-garden and timber town into a major winter resort.

Te Porere A tussock fort, built by Te Kooti in 1869, has been restored by the Historic Places Trust.

Waiouru A major Army camp uses much of the volcanic plateau for military exercises. The Queen Elizabeth II Army Memorial Museum traces the country's involvement in conflict.

TE HEU HEU TUKINO IV A bust of the paramount chief of the Tuwharetoa stands in the park headquarters. It was he who led the Taupo forces into battle against the Pakeha in the Waikato and who later supported Te Kooti. Alarmed at the prospect of his tribe's sacred mountains being used as trig stations, he succeeded in preserving their tapu by ceding them in 1887 to the people of New Zealand as the country's first national park.

ASPECTS OF RUAPEHU *The Pinnacles* (above) *and a ski lesson* (below).

OHAKUNE TOWNSHIP *The focus for recent development of Ruapehu's southern slopes, Ohakune is alive with activity in the winter months.*

Taranaki

MOUNTAIN AND MILK *Mt Egmont viewed from Inglewood, with the inevitable and ubiquitous dairy herd in the foreground. Mt Egmont is often compared with Japan's Fujiyama.*

PUKEKURA PARK *The showpiece of New Plymouth's central-city gardens.*

RICHMOND COTTAGE (1853) *An early New Plymouth home.*

The lone sentinel of Mt Egmont visually and climatically dominates a lush, verdant region. Her 2,518-metre peak sweeps symmetrically from a low coastal landscape to precipitate rain from moisture-laden westerly breezes: this falls on a lowland area floored with ash deposits from the dormant volcano. On this combination of blessings Taranaki's prolific dairy industry is based, with dairy cows in milk in some areas outnumbering sheep shorn by more than two to one. The cows themselves are among the country's most productive.

The discovery of vast fields of natural gas both on and offshore has given a new purpose to the region's development, with New Plymouth, its urban heart, at last reaping the benefits from hydrocarbons which for over a century had proved elusive. These finds have helped afford some modest cushioning to the country's economy in recent times, but their full exploitation calls for an unprecedented level of investment, most of it in foreign currency. Much of this will be spent in the Taranaki region, giving it a bright economic outlook.

Egmont National Park The sacred mountain of the Taranaki was returned to the tribes in 1978 in a symbolic gesture, to enable them to give it voluntarily to thd people of New Zealand. The peak's magic pervades a wide surrounding area; it served as a burial ground for chiefs and such was its tapu that guides would only accompany the first European climbers as far as the perpetual snowline, and then pray for their safe return. Three "mountain houses" serve as bases for visitors – Dawson Falls, Stratford Mountain House and the North Egmont Chalet. There is a variety of good walks and the climb to the summit is an easy one in good conditions.

1.

2.

3.

OIL AND GAS New Plymouth was quickly in the oil stakes: the first find in the British Empire was made here in 1856, barely seven years after the world's first commercial strike had been made in the USA. With the advent of the motorcar came "Peak", the city's own brand of petrol which was refined here from local oil. Only one pump remains from the old field (*2, above*), in Bayly Road. In 1969 came a gas strike at Kapuni (*3, above*), from where gas is now piped to many parts of the North Island. This in turn was eclipsed by massive offshore finds (*1, left*). These require the skills perfected in Europe's North Sea to bring it ashore, and give the country so much gas that it has taken some years for decisions to be made on its exploitation.

CHEESE *Still a major cheddar producer, Eltham now makes many varieties – such as this blue vein cheese.*

SHOPPING IN STYLE *New Plymouth's Devon Street Mall, an indication of the region's growth and prosperity.*

MT EGMONT The isolation of Egmont from other mountains gives it a distinctive flora, but the mountain (viewed here from Dawson Falls) is in fact part of a chain of volcanic peaks which stretches to the Sugar Loaf Islands, offshore from New Plymouth. A sustained series of eruptions built the symmetrical cone. The myth explaining the mountain's solitude is recounted on p. 82.

New Plymouth The country's "oil boom" city exploded into prominence with the discovery of vast fields of natural gas both on and off shore. These, and subsequent finds of oil, came when fuel costs were biting heavily into the highly mechanised farming industry and rapidly eroding returns from exports. Hitherto "Taranaki" had been synonymous with "cheese" and New Plymouth was the world's largest exporter of cheddar – a title lost when the EEC closed New Zealand's access to the British market.

Pukekura Park is one of the country's finest gardens, with neighbouring Brooklands Park affording an elegant setting for outdoor performances. A small lake in front of the stage mirrors the performers. Some 29 kilometres away is the 360-hectare Pukeiti Rhododendron Trust, nestling between the Kaitake and Pouakai Ranges. Duncan & Davies nursery (*Westown*) exports native plants all over the world. The museum (*cnr Brougham and King Streets*) and art gallery (*Queen Street*) house excellent collections. St Mary's Church (1842) (*Vivian Street*), backed by Cherry Blossom Walk and the lookout on Marsland Hill, is the oldest stone church in the country. Richmond Cottage, by the museum, is one of the city's earliest buildings.

Hawera The principal town of South Taranaki boasts a spectacular dairy factory. The pre-European pa site at nearby Turuturumokai is also worth a visit.

Manaia The township centres on a war memorial while on its golf course stand two well-preserved blockhouses built by the Armed Constabulary during the Land Wars. To the north, at Kapuni, lie gasfields which feed the North Island grid.

Opunake A modest dairying centre where cheese for export was first produced in Taranaki. Nearby, at Oaonui, is the on-shore treatment station for gas from the Maui field. Condensate is extracted for refining at Whangarei before the gas is fed to Kapuni and into the North Island pipeline grid.

Waitara Scene of the outbreak of the Land Wars between Maori and Pakeha, the former Maori riverside stronghold has a huge freezing works. Nearby Motonui is the site of the world's first plant to produce petrol from natural gas using Mobil's advanced catalystic technology.

MANUKORIHI PA At Waitara stands a memorial to Sir Maui Pomare (1876–1930), a Maori leader who did much to restore the fortunes of his people after the Land Wars. It was at Waitara in 1860 that land tensions between Maori and settler erupted into war after the government used troops to enforce a patently defective transaction. Fighting engulfed much of the North Island and provided the pretext for further land confiscations. Pomare is likened to the legendary Maui (who fished the North Island from the ocean) as he "fished" compensation for the land from a sea of sorrow.

GAS-FIRED STATION *New Plymouth.*

IRONSAND At Waipipi, deposits are extracted from poor land, turned into a slurry and pumped out to tankers for shipment to Japan.

PUKEITI RHODODENDRON TRUST *Azaleas, rostas and, of course, rhododendrons abound.*

The dairy industry

The New Zealand dairy farmer ranks as the world's most efficient. For although the national dairy herd of about two million is only twelfth in size compared with those of other countries, New Zealand ranks as the foremost exporter of butter, cheese, milk powders and casein – and at the lowest prices.

Much of the credit for these achievements belongs to the industrious and enterprising dairy farmers and their capacity to organise, both individually and collectively. Their highly mechanised, one-person, "herring-bone" milking sheds can push cows through at the unbelievable rate of one per minute, and their co-operative dairy factories are envied the world over. However, the trigger to the blossoming of the industry lay in the application of artificial fertilisers. Dairy farmers were quick to exploit the possibilities afforded by the advent of refrigeration, but it was only at the turn of the century that the industry boomed to its present dominance.

Stock are not housed during the winter, and pasture provides most of their feed the year round. This gives local butter a high carotene content, making it much yellower than that produced in countries where cows are fed indoors for much of the year. But the feed requirements for a dairy farm are much more demanding than those for sheep. A herd is in milk for about ten months of the year, when feed needs are at their highest, whereas sheep can have their lambs sold at four months and so be off a property before feed becomes scarce either from a dry summer or from a prolonged winter. Thus the country's dairy farms are concentrated overwhelmingly in the North Island, and generally in the rich, fertile lowlands to the north and west where summer rainfall is high and the winters short. Well-drained soils there can stand up to trampling by cattle, and in such a setting the relative economics of dairying and sheep-farming usually enable dairy farmers to outbid their competitors for available land.

The general pattern is slightly modified by those who supply town milk. Here, the whole herd may not be able to be "dried off" for the winter (by timing their calving for the spring) and a greater degree of feeding-out is necessary.

Almost all dairy produce is manufactured in co-operative factories owned and managed by the dairy farmers. Many of these are world leaders in the technology of milk processing. Ubiquitous milk tankers call to collect milk and cream from the farm gate and trundle it to the factories for processing into butter, cheese, casein or milk powder. The factories pay the farmer on the basis of the weight of the butterfat supplied, and the performance of each herd is carefully monitored. The resulting products are marketed by a central body, the New Zealand Dairy Board, whose sales-people scour the world for export markets and whose consulting officers advise on herd improvement, test each herd and run an artificial breeding centre.

Wanganui and environs

A DEEP, GREEN, LIMPID RIVER *A gorge on the Wanganui River, just one of the series of elegant scenes that awaits the traveller.*

TE KOOTI'S BATTLE-FLAG *The wily rebel's flag now reposes in Wanganui's museum.*

VICTORIAN FACADES *Wanganui's Victoria Avenue.*

AT PEACE *River wildlife is little disturbed.*

The city of Wanganui exudes a mellow air, which derives both from its origins as one of the earliest of the New Zealand Company's settlements and its superb site near the mouth of the wide Wanganui River. Inland the river is narrower, flowing down from the volcanoes of the Tongariro National Park and winding through virgin bush and spectacular scenery before broadening to enter tidal reaches. In mythology the river's course was hewn by massive Mt Egmont as it retreated to safe ground, badly wounded, after losing a lovers' battle with the fiery Tongariro.

In pioneer times boats of settlers and Maori canoes shuttled to and fro, trading up and down the river, but the Wanganui is no longer the major waterway it once was, and the demise of coastal shipping has stilled a once-busy sea port. The city is now established, if not wholly secure, in the role of manufacturing centre, but it has suffered from its proximity to other centres now better served by transport.

Added character is lent the city by Putiki pa, a riverside Maori settlement within the city limits, which has a splendidly decorated church. The Maori treasures in the city museum, too, are among the finest of any provincial centre.

JERUSALEM *An agreeably named Catholic mission station, where an international nursing Order began, situated downriver from Pipiriki.*

MAKER AND MADE *Mt Egmont, viewed from near the Wanganui's source, is said to have gouged out the river bed on its journey west.*

CITY AND RIVER *Wanganui city, its suburbs and river viewed from Durie Hill's tower.*

RESTORED RIVERBOAT *Now a ferry for sightseers up and down the Wanganui River.*

Bulls The oddly titled junction town by the Rangitikei River has a name which honours an artist rather than its dairying activities. The carver James Bull established the hotel and store around which the town eventually formed after having done work on the British House of Commons at Westminster. Nearby are Flock House, an agricultural college whose graduates have made significant contributions to the country's agriculture, and the New Zealand Air Force base at Ohakea.

Marton A prospering farming town, with several nationally known schools, Marton was re-named for Captain Cook's birthplace more out of desperation than from any desire to honour the navigator who was never anywhere near here. Its shocked residents had discovered that its sonorous Maori name of Tutaenui actually meant "dung heap". Splendid homesteads abound, the finest being "Westoe" (1874), built by Sir William Fox, who was four times Premier but is today better remembered for his watercolours than for his political achievements. The town of Foxton is named for him.

Raetihi Originally built as a timber town, which has since broadened into sheep- and cattle-raising as well as some dairying and market gardening, Raetihi first developed on a level clearing where wagoners could overnight on the way to and from Pipiriki, the point on the Wanganui River that then served as the district's principal point of access.

Ratana The country's only religious settlement of substance was founded by followers of Wiremu Tahupotiki Ratana who, in 1918, here experienced the vision that was to change his own life and that of countless thousands. His vision led him to found the Ratana religion, and so kindle a revival of Maoridom that over 60 years later continues to blaze. The movement, initially conceived simply as a catalyst to draw Maoris into the established Christian churches, developed into a Church in its own right. The Ratana Temple here is heavy with symbolism, and a museum (which can occasionally be visited) contains the crutches and other aids of invalids cured by Ratana, whose prowess as a faith-healer has few equals.

Wanganui The "River City" sprawls across the tidal reaches of the Wanganui River, a city with a feeling of substance that derives from its origins as one of the first New Zealand Company settlements. Queen's Park is its cultural centre, with a good small art gallery and a museum that has a particularly strong Maori collection. The suburb of Putiki, by the river, marks the site of the original Maori settlement and has a fine carved meeting house, an old *pataka* (storehouse) and a flamboyantly decorated Maori church. At Cooks Gardens, Peter Snell in 1962 set the first of his world records for the mile, and on St John's Hill, surrounded by the gardens of the city's most exclusive suburb, is the showpiece of Virginia Lake. The best beaches are at Castlecliff (*8 kilometres*) and Kai-Iwi (*16 kilometres*).

MEMORIAL LOOKOUT *On Durie Hill.*

Wanganui River Trips on the river range from the leisurely to the rapid, but to see the scenery to advantage it is necessary to venture up beyond Pipiriki. The river is navigable by small craft – from organised jet boats to canoes – for some 230 kilometres.

Waverley A farming centre close to the border with Taranaki, Waverley is known for curious Maori rock drawings (at Kohi) and the exploitation of coastal ironsands.

WAR CANOE *In the Wanganui Museum.*

VIRGINIA LAKE *A tranquil city haven.*

PUTIKI CHURCH (1937) *One of the country's finest Maori churches.*

RIVERSIDE SCENE *Tree ferns and waterfall.*

Manawatu

RANGITIKEI RIVER *Pictured near Ohingaiti, the river is noted for its fertile, intensively farmed terraces and steep-walled gorge.*

THE SQUARE *Te Awe Awe presides over Palmerston North's heart, with the Civic Centre in the distance.*

The Manawatu encompasses the largest plains to be found in the North Island, sweeping from the greywacke ranges of the Tararuas and Ruahines to lap the Tasman Sea. The ranges are cleaved by the imposing Manawatu Gorge, a cleft illogical in that here a river that rises on eastern slopes has turned about and cut its way through the range that gave it birth in order to reach the sea to the west. Elsewhere, by comparison with some other regions, the prospect appears to lack visual drama. However, closer acquaintance reveals the several rivers that formed the alluvial plains and a variety and intensity of farming activity that matches anything elsewhere.

Economically the region divides between dairying on the plains and fat-lamb production and the breeding of stud sheep on the downlands to the north-east. It focuses on Palmerston North, once a clearing in the bush, later a major rail junction, and now a city which ranks only behind Hamilton as the country's second largest inland metropolis. With Hamilton it shares international importance as a centre for agricultural research.

Manawatu's open, surf-swept beaches provide good fishing, but bathing in unpatrolled areas calls for caution. Rather, the region's opportunities for recreation lie inland, with fishing for trout in the rivers and tributaries or tramping in the foothills. The rivers also provide good settings for jet boating and for canoeing.

SUMMER NEAR MANGAWEKA *Dense forest has made way for peaceful pasturelands.*

TREE-LINED *Massey University's campus.*

OVER THE TOP *Palmerston's Civic Centre.*

1. 3

HALL OF RUGBY FAME Appropriately sited in the capital of a rugby stronghold, the collection of ephemera engendered by the national passion grows steadily. 1. One of the immortal (1905 All Black) Billy Wallace's international rugby caps. 2. The coveted All Black jersey. 3. A rare French rugby poster. 4. The boot with which Geffin kicked five penalties in 1949 to deprive the All Blacks of a well-merited victory over South Africa.

2. 4

Feilding The rich downlands around Feilding support many prized stud flocks and give the town a substance other farming centres close to major cities generally lack. Curiously, its layout is modelled on the English city of Manchester.

Hunterville A tiny sheep-farming centre whose spruce pastures were won from the bush, only fragments of which remain in Bruce Park and on Vinegar Hill.

Manawatu Gorge A grand canyon twisting through the ranges to link with Woodville and southern Hawke's Bay. Theories abound as to how the Manawatu managed apparently to defy the logic of geography in this extraordinary way. Perhaps the most likely explanation is that the ranges, which originally lay under the sea, sagged and then slowly rose out of the water so that the gap was gradually chiselled deeper to form a natural watercourse, to which the river adapted itself.

"WATERFALLS" *A painting by New Zealand artist Colin McCahon which hangs in the Manawatu Art Gallery, Palmerston North.*

FEILDING'S STOCKYARDS *Overseas as well as local buyers gather here for the Friday stock sales.*

Palmerston North The city lies by the Manawatu River, close by the ranges that assure the region's rainfall. The bush that once clothed the plains has long fallen to the settler's axe, but abundant parks and a huge square are compensations. The city, in which education is the single most important industry, has long been at the forefront of agricultural training and research – Massey University has trained farmers for over 50 years, and comparatively recent expansion into other disciplines has helped give the city a vibrance it once lacked. The university, which includes the country's only veterinary school, has a research role but is dwarfed in this by the Grasslands Division of the Department of Scientific and Industrial Research, a seed-testing station, and both the Dairy Research Institute and the Dairy Board's artificial breeding centre at Awahuri. The city also boasts an impressive art gallery with an excellent contemporary collection. Museums include Totaranui (*Church Street*), the Hall of Rugby Fame (*Grey Street*) and a steam engine museum at Tokomaru.

Sanson A tiny junction settlement close by the Mount Lees Reserve, a rich and verdant setting in which to wander and to picnic amongst native and exotic plants.

Taihape There are some North Island towns marginally farther from the sea, but none with quite the same landlocked feeling. To the north of this once-railway town lies the wild Volcanic Plateau; to the east, the inland Patea route through the North Island's largest sheep runs to Hawke's Bay.

HISTORY PRESERVED *A vintage steam engine pictured at Feilding.*

PLAIN PEDALLING *An easy mode of transport in a flat, unhurried city.*

TEACHER'S TRAINING *A marae and meeting house at the Palmerston North Teachers' College.*

MAIZE FIELD *Croplands near Marton.*

The Kapiti Coast and Horowhenua

THE CURL OF THE COAST *The shoreline and Kapiti Island viewed from the Paekakariki Hill. Kapiti served as the base for the warrior-chief Te Rauparaha, and as a shore whaling station.*

The curve of Tasman coastline arching north from Wellington enjoys a special place in the hearts of the capital city's inhabitants. An hour's drive (or less) from the heart of the city lies an unbroken stretch of grey sand beach, which not only provides year-round recreation but also enjoys a unique micro-climate for commercial and private gardeners and the thousands of weekend "bach" owners who swell the Kapiti Coast's otherwise small permanent population. The several small seaside towns are a hive of weekend activity and together with those of the Horowhenua provide a focus for the rich market gardens and lush dairy farms which dominate the hinterland.

ROADSIDE BARGAINS *Fruit and vegetable stalls abound, with offers of "pick-your-own" a special temptation.*

Wedge-shaped between the sea and the mountainous Tararuas and dissected by a number of rivers – the Waikanae, Ohua, Otaki and Manawatu – the alluvial coastal plain tapers from the broad expanses of Horowhenua to a bare roadwidth which, in the early days of Wellington, provided a natural defensive position. Its history is dominated by Te Rauparaha (*c.* 1768-1849), the Ngati Toa chief who, after being driven out of the Waikato, migrated to Kapiti Island where he traded with whalers and flax merchants for the guns he needed to ensure his domination not only of the immediate area but also of much of the South Island. His notoriety was a constant provocation to the Wellington settlers who, typical of their time, both misunderstood and undermined his personal *mana* and genuine attempts at reconciliation.

SOUTHWARD CAR MUSEUM *A unique museum complex situated at Otaihanga, between Paraparaumu and Waikanae, combines restaurant, conference and theatre facilities with a superb display hall containing over 120 vintage and classic cars dating back to 1895, as well as antique motor cycles, cycles, traction and fire engines. First opened to the public in 1979, it is one of the largest private collections in the world. Amongst the several exceptional exhibits is the Stutz Indianapolis racer (*picture inset*), one of only five ever made and thought to be one of only two still in existence.*

Foxton The town divides between the beach and the main road, reflecting its origin as a port and its life-blood since the port closed.

Kapiti Island Te Rauparaha's fortress is now largely a bird sanctuary, with a small area grazing sheep. It can occasionally be visited (permits are required). The surrounding seabed enjoys a high reputation with skin divers.

Levin The Horowhenua's principal centre, Levin is circled by prolific market gardens and is home to a variety of light industries. Lake Horowhenua is a pleasant picnic and boating spot, and Waitarere and Hokio beaches are also popular.

Otaki The oldest and most fascinating of the settlements, Otaki was Te Rauparaha's mainland base and has long been populated. There is a small but interesting museum, an old Roman Catholic mission, a good beach and a comparatively new carved meeting house (a feature of the area generally is the number of small meeting houses seen from Highway 1). Pre-eminent is Rangiatea Church – built in 1849 and probably the finest of all the Maori churches. A drab exterior masks a breathtaking interior where full but considered reign is given to traditional Maori design. The ridge-pole is reputed to have been over 30 metres long before a local missionary, terrified that the building project would end in calamity, one night secretly sawed off about a tenth of its length. Opposite the church are memorials both to the Ngati Toa chief and to the coming of Christianity.

AKATARAWA VALLEY *The picturesque alternative route between Waikanae and the Hutt Valley and Wellington.*

Paekakariki, Paraparaumu and Waikanae A chain of seaside settlements faces out to Kapiti Island. With its rich soil, Waikanae is particularly favoured as a place to which to retire. Spectacular sunsets silhouette the distant South Island.

NETTING AT NIGHTFALL *One of the many groups who gather at Paekakariki Beach to net flounder.*

WAITARERE'S WRECK *The skeleton of the sailing ship* Hyderabad *has adorned the beach for over a century.*

Wairarapa

SUNRISE OVER THE WAIRARAPA COAST *A generally wild stretch of coastline is broken here at Castlepoint.*

CENTREPOINT *Masterton's modern mall.*

THE GOLDEN SHEARS The world's leading shearers gather in Masterton every March to pit their skills against each other in the country's premier shearing competition.

The well-groomed, prosperous Wairarapa Valley thrusts southward from Hawke's Bay to meet the sea prematurely in the broad but shallow Lake Wairarapa. The lake in turn drains into the smaller Lake Onoke, separated from the pounding Pacific Ocean by no more than a bar of shingle. To the west rises the bush-draped Tararua Range; to the east rolls hill country which drops, often precipitously, to the sea.

The lower valley was a grassy open plain that readily lent itself to sheep: the country's first pastoral farming took place here, on the eastern shores of Lake Wairarapa. Further north, however, the land was locked in forest and the familiar struggle was joined between hopeful, ill-prepared migrants and a relentless, unyielding terrain. Today's trim pasturelands and orchards are legacies of considerable struggle and heartbreak.

HOMEWARD *A herd of milking cows makes its twice-daily trek to the milking shed.*

STRONG-HEARTED AND TOUGH *A restored traction engine near Carterton.*

SHEEP COUNTRY *A typical Wairarapa landscape.*

PREPARING FOR THE STARTER *Castlepoint's annual beach races attract a festive crowd, who picnic and punt modestly on an equaliser which lets you know your horse only after you've placed your bet.*

Carterton Set in wide plains and graced with substantial market gardens and orchards, Carterton began as a bush settlement, and today's open spaces were wrested from the forest with considerable hardship. To the west rise the Tararuas, in which the Tararua Forest Park and its Mt Holdsworth Reserve and Waiohine River Gorge are particularly appealing spots. The Tararua Range as a whole is much used by trampers, both local and from Wellington.

Castlepoint A rare beach settlement on an otherwise generally bleak and wild stretch of coast, Castlepoint was named for a bastion-like rock, not for its fortress-like lighthouse. Beneath the light is a huge sea cave where a giant octopus is said to have hidden in a vain attempt to escape from the Polynesian explorer, Kupe, before it was chased around Cape Palliser and out into Cook Strait. The Maori used legendary tales to detail geography, and the tale served as an oral map to the region. The settlement is periodically the setting for entertaining picnic beach races.

Eketahuna On perhaps the prettiest site of all the Wairarapa townships, Eketahuna sits above the gorges of the Makakahi River.

Featherston Featherston nestles beneath the Rimutakas which divide the Wairarapa from the Hutt Valley. Nearby is the sweeping expanse of Lake Wairarapa. A sign on the Rimutaka Hill road reads simply: Beware of Wind.

Greytown Picturesque Greytown, an orcharding and market-gardening town, rests on rich river loam.

Martinborough A farming centre, whose main streets are in the shape of the Union Jack.

Masterton The hub of the Wairarapa reflects the affluence of the region and houses increasing industry. The generous grounds of Queen Elizabeth Park incorporate a boating lake and a memorial recording the traditional friendship between Maori and Pakeha in the region. The vigorous Wairarapa Arts Centre *(Bruce Street)* and the Mt Bruce Native Bird Reserve (*24 kilometres north*) are worth visits.

Pahiatua The centre for the upper Wairarapa has a broad street set aside by planners for the railway but never used by it.

Riversdale A sandy surf beach with swimming, fishing and a growing number of holiday baches.

MOUNT BRUCE RESERVE Efforts to save the takahe (*pictured*) and other rare bird species are made at the Mt Bruce Native Bird Reserve, 24 kilometres north of Masterton. Visitors are welcomed.

A WAIRARAPA BACH *Clusters of holiday cottages huddle wherever by-laws allow.*

FEATHERSTON'S FELL ENGINE Before a tunnel was driven through the Rimutakas, these nuggety little engines, with horizontal wheels to grip onto the sides of the rails, were used to haul trains over the range to and from Upper Hutt. Added to the steep grade was the furious wind, which once actually blew a passenger train from the tracks.

TARARUA BUSH *The Mt Holdsworth Reserve.*

The Hutt Valley

A DAY AT THE RACES *Trentham's racecourse is a focal point for Wellington's sporting (and social) life, as is the nearby Heretaunga Golf Club.*

The broad expanse of the Hutt Valley has absorbed much of the capital city's expansion of the past thirty years. Once devoted to market gardens and dairy farms, its rich soil now sprouts two cities – Lower Hutt, very much the larger, and Upper Hutt, farther up the valley – and a bewildering variety of industry. The seafront village of Petone might well have become the nation's capital had not the river's flooding forced the first settlers to move to Wellington.

VIEWS FROM THE HILL *The Hutt River lazily reaches Wellington Harbour.*

VIEWS FROM THE HILL *Overlooking Petone, oldest of the settled areas on the harbour.*

THE HUTT RIVER *The upper reaches, north of Upper Hutt, are popular with fly-fishermen.*

Eastern Bays Historically it was to the warmth of Eastbourne and Days Bay that Victorian and Edwardian gentlemen would move from Wellington for the summer's sun. Today the bays are commuter hamlets, crowded on sunny weekends. "Gentlemen" seek sun further afield.

Lower Hutt Bounded by sharply rising hills to west and east, the city spreads right across the valley floor and, on land reclaimed for industry, southwards out on to the old harbour bed. It houses a number of industries of national importance. Pre-eminent are major units of the Department of Scientific and Industrial Research, among them the Soil Bureau, the Dominion Laboratory, the Geological Survey and the Institute of Nuclear Sciences.

Petone Still with very much of a village atmosphere, despite its urban surroundings, Petone's spirit is traditionally demonstrated on the rugby field, where its club team has defeated all comers. On the foreshore landed Wellington's settlers from the "first four ships", an event recorded in a museum in the waterfront Provincial Memorial.

Three views from Wainuiomata Hill. Pictured left and right are three segments of the magnificent panorama which presents itself on the road from Lower Hutt to Wainuiomata. On the extreme left is the industrial area of Gracefield, with Somes Island and Wellington beyond; progressively, the pictures pan to the Western Hills. This steep-faced range and the line of the Hutt River mark the Wellington Fault, a major fracture in the earth's crust that follows the line of the Southern Alps through Wellington and up the Hutt Valley to continue along the length of the main North Island mountain chain. The fault, which sweeps through Wellington city and follows the curve of the Hutt Road round the harbour before turning up the valley, is even more pronounced from the air.

EASTERN BAYS *To swim, to sail, to laze. . .*

Upper Hutt A newly created city, Upper Hutt seeks an identity independent of its much larger neighbour. The yearling sales at Trentham racecourse attract international interest.

Wainuiomata A dormitory suburb for Wellington and the Hutt Valley. Its commuters enjoy magnificent views.

DOWSE GALLERY *"It's an illusion" exhibition in Lower Hutt.*

TUTIKIWI ORCHID AND FERN HOUSE This attractive building, in Myrtle Street, Lower Hutt, was designed to house the outstanding orchid collection of horticulturalist Herbert Poole and ferns from the Jubilee Park Fernery.

TUI *After the kiwi, perhaps New Zealand's most loved bird.*

EASTBOURNE *A colonial terrace house finds new life.*

LOWER HUTT *Flowers in the city's centre.*

VIEWS FROM THE HILL *Looking towards Lower Hutt city and the Western Hills.*

PIONEERS' LANDING-PLACE *Petone.*

Political life

New Zealand's political life turns on its capital, Wellington. Through its airport a steady stream of parliamentarians, commuting between their constituencies and the centre of government, is joined by representatives of myriad pressure groups journeying either to press a case for governmental action or to make representations to the unceasing round of committees as special interests are consulted on aspects of proposed legislation.

Although modelled closely on the Westminster style of government, there is now only a single House of Representatives, the Upper House (the Legislative Council) having been voted out of existence in 1950. Like Britain, there is no "written constitution", the relevant provisions being scattered through a number of Acts of Parliament, some of which are "entrenched" (such as the term of Parliament) so as to render their amendment in effect impossible in the face of significant opposition. However, the combined absence of a written constitution and of an Upper House has led to calls for constraints on a process that has come to be so dominated by the system of party "whips" that it is now a rarity for a Government Member even to abstain, let alone to vote with the Opposition. Curiously, the same loyalty has not been shown where it is, by convention, required. Members of Cabinet, the Ministers who in theory "advise" the Crown in the exercise of executive powers, must support Cabinet decisions collectively – no matter that they may have argued against them – or else resign. In recent years few Ministers have done either.

Parliament has a maximum life of only three years, the shortest of any democracy. Though some see this as too brief an interval for coherent policies to be pursued, when offered the option of a four-year term in a referendum in 1967, the voters rejected it overwhelmingly.

The titular Head of State is the Queen of England, as she is in about 15 other Commonwealth countries, with the Governor-General (appointed by her on the advice of the Prime Minister) acting in her general absence. The Head of Government is the Prime Minister, the leader of the block supported by the majority of the Members of the House of Representatives. There are some 92 of these, four of whom are Maori Members elected by those Maori who choose to enrol on the Maori (as opposed to the General) voters' roll. Because in recent years increasing numbers of Maori have been elected to represent general constituencies, the same need for the seats to ensure representation by Maori no longer exists, although there is an argument in favour of their retention. The general constituencies are so overwhelmingly Pakeha in composition that it would be difficult for their Members, who might happen also to be Maori, to advance a consistently Maori viewpoint.

SYMBOL OF ROYAL AUTHORITY *The golden mace, carried in the Speaker's procession by the Sergeant-at-arms before each sitting of Parliament, and on the occasion of the opening of Parliament when Members proceed to the Council Chambers to hear the Speech from the Throne.*

Wellington

MEANDERING LAMBTON QUAY *The street records in name and configuration the original shoreline, before reclamation began.*

PARLIAMENT'S BEEHIVE *The statue of "King Dick" Seddon is in the foreground.*

ALEXANDER TURNBULL'S HOME A wealthy bibliophile's home in Bowen Street is now a gallery and restaurant.

Its houses sprinkled on the steep green slopes which skirt a splendid natural harbour, Wellington enjoys an incomparable setting of ever-changing mood. The beauty of the city on a clear, still day lingers in the memory and suggests that such days are of great frequency. Unfortunately boisterous winds well earn it the epithet "Windy Wellington", a reminder that the city is in the "roaring forties" and on the only break in a chain of mountains over 1,400 kilometres in length. The downtown area is largely reclaimed, somewhat discordantly, from the harbour, a process that has been continuing for over a century as a shortage of flat land bedevilled the settlement from the outset. To compound the problems of constructing high-rise buildings on reclaimed land is the fact that a major earthquake fault runs right through the commercial area, necessitating special design to accommodate the occasional tremors.

RISING HIGH *Economics dictate the balance between further reclamation and buildings rising higher. Of all New Zealand's cities, Wellington has the most spectacular skyline.*

HOME GROUND *The New Zealand Symphony Orchestra, based in Wellington, tours the country and beyond.*

EARLY MORNING AT EVANS BAY *A still dawn too frequently heralds a breezy day and tricky sailing for the yachts. On fine days these freckle the harbour, risking an upsetting from a sudden squall.*

The Maori likened the North Island to a fish – "the great fish of Maui" – and depicted its emergence from the sea as the "catch" of that great Polynesian hero. With its tail extending along Northland to Cape Reinga and with Taranaki and Hawke's Bay as its fins, the "great fish" has its head at Wellington. The country's capital rests on its nostrils.

The Wellington Peninsula is traversed by a number of faults, all recently active, several of them continuations of the fault lines that cross Cook Strait from Marlborough. The sharply rising hills dictate the city's layout and hamper communications with the northern hinterland. A solitary main road threads along the harbour shore out of the city, branching at Ngauranga to commence Highway One's journey north, and continuing around the harbour to the Hutt Valley.

Cook Strait, the only cleavage in a series of mountains that stretches from the southernmost South Island to East Cape, acts as a funnel through which a concentrated flow of air is forced, earning for Wellington its reputation for windiness. Gales of up to 100 km/h are experienced on about 30 days each year, most frequently in summer and in spring.

A QUIET FISHING SPOT *Evans Bay wharf.*

CUBA MALL *Setting for a water-mobile.*

RUGBY UNION'S HEADQUARTERS *Athletic Park, scene of epic encounters, is the national sport's home.*

A HEAVILY STYLISED OPERA HOUSE *The New Zealand Opera Company performs Puccini's* La Bohème *at the Wellington Opera House.*

ECHOES OF THE PAST *The Village shopping complex, Willis Street.*

PIGEON PARK *Courtenay Place affords a lunchtime resting place.*

Marine Drive Wellington's harbour is sprinkled with rocky coves rather than sweeps of sandy beach, but as compensation there is a magnificent marine drive of some 40 kilometres, which can be extended to 90 kilometres by including the run out around the harbour to Eastbourne. Start at Oriental Bay (a popular lunchtime spot with office workers) and drive with the sea on the left to skirt Miramar Peninsula until finally Island Bay and Owhiro Bay are reached. Return by way of Happy Valley Road. The drive passes Wellington airport.

Viewpoints The city is one of hills and vantage points. Of the many, the pick are Mt Victoria (which offers a sweeping panorama and whose Maori name indicates that they, too, used it as a lookout) and Tinakori Hill (festooned with wireless masts and affording an even more sensational view). From Lambton Quay the famous cable-car lifts pedestrians to Kelburn and a pleasant corner of the Botanic Gardens from which to savour both the city and the harbour. Rather than return to the city the same way, one may walk down through the Gardens and emerge a little distance from Parliament Buildings.

Some beaches The pick of the city's inner harbour beaches are Oriental, Worser and Scorching Bays; of the ocean beaches, Lyall and Island Bays are well-suited for surfing. More distant beaches to entice Wellingtonians are sun-drenched Eastbourne and Days Bay across the harbour, and the endless tract of sand up the Kapiti Coast, visited by thousands each summer weekend.

MANSFIELD MEMORIAL New Zealand's most famous writer, Katherine Mansfield (1888–1923), is inadequately remembered in Murphy Street, but she herself could scarcely wait to leave her homeland, reflecting the negative view of New Zealand culture that has mellowed only in relatively recent times. Wellington she wrote, was "Philistia itself". Yet curiously her most enduring short stories all have a Wellington setting: "Prelude" (set in Karori), "The Garden Party" (at 25 Tinakori Road) and "At the Bay" (Days Bay). In Europe, Katherine Mansfield was closely associated with Virginia Woolf, D. H. Lawrence and other literary giants of the day. However "the one peacock in our literary garden" in no way interpreted her country to its people.

BASIN RESERVE *New Zealand cricketers engage with India in a rare New Zealand victory. The ground, once waterlogged, was raised in the 1856 earthquakes.*

THE SCENE AT MAKARA *In the distance is Mana Island, birthplace of the sheep industry, where 102 Merinos were landed in 1834 and from where the first wool was exported the following year.*

Hutt Valley Wellington's harbour fills a sea-drowned rivermouth, carved by the Hutt River along the line of the Wellington Fault. The valley, which provided the first extension of a land-starved city, has now blossomed into the cities of Lower and Upper Hutt.

Kapiti Coast A chain of sunny beaches and warmer settlements within comfortable commuting distance of the capital.

Makara A shingle beach on a wild stretch of coast with good fishing and diving is reached beyond the suburb of Karori. Makara Radio is the country's major receiving station.

Paremata An attractive seaside township, with the remains of a fort (1847) built to protect Wellington from the menace of Te Rauparaha's belligerent nephew Te Rangihaeata. His pa was by pretty Pauatahanui Inlet (where a host of yachts now ride) on the site occupied by the tiny church of St Albans.

Plimmerton A pleasant commuter settlement. On its beach Te Rauparaha was kidnapped by British troops at dawn.

Porirua A much-maligned city, the product of inept post-war planning, but one assuming its own special multicultural character.

Somes Island The larger of the harbour's islands seems to beckon but is in fact a quarantine station for imported animals. Its shore is less hospitable than distance suggests.

VIEW FROM NORTHLAND *Long overlooked by home buyers, the suburb has a sunny aspect.*

SURF LIFESAVERS AT LYALL BAY *The country's ocean beaches should be treated with respect.*

KELBURN'S CABLE-CAR *Originally horses hauled the carriages up from Lambton Quay.*

PARLIAMENT High Court judges in full-bottomed wigs parade for the formal opening of Parliament. New Zealand's legislature lacks an Upper House but – from its unwritten constitution and its procedures to the naming of the Members' restaurant – it is closely modelled on "the Mother of Parliaments" at Westminster.

TRADE FAIR *Newtown's Show Buildings.*

LADY NORWOOD ROSE GARDENS *A short walk from the city's centre and adjoining the Botanic Gardens, a profusion of colour and smells awaits the visitor.*

TOWARDS RED ROCKS *On the wild south Wellington coastline, a good walk from Owhiro Bay leads to both a seal colony and a curious upthrust of reddish volcanic rock.*

Even from 21,000 kilometres away, in London, it was apparent that Wellington, sited in the geographical centre of the country, was the logical place for the capital city. It was thus a priority for the New Zealand Company, under its "Wakefield Scheme", to establish a settlement here. Even before the Treaty of Waitangi was signed in February 1840, the first shiploads of migrants had arrived to establish themselves on the harbour shore at Petone. The Governor, though, had other plans, and there was a stormy relationship between these pioneers and the Auckland-based administration until, 25 years later, the seat of government was moved south. However, this was less the product of logic than the result of pressure from gold-rich Otago and a booming Dunedin, whose inhabitants could not accept a situation in which their only form of communication with the (much smaller) capital in Auckland was by way of Sydney. Even then the location was decided not by envious competing provinces but by a delegation appointed by the Australian State Governors! The move has now effectively reversed the situation: Otago's gold dwindled and today it is Auckland that resents being governed from Wellington, with Dunedin as remote as ever.

The new settlers were fortunate to find that the winds which so battered their first makeshift homes had deterred substantial Maori settlement on the harbour. The Hutt Valley, too, was lightly peopled with the main concentrations of Maori population on the warmer and more hospitable coastal plains to the north. These lands were dominated by the "Maori Napoleon", the chief Te Rauparaha, from his base on Kapiti Island at the northern entrance to Cook Strait.

Although there were some skirmishes in the Hutt Valley, and the presence of the Ngati Toa war chief on Kapiti and at Paremata was unsettling, most local chiefs were willing to sell land, and the region was largely spared the conflict between Maori and Pakeha that so marred the early history of much of the North Island. The settlers were alarmed when Te Rauparaha was involved in an ugly incident in Marlborough in 1843, when an armed party of Nelson settlers misguidedly and illegally attempted to imprison him. He had signed the Treaty of Waitangi but did not regard this as offering an open door to European immigration. Later, after the aging chief had retired to Otaki and professed belief in Christianity, the newly arrived Governor, Sir George Grey, felt unsure of Te Rauparaha's intentions, and in July 1846 used troops to abduct him to Auckland, where he was held without charge until 1848.

A combination of political importance and a sheltered anchorage assured Wellington's steady growth over the years, though in more recent times the burgeoning of Auckland had taken its toll. With most of the country's population now living north of Lake Taupo, more and more head offices have moved north, and the region's relative importance as a manufacturing centre has similarly declined. As the seat of government, Wellington is home for the head offices

WOODEN COLOSSUS *"Government Buildings" (1876) is the world's second-largest timber building.*

LYALL BAY *A highly rated surf beach where even in the winter surfers brave the waves in wet-suits.*

COAT OF ARMS New Zealand's arms atop the wooden Government Buildings.

of international organisations and for representatives of foreign and Commonwealth governments. Based here, too, are numerous scientific, cultural and agricultural bodies.

Like no other New Zealand city, Wellington is a jumble of Victorian wooden buildings and modern high-rise office blocks, a mixture of colonial and computer eras. The houses perch at times precariously on the steep harbour wall, while the small apron of level land by the water is crowded with ever-taller commercial buildings. Parliament Buildings (*cnr Lambton Quay and Molesworth Street*), built in 1922 of grey Takaka marble from across Cook Strait, reflect the same contradictions, bridging the effervescent Gothic of its library wing (1897) with the recently completed "Beehive" (1980). Arguments surrounding the building of the Library wing culminated in Prime Minister Seddon summarily ordering that the third storey be left off to save money. In fury, the architect had his own name removed from the foundation stone which, almost a century later, echoes his mute protest at the decision to "spoil the Architectural appearance of the edifice".

The site goes back to the settlement's origins, when it served as the home for the leaders of the New Zealand Company settlement. (Guided tours of the building provide a glimpse of the working of a Westminster-style of government, and it is possible to attend debates. The debates have been broadcast continuously since 1936, when the first Labour Government introduced the innovation as a way of countering what it saw as biased newspaper reporting.)

Behind Parliament Buildings stand more modern appurtenances of government, which in turn adjoin an historic pocket of Old Thorndon where quaint cottages in delightful disarray line pedestrian paths. Nearby, in Mulgrave Street, is Old St Paul's, a "Selwyn" church which for a century served Wellington's spiritual needs and is now a tranquil setting for drama and concerts.

Lambton Quay, which has been progressively modernised over the last decade and is now a maze of hidden shopping malls and arcades, marks the original beachfront before reclamation pushed back the sea.

To the south of Lambton Quay sprawls the expanse of Government Buildings. Built of kauri and the second-largest wooden building in the world, it continues to house government departments more than a century after it was accorded a very quiet opening ceremony for fear of drawing attention to the fact that it had run wildly over its budgeted cost. Turnbull House (*Bowen St*), once the home of bibliophile Alexander Turnbull, is used by community groups. The Alexander Turnbull Library itself, the core of which Turnbull bequeathed to the nation, is to be housed in the National Library. The Library's collections of Pacific material and of Milton's works are world-renowned. Some distance away is the National Museum and Art Gallery *(Buckle Street)*. Special amongst its wild range of collections is a botany section dating back to specimens gathered by Cook's naturalists and others collected by the missionary-botanist Colenso. Included in excellent holdings of Maori material is the carved meeting house Te Hau-ki-Turanga (c. 1842). The finest surviving example of its kind, it was purchased from a Poverty Bay tribe in the euphoria of goodwill that followed the waiver in 1867 of some arbitrary confiscations of land in their area.

Across the Basin Reserve from the Museum lies the official residence of the Governor-General, the Queen's representative in New Zealand. New Zealand is one of more than a dozen independent countries which recognise the Queen of England as their formal Head of State.

The capital's architecture is a jumble of old and new, with highly organised pressure groups battling commercial interests (and occasionally the government) to preserve pockets of the city's colonial heritage. Particularly in Thorndon, old wood continues to defy modern concrete.

INNER-CITY RESIDENCES *Sydney Street, Thorndon.*

CONTRASTS *Plimmer House* (c. *1872), Boulcott Street.*

OLD ST PAUL'S CATHEDRAL (1866) *Mulgrave Street.*

The South Island

Marlborough

THE MARLBOROUGH SOUNDS *River valleys, formed during glacial periods and subsequently drowned by the sea, probe deep into the mainland.*

EDWIN FOX *The hulk of a fully rigged clipper lies in Shakespeare Bay.*

VINTAGE TRAVEL *A surprise find on the Grove Road, Picton's coastal route to Havelock. Vintage car rallying has a large following nationwide.*

In Marlborough, sea and land are intertwined. A boisterous past, when whaling stations flourished on the shores of Cook Strait and local Maori were locked in a series of devastating encounters with invaders from the north, has since given way to rather more placid times. Seaward reach the arms of Marlborough Sounds, enclosing Queen Charlotte, Pelorus and Kenepuru Sounds as well as Port Underwood. On land the pattern is mirrored in the ridges of the mountain ranges which splay like the fingers of a hand. Both inhospitable mountain country and the steep sides of the Sounds render farming difficult where not impossible, and only the Wairau and Awatere Rivers have built up any extensive areas of flat land in the form of broad alluvial plains.

It is the Sounds and the plains which catch the visitor's eye, and it is easy to overlook the vast hinterland of tussock country behind the bush-clad hills. So vast is this back country that the nation's largest sheep run, the 182,000-hectare Molesworth station, lies at the head of the Awatere Valley.

Blenheim Marlborough's main centre occupies a sun-drenched site on the Wairau Plains. But it is a site bought with blood. Early settlers at Nelson, hampered by lack of easy land, envied the Wairau and tried to enforce a dubious sale from its Maori owners. The bodies of the 22 Europeans who died in the attempt lie at Tuamarina, a short distance on the road to Picton. The cannon, said to have been the purchase price of the land, is mounted on the corner of High and Seymour Streets.

FORBIDDINGLY BEAUTIFUL *The coastline north of Tory Channel. It is near here that successful Strait swimmers have come ashore.*

HEADING EAST *The inter-island ferry* Aratika *enters Cook Strait from Tory Channel. The North Island is in the distance.*

PICTON FROM THE AIR *More usual is the approach to Picton by sea or land.*

WAIKAWA BAY *This was where local Maori moved after selling the site of Picton.*

LAUNCH LIFELINE Isolated farms around the Sounds receive their supplies and mail regularly by launch from Picton and Havelock.

French Pass The pass which cleaves D'Urville Island from the mainland was first traversed by the French explorer, Dumont D'Urville, in 1827. The feat was extremely hazardous, and part of the keel of his ship *Astrolabe* was lost. Even today the stretch of water is a treacherous one for boatspeople.

Havelock From this pretty hamlet, which rests at the head of Pelorus Sound, one may join launches which supply the outlying farms and houses with stores and mail, and also arrange to be dropped off to camp in deserted bushland settings. The local youth hostel is named for Lord Rutherford, the "father of the nuclear age", who received his early schooling in the building.

Pelorus Sound A favourite with campers, picnickers and walkers, the Sound is studded with reserves, most of them accessible only by launch from Havelock. The largest reserve, at Tennyson Inlet, can be reached by way of the Rai and Opouri Valleys. Line fishing, especially for cod and gurnard, and scuba diving are excellent here (as they are in the other Sounds).

TUATARA *This "living fossil" finds sanctuary on Stephens Island.*

Port Underwood Tucked away to the east and seemingly part of Cloudy Bay, it is geologically still a "sound".

Queen Charlotte Sound A favourite with the explorer Cook, who came no fewer than five times, Queen Charlotte is still the best known of the Marlborough Sounds because the Cook Strait ferry traverses its length. Cook's imprint is nevertheless still alive at Ship Cove, where he planted vegetables and released animals to stock the area for future visitors. Cannibal Cove, too, he named after discovering that here the Maori did indeed observe the practice.

Stephens Island A remote spot north of D'Urville Island, it is zealously preserved as the home of the country's largest population of tuatara (sole survivor of the species which included the dinosaur) and of the unique Stephens Island frog (which does not swim and is the ancestor of all other frog types).

"THAR SHE BLOWS" A sometimes thriving whaling industry operated until relatively recently from Whekenui, near Tory Channel. The name means "big octopus" in Maori.

MARLBOROUGH VINEYARDS *The newest of the country's wine-growing areas is also one of the largest. Red and white wines are produced largely for local consumption, although international recognition of their quality has not been long in coming.*

SALT FROM THE SEA *Salt water is pumped to feed concentrating ponds at Lake Grasmere, south of Blenheim. Good sunshine and drying winds combine to make this New Zealand's only source of solar salt.*

Kaikoura, Lewis Pass and North Canterbury

LESLIE DOWNS *Here begin the downs which characterise much of the district yet contrast sharply with the extensive plains to the south and forbidding mountains to the north.*

The broad alluvial plains of Canterbury are bounded north and south by downland and easy hill country, which finally builds into upthrusting, near-parallel ranges and fault valleys. These follow major fault lines and continue north of Cook Strait. Here the contrasts are vivid: rich rolling land, closely grazed, is backed by eroding mountain slopes. But nowhere are they more astonishing than where the Kaikoura Ranges rise sheer from the sea to preside over a wild and inhospitable coastline.

The downland is characterised by low ranges enclosing wide valleys and extensive basins. In the last 35 years or so it has responded well to improved farming techniques. Topdressing, drainage and stock control have mastered much of the land which was previously difficult to manage, rendering it highly productive. Indeed, the region's most famous resident, double Victoria Cross-winner Charles Upham, refused the lucrative offers of an admiring public and participated in this process as just one of many resettled returned servicemen. Some areas, however, remain relatively poor and stony, though much of the largest area, the Culverden Basin, is part of the Balmoral State Forest.

From here, too, runs the Lewis Pass, the easier of the Canterbury routes over the Main Divide – a wonderfully scenic drive, though lacking the alpine awe of Arthur's Pass and Haast Pass to the south.

As a whole, the region is comparatively overlooked by the visitor, though the beaches are good and there is much to intrigue those who explore the byways, including fascinating Maori rock drawings.

CANNIBAL GORGE *An unlikely setting, but one where famished Maori greenstone parties would despatch the slaves taken to act first as bearers, then as fodder.*

WAIAU RIVER *Here shadowed by deep gorges near Hanmer.*

A WILD COASTLINE *The dramatic but inhospitable Kaikoura coastline affords good catches but little shelter to the local fishing fleets.*

Cheviot Late last century the retention of vast estates in private hands was "an obstacle to enterprise, a barrier to settlement, a social pest". The description was accepted as valid and Land for Settlements Acts were passed by Parliament. However, the great Cheviot holding fell to Government hands almost fortuitously. Trustees had challenged the land-tax valuation of its 84,000 acres (34,000 ha) of fine pastoral country and the Government had either to accept the trustees' lower figure or buy at its own. The Government did not falter and what legislation had hitherto failed to achieve, the land-tax system in 1892 delivered. Competition for farms and sections in the new "McKenzie township" (now Cheviot) was fierce. Within a year there were over 650 people on the estate and, after a hesitant start, the Government's involvement in land resettlement began to flourish.

The estate had been owned by the magnificent "Ready Money Robinson", reputed once to have tendered a wheelbarrow-load of cash after his cheque had been declined. A memorial to McKenzie, the Minister of Lands responsible for breaking up the run and creating the town, stands near the post office.

Culverden Like Cheviot, Culverden perpetuates the name of a famous run broken up by Government action. But Culverden, in 1908, was to prove to be the only forced acquisition in Canterbury, and one which won the Government few admirers. For, contrary to the wishes of its more radical supporters, the estate was divided into large units, which were within the means only of those quite able to look after themselves. To the south lies the Balmoral Plantation, a broad area of forest where planting began in 1916 with just ten men planting over 250,000 trees.

Hanmer Sited just a little away from through-routes, near wonderfully varied forests which paint a spectacular scene in autumn, the hot springs here make a refreshing adjunct to long walks in the forest. Hanmer gave rise to a sanatorium, and blossomed as a health resort; however, hydrotherapy has now given way to pleasure bathing and the sanatorium is now used as a clinic for alcoholics.

Kaikoura Even the rapid through-traveller should be able to pause to take advantage of a place whose name means "to eat crayfish" – especially when, in season, cooked crays are sold by the roadside. Another highlight is the detour out along the peninsula which juts into the Pacific from under the shadow of the towering seaward Kaikoura Mountains. In mythology, this was the thwart on the giant canoe from which Maui "caught" and dragged to the surface the North Island, "the fish of Maui". The peninsula has the feel of legend, trapped as it is between soaring mountain and wild ocean, with a narrow, impressive coastline running north and south. As an oasis it was long inhabited by the Maori, and it also witnessed the comings and goings of bay whalers. Relics of both can be seen, along with a colony of seals on the tip of the peninsula.

Chilled crayfish

1 cooked crayfish
1 cup cream
1 tsp paprika
squeeze of lemon juice
¼ tsp sugar
¼ tsp salt
black pepper

Split cooked crayfish in half and remove internal flesh. Leave legs on, cracking shells of larger legs so that flesh can be easily obtained. Mix all ingredients together adding sufficient lemon juice to sour cream. Mix together with flesh and replace in shell. Serve cold, decorated with parsley.

KAIKOURA *The township rests on a rare protrusion on the eastern coastline.*

NEARING THE SUMMIT *The Lewis Pass Highway, seldom closed by winter snow, is a tranquil prospect in summer.*

Lewis Pass Lying at 863.7 metres on the Main Divide, the Pass, although forested, is more open and less dramatic than those to the south. As a result, it serves as the principal passage for road traffic between Canterbury and the West Coast. The route from Canterbury lies up the Waiau and Lewis River valleys, then over the pass to the Maruia River.

Ostensibly named for the surveyor who "discovered" it in 1860, the pass had, of course, long been used by Maori parties as they journeyed from Canterbury to gather greenstone from the environs of Hokitika. With protein scarce and little food to be had on the wild West Coast, the parties took food with them that included slaves captured in war. They were useful not merely as porters but served another purpose. On the return journey, the worst of the trip behind them and food running low, they were consumed here on the pass, and their remains flung into Cannibal Gorge. Nor is the name merely a European invention: to the Maori it was Kapai-o-Kaitangata ("good feed of human flesh"). What *is* Pakeha fable concerns prettily named Magdelene Valley, where rumour would have it there lies a French monastery, crumbling to ruin amidst grape vines run wild.

To the west of the Pass lie Maruia Hot Springs, where the traveller with time in hand may luxuriate in the natural hot waters.

KAIKOURA PASTORAL *The mountains rise to edge every inland view.*

WEKA PASS *Limestone rock shelters in the vicinity contain ancient Maori rock art.*

MORRIS DANCERS *No surprise in an English village, the customary six dancers are equally at home in Canterbury, with its passionately English traditions.*

Oxford A farming centre on the edge of the hill country, the town is only about 14 kilometres from the spectacular cleavage of the Waimakariri Gorge, where the character of a great river changes dramatically as it escapes the confines of the hills.

Rangiora Almost as old as nearby Christchurch, it serves dairy and sheep farms, orchards and a nearby state forest.

Waiau This tiny, mellow farming village rests by the braided Waiau River.

Waikari This small junction settlement serves as a landmark from which to find the famed Timpendean Shelter, which holds some of the first Maori rock drawings to be discovered by shepherds of pioneer runholders. Like all people through the ages, the early Maori drew and scratched pictures on inviting plain surfaces, and there are many limestone overhangs that have been decorated in this way, perhaps in some instances by travellers sheltering there from the rain. A considerable number must have been lost, either from weathering or from being rubbed off by sheep with itchy backs. Others have been reduced in archaeological significance (although made more spectacular for the casual visitor) by being painted over with oil by a well-meaning if misguided early enthusiast anxious to enhance the photographic record he was making. The Timpendean Shelter is a spectacular example of old Maori rock art which, though found throughout the country, is best seen here and in the vicinity of Timaru.

Waipara Another junction settlement, Waipara recalls another of the region's vastly wealthy runholders – "Scabby" Moore, so called as he was too mean (though otherwise not too shortsighted) to dip his sheep for scab (a potentially fatal parasite).

CHEVIOT HILLS DOMAIN *The ruins of "Ready Money" Robinson's 40-roomed mansion rest in a well-wooded setting.*

HANMER *An early walk on a crisp, frosty morning can tempt even the most house-bound.*

THE FUN OF THE FAIR *Entertainment and education blend happily at an A & P (Agricultural and Pastoral) summer show. Summer shows are held each year, in 100 or so different centres, when the country comes to town to display its wares, to socialise and to give townspeople a chance to learn something of life on the farm.*

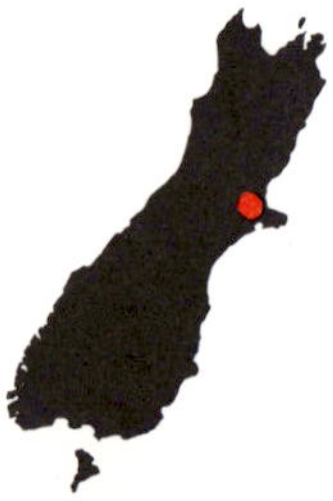

Christchurch

CATHEDRAL SQUARE *An open-air flower stall in the heart of the city adds further blossom to that of the extensive parks and gardens.*

The South Island's largest city sprawls on the lip of the Canterbury Plains, backed by the Port Hills and decorated with some of the country's prettiest homes and gardens. Even today, over 125 years later, Christchurch remains true to its origins as a Church of England settlement. Its claims to being "the most English city outside England" have over the years been cherished and, more recently, denied, perhaps as a sign of growing national confidence. Yet in many respects its inheritance still has strong hold. The country's most elegant Anglican cathedral towers over a broad square. Hagley Park bears similarity to London's Regent's Park. The baronial flamboyance of the old Provincial Council Chambers; Christ's College, self-consciously modelled on English counterparts: these "monuments" are matched by the fierce pride of those descended from the pilgrims who arrived aboard the revered First Four Ships.

FERRIER FOUNTAIN *A feature of the town hall, on the bank of the Avon.*

JOHN ROBERT GODLEY The man who led the first settlers presides over Cathedral Square.

LUNCH BY THE AVON *A place for dreaming or picnicking, comfortably close to the office.*

"THE WIZARD" *A local character, now a national institution, on his podium in the Square.*

LANCASTER PARK *A major rugby venue, and also the nation's cricket headquarters. It was here, too, that Peter Snell set world records for the 800 metres and 880 yards in 1962.*

The settlement at Christchurch was seen in grand terms by John Robert Godley, a young Tory who feared an age of equality and the collapse of church and civilisation. His Canterbury Association would redress this by firmly establishing both in the New World. In conjunction with Edward Gibbon Wakefield, migrants were selected, certified by their ministers as being sober, industrious, honest and respectable, and were shipped out – the first ships dropping anchor at Lyttelton in December 1850. Of course the grand design proved unnecessary, but the local citizenry has long enjoyed the reputation of being highbrow in cultural matters. For its part, Wakefield's scheme, dreamed up in an English prison, proved unworkable. He stressed the need to keep the population close-knit: indeed the *Westminster Review* added that any dispersal of settlement would "convert the nation, in short, into a horde of wandering Tartars, living upon milk and flesh and getting drunk on fermented mares' milk". But disperse the settlers did, for had they not there would have been no export trade. An age of great sheep runs followed, aided by an influx of Australian squatters with their flocks. Today there are still several vast runs in the high country, though those on the plains have since been systematically broken up as a result of action by successive governments aimed at "putting the small man on the land".

AN ENGLISH TRANSPLANT *Terraced housing is rarely found elsewhere in New Zealand.*

HAGLEY PARK *Created to soften a "treeless, featureless" landscape.*

SIGN OF THE TAKAHE *A Tudoresque roadhouse intended as just one of a series on the Summit Road. The Sign of the Kiwi, less ornate than the Takahe, but also of stone, is at the top of the road.* Below left, *interior of Sign of the Takahe;* below right, *typical stained glass window.*

SCHOOL OF ENGINEERING *Canterbury University has a long tradition of training the country's engineers.*

LORD RUTHERFORD'S DEN *Here the "father of the atom" began his career.*

MODERN PIONEER *Bill Hamilton's jet boat invention is used the world over.*

MONA VALE *The gatehouse entrance.*

MONA VALE *An imposing home, built in 1905 by one of the country's wealthiest women, the mansion has a splendid garden through which flows the Avon. Its builder, Annie Townend, inherited a fortune from her father, "Scabby" Moore of Glenmark, an early runholder. Today her one-time home in Fendalton Road is used for receptions, exhibitions and the like.*

Canterbury province Christchurch, "capital" of Canterbury, presides over a region as distinctive as any. Here the broadest area of plains in the country merges with its highest mountains. In the high country the nation's largest flocks of sheep graze the greatest of its runs, while on the seemingly endless sweep of plain the introduction of the double-furrow steel plough and the construction of water races has wrought astonishing change, transforming a vast desert of tussock into a mosaic of closely worked holdings. Unlike other South Island regions, Canterbury experienced no gold rush to generate local wealth. Large rewards for payable discoveries were left to languish, and provincial investment designed to capture for Christchurch some of the pickings from the West Coast goldfields resulted in the rapid construction of the Arthur's Pass road but saw precious little gold brought back along it. Instead the Canterbury settlers were left to work out their own destiny: a highly prosperous agricultural economy based on wool and, in more recent years, the intensive arable agriculture of the fertile alluvial plains.

GLAZIER AT WORK *A resurgence of interest in stained glass has encouraged the revival of an ancient craft.*

Christchurch city First and foremost, Christchurch is a garden city, and one in which as nowhere else in New Zealand seasonal changes are vivid. At its heart lies the wide expanse of Hagley Park and the River Avon, which casts a ribbon of green as it meanders seaward. In its wanderings, the Avon softens a sternly rectangular street pattern – as much a product of the city's flat topography as of the intentions of its first surveyors. Originally bounded by Salisbury, Barbadoes, St. Asaph and Antigua Streets, the infant settlement's limits were soon extended to the four broad avenues that are so much a feature of the city today – Bealey, Fitz-Gerald, Moorhouse and Rolleston Avenues, named after the first four superintendents of Canterbury Province. Tempering further the grid pattern of streets are Oxford and Cambridge Terraces, which flank the sinuous bends of the river. (Diagonal Victoria and High Streets were later additions.)

If arguably the country's most "English" city, it is undoubtedly its most level, standing as it does on the edge of New Zealand's largest plain and bounded to the east by the volcanic hills of Banks Peninsula and looking inwards to the distant and soaring Southern Alps. It is over these mountains that the distinctive "nor'west arch" forms to herald the onset of a dry, warm north-westerly wind that periodically howls across the plains to enervate the city's population.

In any season, a walk around the city is a rewarding experience, not only for the parks and gardens, but also for the splendid old buildings, many of them in stone and often with unexpected detail to delight the eye. Highlights include the old Gothic university (*Rolleston Avenue*), where one may see the den where the student Lord Rutherford did his early work; the Provincial Council Chambers (*Armagh and Durham Streets*); the stone of Christchurch Cathedral (*Cathedral Square*), and the wood of St Michael and All Angels (*Durham Street*) are all well over a century old: more recent is the High Renaissance of the Roman Catholic Basilica (*Barbadoes Street*), dating from the turn of the century, and the much-admired Town Hall complex (*Victoria Square*).

Statues of the early leaders are much in evidence: John Robert Godley (who led the first band of "pilgrims") stands by the commanding cathedral, and within short walking distance are Fitz-Gerald, Moorhouse and Rolleston. These are augmented by those of Queen Victoria, Captain James Cook and Captain Robert Falcon Scott. The last-named is much remembered, for he called on and won many friends here in 1910 on his way to the South Pole – and to his death. Displays in the museum also recall the city's special links with Antarctica, more recently renewed by the U.S. Operation Deep Freeze.

The museum has a special place in local life: traditionally locals have revelled in tracing their descent from the first four ships of pilgrims, and the museum's holdings have played a major role in "grandparent hunting". This passion for roots gives rise to the impression that the city's inhabitants may not be quite as mobile as those in other parts of the country. This reluctance to move is readily understandable. With a garden city set on alp-backed plains, with the beaches and crannies of Banks Peninsula close by for swimming and sailing, and with some of the country's finest climbing and skiing within easy reach, residents here are better placed than most to enjoy the outdoors, whilst Christchurch also has strong musical and artistic traditions. As befits the most "English" city, it is here, too, that the country's Cricket Board of Control has its headquarters.

SCOTT OF THE ANTARCTIC *A memorial sculpted by his widow.*

FIRE! *Ferrymead Historic Park displays a wide variety of early technology.*

ANTARCTIC LINKS *Christchurch farewelled many Antarctic explorers, among them Robert Falcon Scott and Edmund Hillary, who used this tractor displayed in the museum.*

A THRIVING ARTS CENTRE *Time-worn university buildings escaped demolition to house cultural activities.*

CHRIST'S COLLEGE *One of only two schools in the country to be endowed on the English model, and traditionally a school for the sons of the gentry, it has only comparatively recently abandoned the famed straw boater as part of its uniform. However, gentility should not be assumed: double Victoria Cross winner Charles Upham was educated here.*

ARTISTS' QUARTER *An Oxford Terrace craft centre.*

WEAVER AT WORK *Modern practitioners have won an international reputation.*

A QUIETER MOOD *Browsing in one of the city's shopping arcades.*

"GOLDEN HALF-MILE" *A busy New Brighton mall.*

COB COTTAGE The early settlers were forced to build their homes from whatever material was nearest to hand. Timber was preferred for quick and easy handling, but the broad and treeless plains, coupled with the economics of cartage, effectively denied this option to many. Stone, too, was scarce, so the settlers fashioned their cottages from puddled clay and straw, and used sticks for reinforcement. These "cob cottages" served the settlers well, being cool in summer yet cosy in winter.

Arthur's Pass The direct route from Christchurch to the West Coast lies along a splendid scenic drive over the alps.

Banks Peninsula A curious volcanic peninsula abutting an alluvial plain adds interest and contrast to the region.

Burnham Sited on billiard-table flat plains, the military camp here appears unremarkable, yet it stands on a site once occupied by a borstal whose most famous inmates were enshrined in the book *Borstal Boy* by the irrepressible John A. Lee. It was here also that the country's most celebrated soldier, Captain Charles Upham, VC and Bar, began his brief but spectacular military career – by helping lay the camp's lawns!

Lake Coleridge The lake lies in a tussockland setting of a glacier-gouged bed, some 103 kilometres west of Christchurch. It is a pleasant picnicking and fishing spot, and nearby Lakes Ida and Lyndon are winter venues for ice skating.

CAPTAIN COOK *In Victoria Square the Yorkshire navigator rues his mismapping of Banks Peninsula?*

"CONCORD" *Architectural detail on the Chamber of Commerce Building (1887).*

SUMNER BAR *A view from the hills above Redcliffs. Moa Bone Point Cave at Redcliffs has proved to be a major archaeological site, and was apparently occupied for over 600 years.*

Lake Ellesmere The lake is essentially a coastal lagoon, cut off from the sea by a long gravel spit which has built up gradually as the result of erosion further south. Although in area the country's fifth largest lake, its depth does not exceed about two metres. The lake abounds with fish and birdlife: predominantly black flounder, eels, black swans and Canadian geese. There is no permanent outlet to the sea, and to control flooding a cut is periodically bulldozed at Taumutu, its narrowest point. In season the lake is a favourite with duck shooters.

Kaiapoi Now a satellite centre for Christchurch, Kaiapoi once enjoyed the fruits of a river port on the mouth of the giant Waimakariri River. Its name is traditionally associated with woollen products, but originates from Kaiapohia, the name of a major fortified pa site some ten kilometres north. The pa was set in marshlands which afforded natural protection, but these have been so drained as to alter the scene beyond recognition. However, a tall column serves as a memorial to the place where, in 1831, the "Maori Napoleon", Te Rauparaha, swept south from his Cook Strait fortress to annihilate local Ngai Tahu and so avenge the death of his uncle here some years earlier. The attacking Ngati Toa had piled up huge amounts of debris, planning to start a bonfire which would burn down the palisade defences. But the Ngai Tahu took the initiative and themselves set alight to the pyre at a time when the north-west wind should have carried the flames harmlessly away from the pa. However, just as the fire had taken a firm hold the wind swung abruptly to the south and fanned the flames and smoke through the pa where the fate of the luckless Ngai Tahu was sealed.

Lincoln The agricultural college here has been a centre for agricultural training and education for over a century, and was among the first in the world to be established. Indeed, plans for the college were made by the first pioneers, who had been swift to realise that the prosperity of the new nation would depend on progressive and inventive farming. From these very early beginnings have developed farm advisory services within the Department of Agriculture by which farmers are kept abreast of general developments in relevant aspects of farming and farm management. Advisory officers can also assist both on a day-to-day basis (e.g. by helping draw up budgets, etc.) and with forward planning (e.g. by assessing the potential for local irrigation schemes).

Lyttelton The port serves as the "gateway" to Christchurch. Today access is via a tunnel through the Port Hills.

New Brighton As its name suggests, the seaside town was envisaged as a counterpart to England's Brighton, and it even once enjoyed its own entertainment pier. Today the facilities at Queen Elizabeth II Park, a complex built for the 1974 Commonwealth Games, provide entertainment on a different scale, though perhaps no other event has yet matched the excitement of the epic clash between New Zealand's John Walker and Tanzania's Filbert Bayi in which both athletes broke the world mile record.

Port Hills Over these hills, which mark the edge of Banks Peninsula, the Canterbury pilgrims walked along a bridle path now so well used as to be etched permanently into the hillside.

Rangiora A mature market and commuter town which is almost as old as Christchurch itself.

Sumner The beach here, characterised by unique Cave Rock, is popular for family outings.

Waimakariri River From its sources in the Southern Alps, the river, in a dramatic change in character, cuts through a spectacular gorge to debouch across the plain. Braided and lazy, it reaches the sea at Kaiapoi. Flood control depends on the ability to manage the vast quantities of shingle which the river sweeps down from the mountains. A jet boat ride from Kaiapoi can be a memorable experience.

Wigram The principal training base for the country's Royal Air Force is named for the man who pioneered aviation in New Zealand.

LYTTELTON HARBOUR *From the Summit Road, with Governor's Bay in the foreground.*

WOODLAND PARK *In spring the city is ablaze with daffodils.*

The arts

New Zealanders' much-vaunted prowess in the international sports arena has tended to overshadow their achievements in the fields of the visual and performing arts. This has deprived not only the nation's artists of the recognition they deserve, but also visitors to New Zealand of rich sources of entertainment and insight. For to appreciate that which is unique and vital in New Zealand's cultural life is to understand something of the country itself: the land, its influences and resources; the people, both Maori and Pakeha; the history, from a highly developed stone-age culture, through colonial rule to independence.

As a young country, with no single wellspring of tradition to guide its cultural development save that of the Maori (see pp. 62–63), both the range of artistic media and the freedom with which they are given new expression are remarkable. What many of them have in common, however, is a firm basis in the country's natural resources: pottery and ceramics from local materials; weaving from local wools; sculpture, wood carving, bone and jade carving; textile printing and manufacture from local fibres and dyes. In painting, the influence of the land is reflected in a surprising absence of portraiture and an exciting use of colour and texture evocative of the natural environment. The use of Maori motifs (as in the painting by Gordon Walters, *pictured*) is another characteristic of several of New Zealand's best painters and printmakers.

Similarly, in the performing arts the dominance of British and European works has in recent years been increasingly replaced by performances of local works which, like many innovations, are often controversial and even provocative. Professional theatres have been established in all the major cities, and amateur dramatic groups are active in nearly every small town. Large-scale, big-budget media like opera and ballet have enjoyed a more chequered history, although individual performers have gone on to achieve enormous success abroad; the New Zealand Symphony Orchestra, however, has (under a variety of names) been a part of New Zealand's cultural life since 1946. Today it tours regularly throughout the country, performing both classical and contemporary works, some by local composers.

Perhaps one of the most striking features of New Zealand's artistic life, however, is the extent to which amateur practitioners in a wide variety of fields have developed and refined their skills to become instrumental in spearheading new trends and stimulating interest from their audiences. Few New Zealanders would not at least have tried their hand at a medium suited to their inclination or taste, and this in turn has encouraged demand and expertise. Recognition may not be the reward of all, but for most the act of participation is reward enough in itself.

"PACIFIC" *Sea and sky merge in John Drawbridge's 510 × 510 mm design for a much larger watercolour mural.* From the private collection of John and Irene Zohrab.

CERAMIC PLATE (*Top left*) *Pottery by Len Castle.*

"RONGOTAI" *(Bottom left) A painting by Gordon Walters incorporates the traditional koru pattern of Maori carving and rafter painting.* From the collection of Michael Dunn.

THE DEPOT *(Right) A performance of a New Zealand play at Downstage's "alternative" theatre in Wellington. The Depot aims to provide a permanent venue for the production of local and lesser-known contemporary works in an intimate, informal environment.*

Banks Peninsula

HOME FROM THE SEA *Fishing boats ride at anchor from the wharf at Akaroa, a flooded volcanic crater.*

Banks Peninsula seems at odds with its setting. An abrupt volcanic upthrust, it is encircled by the sea and the vast alluvial plains that trapped the most astute of observers, Captain James Cook, into charting it as an island. Its much-indented shoreline and the vast flooded craters of Lyttelton and Akaroa afford shelter rare on the country's east coast, and it was Lyttelton's harbour rather than the plains which attracted the Church of England settlement to Christchurch. Between the harbour and Canterbury's "capital" rise the steep Port Hills, over which the first settlers toiled along a Bridle Path which their descendants still walk each December in memory of the revered "First Four Ships". The peninsula's elegance is enhanced by its French connections, most conspicuously at Akaroa, where France attempted to found a colony until a British gunboat helped put paid to the venture.

TIMEBALL STATION (1875) *For the mariners in Lyttelton Harbour, the station signalled the hour by which to set their chronometers.*

Akaroa Despite its French associations, Akaroa is essentially the best preserved of the country's Victorian townships. Picturesque wooden cottages, the museum house, the old cemetery, a plaque at their landing place and the British ship *Britomart*'s field-gun all recall the French settlers and the "race for Akaroa". At the northern end of Akaroa Harbour is Onawe Peninsula, scene of a dramatic tribal battle 150 years ago in which many were slaughtered and despatched to the ovens.

RELICS Three trypots at Akaroa, typical of those used to render down whale blubber and separate out the valued oil, recall times when whalers used Banks Peninsula as a natural haven from which to launch assaults on whales migrating along the coast. It was the enthusiasm of a French whaler that led France to attempt the establishment of a colony here. The last station closed in 1964, but whaling has been moribund here for over a century.

COLONIAL FLAVOUR *Akaroa's colonial architecture gives the town a special elegance.*

GALLIC AIR *Cultures meet in Akaroa.*

LYTTELTON *In the background, the Bridle Path over the Port Hills;* inset, *the road tunnel beneath provides access to Christchurch today.*

SHELTERED WATERS *The harbour at Akaroa is ideal for all water sports. Here yachts and small craft usually find a calm haven.*

Banks Peninsula has numerous inviting bays and inlets, among them Le Bon's Bay, Pigeon Bay, Little Akaloa and Okains Bay. To drive or walk around the highest points is to savour a succession of unfolding, almost aerial, views. At Little River is an unusual statue of a Maori chief who led the unsuccessful defence of Onawe pa and who helped provoke the attack by slaying Te Rauparaha's uncle in battle near Kaiapoi. The peninsula was named by Cook to honour the naturalist Sir Joseph Banks, who accompanied him on his first voyage and helped finance the scientific aspects of the expedition.

SWEEPING VIEWS *In a province dominated by plain and alp, the seascapes add enchantment and variety to this corner of Canterbury.*

GUNBOAT DIPLOMACY *The* Britomart's *gun stands guard over Akaroa.*

Lyttelton Christchurch's sea port was named to honour the Chairman of the Canterbury Association, Lord Lyttelton. Its seagoing tradition runs deep and is reflected also in the town's timeball station, the museum and the votive offering of miraculously saved sailors displayed in St Joseph's church. Behind rise the Port Hills and the zig-zag of the Bridle Path which gave way to a coast road and finally a tunnel as the prime link with Christchurch. Two islands in the harbour have unusual backgrounds: Quail Island, the largest, was once a leper colony and also housed ponies and dogs for Antarctic expeditions by Shackleton and Scott, and Ripa Island was constructed as an impregnable fortress during the "Russian scare" of 1885.

WILDLIFE REFUGE *Lake Ellesmere, to the west of Banks Peninsula.*

Mid-Canterbury

THE LEVEL AND THE UPLIFTING *The snow-draped Southern Alps preside over mid-Canterbury's sheep-grazing flats.*

The region is one of broad, braided rivers and wide, sweeping plains backed by sheer, snow-clad alps. It was here, on the native tussock grasses of the plains, that the moa grazed in large numbers in prehistoric times. Today, exotic English grasses have taken over the plains and the moa has long been hounded to extinction. However, the rivers still sweep vast quantities of glacial shingle down from the alps as the process of building the alluvial plains continues unabated. The plains themselves were natural magnets during the pastoral invasion of the 1850s–60s, while artificial fertilisers, water-race construction and the planting of windbreaks have made possible today's level of close settlement and mixed farming. Cash cropping is an important activity: wheat does not dominate as it once did, though Canterbury and North Otago produce most of the country's crop. Lamb, much of which is fattened on the plains here and in Otago, has enjoyed a pre-eminent position on the English market for over a century. It is still exported in larger quantities to the EEC countries than to newer markets in the Middle East, North America and Asia. Tourism, too, has grown in importance, especially with the opening of new facilities at Mount Hutt, New Zealand's fastest-growing ski resort.

ASHBURTON'S CLOCK *The town clock celebrates 100 years of local government.*

Ashburton Set on the rim of what was once described as a "desert", today's town has a well-treed complexion that belies such a past. The surrounding area is closely farmed, and just one of many local labels proclaims it "the granary of New Zealand"

Two local identities remembered in the town are the pioneer John Grigg, whose statue in Baring Square records his achievements as a notable settler farmer, and Edward Jerningham Wakefield, who lies in the cemetery on the corner of Kermode and William Streets. The only son of Edward Gibbon Wakefield, author of the controversial Wakefield Scheme, his contribution to New Zealand's settlement is well remembered – if occasionally exaggerated.

The Ashburton River, some 115 kilometres in length, is formed just above the town. Its northern and southern branches combine to maintain a perched water table only a few metres deep across a large area of the Canterbury Plains. For

RAKAIA GORGE *Here the river debouches spectacularly to sprawl across the plain.*

RAKAIA BRIDGE *The country's longest bridge spans fully 1.75 kilometres.*

THE PAST IN ACTION This restored Rogers engine, recovered from the Oreti River in Southland, once hauled the first Christchurch-Dunedin Express – the first "Kingston Flyer". Thought to be the only one of its type in working order, it can be seen at the Tinwald Domain south of Ashburton.

"IN THE SOUTHERN ALPS" (1881) *Almost entirely self-taught, the artist John Gully (1819–88) produced landscapes even more sought after today than in his lifetime.*

local farmers, the river's benefits are enormous, for without it the water table would be much less accessible.

Barrhill The lingering fragment of a dream. With English and Scottish models much in mind, many pioneer settlers imagined villages on their estates. Seldom were these realised, but occasionally, as here, some buildings linger on in memory of more populous times.

Erewhon A vast high-country sheep station deep in the Main Divide, this was not the setting of Samuel Butler's famous novel, nor was it the writer's home (which is across the treacherous Rangitata River at Mesopotamia). Here the landscape contrasts starkly with that of lush, verdant Ashburton, with treeless wastes of tawny tussock lapping the shingle slides of perpendicular alps.

Remote and much larger than other holdings (Erewhon has some 25,100 hectares), its produce is virtually limited to wool, store stock and some cattle. In summer, the flocks (Halfbred or Merino) are moved up to high ground, but with a comparatively short growing season hampering the production of supplementary feed, few can be carried through winter. The overall economic contribution made by the runs to the nation has occasionally been called into question on the basis that more of the higher land should be retired from grazing in the interests of conservation.

METHVEN'S ALL SAINTS CHURCH *It took all of seven weeks to drag this building from Sherwood to its present site, so strong was the wind.*

Erewhon Park This complex has been developed at Erewhon to cater for the hunter and skier. Accommodation is generally available, but it is wise to book.

Lake Heron An appealing summertime camping spot in a wildlife reserve where there is excellent fishing for both trout and land-locked salmon.

Highbank Power Station Situated on the Rakaia River, the station is fed with water diverted 65 kilometres from the Rangitata. Inverted siphons take the water under intervening rivers. The scheme provides for irrigation as well as power.

Methven This quiet farming township has taken on a new and bustling role as a winter sports centre after local interests combined to develop the Mount Hutt ski field nearby. South facing slopes are angled to the sun's warmth and trap the excellent falls of snow that assure a long and reliable season. The tow to the southern summit (2,756 metres) also operates in summer, whisking visitors up to a magnificent panorama of alp, plain and ocean. In wintry conditions, chains are needed on cars travelling the access road. Methven also hosts an annual floral festival on the first Saturday in November.

Rakaia River Rakaia probably means "to arrange in ranks", and would be a reference to the method used by the Maori to ford such difficult rivers as this. Included in its 2,600 square kilometre catchment area are the Lyall and Ramsay Glaciers and three relatively low passes over the Main Divide to the West Coast – the Whitcombe, the Mathias and the Browning.

Rakaia The town takes its name from the river. There is excellent salmon fishing in the area. Rakaia once bid to become the region's main centre, but lost out to Ashburton in the 1870s.

STUD FARM NEAR PREBBLETON *A popular area for horse breeding.*

South Canterbury

EVENING NEAR FAIRLIE *A pastoral scene as evening falls over rolling countryside. Poplars now grace a once barren landscape.*

Viewed from the air, the contrast within the region is stark. Here the gravel Canterbury Plains, a vast, multi-coloured checkerboard which stretches from a gently arching coast to an upthrusting chain of forbidding mountains, end abruptly as they yield to easy, undulating downland. Behind the downs rise hard-rock ranges enclosing basins created by downwarping, the greatest of which is the Mackenzie, and building to form the country's highest peak, Mount Cook.

This diversity of terrain is reflected in a flexible farming economy, not tied to any narrow range of product or market. Traditionally local wealth has come from sheep in the high country and mixed farming, predominantly cropping, on the lower coastal areas.

KAKAHU KILN *The kiln (c. 1880) was one of several in the area to burn lime for buildings in Christchurch and Dunedin.*

Cave Named after a cave that was once nearby, the township has an intriguing pioneer memorial church built of glacial rock and richly imbued with memories of the early Mackenzie Country.

Fairlie Seat of the Mackenzie, Fairlie's sylvan setting is in stark contrast with the open tussocklands it administers. An old blacksmith's cottage serves as a local museum and there is a cheerful country carnival each New Year.

Geraldine Set on rolling downland, this is the most picturesque of the region's settlements. Picnic spots abound, among them the Waihi and Te Moana Gorges. A vintage car and machinery museum is appropriate in a town which has used trees as milestones.

Mesopotamia Samuel Butler's large sheep station, where the classic novel

STAFFORD STREET, TIMARU *The city's main street.*

TIMARU'S ARTIFICIAL HARBOUR *A haven on a generally inhospitable coastline.*

AN UNSUNG PIONEER AVIATOR On Main Waitohi Road near Temuka, a memorial (*above*) records the place where an eccentric local farmer attempted to fly, arguably before the Wright brothers took to the air. Whether he succeeded is debatable, but he certainly left the ground before his powered craft veered into a hedge. What is beyond doubt is the inventive genius of Richard Pearse who, unaided and working in isolation, fashioned an aircraft and patented designs which were to become standard features in later years. Today Pearse's marriage of farming and aviation has been cemented by aerial topdressing (*below*). Two-thirds of the country's farmland is too steep for tractor-drawn implements and only widespread use of aerial topdressing has enabled the spreading of fertiliser to arrest declining soil fertility.

ROCK ART Many rock drawings survive from the time before sheep, when moa grazed the plains. This early Maori art has inspired tourist designs and even postage stamps.

Timaru The city serves as the region's pivot, standing as it does on a slight deviation on an otherwise unbroken shoreline which has been transformed into an artificial harbour. Caroline Bay is the scene of intense holiday activity in summer, with a three-week carnival held every Christmas. Behind the beautiful beach stretch 12 hectares of gardens and lawns, popular with picnickers. The Pioneer Hall Museum (*Perth Street*) and the Aigantighe Art Gallery (*Wai-iti Road*) are full of interest. The museum's holdings include moa-hunter artefacts and a display which shows the development of Timaru's harbour. Nearby Pleasant Point has an intriguing railway museum, a Pioneer Park and an excellent swimming spot at Hanging Rock Bridge.

Erewhon was conceived, also provided Butler with the wherewithal to devote his life to public debate with Charles Darwin about *The Origin of Species*.

Temuka A mere 18 kilometres from Timaru, splendid trout and salmon fishing facilities and numerous potteries give the town a special identity.

WAITAKI RIVER *As well as trout, the river provides valuable hydro energy.*

RUINED FARM BUILDINGS *Evidence of an earlier pastoral era at Burkes Pass.*

MOUNT PEEL STATION *The homestead at Mount Peel* (above) *and the tiny church close by* (right) *are testimony to the persistence and idealism of early runholders John Acland and Charles Tripp who, undeterred by rumours of how bleak their prospects would be there, arrived in New Zealand in 1855 to re-create an essentially English environment. Acting on the principle that "the worse account you hear of unoccupied country the greater the reason for going to look at it", they came, stayed, and prospered. The Acland family, who continue to farm the Mount Peel station (on part of the original joint holding), have preserved the beautiful pitsawn and brick homestead as its founder would have wished. The Acland family church contains appropriate memorials and headstones.*

Close by, Peel Forest Park, and especially Agnes Mills Bush, are rendered the more inviting by the comparative absence of bush in the area.

The Mackenzie Country

THE MACKENZIE BASIN *The basin presents a seemingly limitless panorama of tussockland.*

The Mackenzie Country has a magical quality. Here history and legend merge in a setting as grand as it is distinctive. In a vast basin, an inland sea of tussock is broken by perpendicular alps. Lakes of infinite elegance, whose beds gouge deep below sea level, taper back to glacier-fed streams.

Slowly this huge area is yielding to agricultural advances, and the land where the fabled sheep-stealer James McKenzie once planned to graze his stolen flock in secret is giving way to irrigation and the slash of hydro canals. In time, the character of the region will change markedly as English grasses replace the tussock. But the region experiences some of the country's harshest winters, and this factor has helped preserve its unique character for so long.

TEKAPO B POWER STATION One of five planned for the Upper Waitaki, the station is part of a scheme which will incorporate nearly 60 kilometres of canals. Water from the Tekapo River is diverted here for discharge into Lake Pukaki.

Burkes Pass A startling entry to the Mackenzie Country, as a green and well-wooded landscape abruptly gives way to mountain-backed tussock.

Lilybank This high country sheep station at the head of Lake Tekapo has drawn considerable numbers of tourists seeking the hunting trophies that a combination of alp and helicopter can provide. In common with several other such runs, access (and so station life) is ruled by an unpredictable river crossing.

LINDIS PASS *The pass between the basin and Central Otago links markedly dissimilar regions.*

CHURCH OF THE GOOD SHEPHERD, TEKAPO *A memorial to early pastoralists.*

CONTRASTS *Dry tussock contrasts starkly with the sparkling blues and whites of the alps' foothills which rise up in the background.*

TWIZEL *Unmistakably a Ministry of Works town. The local hotel sign* (left) *depicts James McKenzie, attributed with the discovery of the basin in 1851 after an heroic if illegal attempt to stock it. McKenzie was captured, tried and convicted, but oddly enough (for those were the heady days of the sheep barons) he was subsequently pardoned and disappeared from history. Many tales surround him – none authenticated.*

Lindis Pass The road which provides access to Central Otago follows a trail used by early Maori travellers. Not only were Otago's first deer liberated near here, but the pass also witnessed Otago's very first gold rush – one soon eclipsed by more spectacular finds elsewhere. As the diggers were drawn to richer fields, the promise of the Lindis was forgotten – along with the reward that was rightfully due to the hapless discoverer of Otago's first field.

Mackenzie Pass Here, on the spot where James McKenzie was captured with his stolen flock, stands a memorial to the region's enigmatic founder. Even today a controversy continues as to whether the Gaelic shepherd was self-motivated or set up by someone else. After his conviction he continued to protest his innocence, and after a series of escapes from gaol he was pardoned.

THE PIED STILT *A migrant visitor to the lakes of the Mackenzie Country.*

Mount Cook station Situated at the head of Lake Pukaki, the station is unusual in that it is still run by descendants of the family which founded it in 1856.

Mount John Here, above Lake Tekapo, an observatory and a United States satellite station testify to the region's extraordinarily clear atmosphere.

Lake Ohau That the lake marks the boundary between Canterbury and Otago is of little relevance today, but its affiliation was keenly contested in times of provincial government, when both provinces laid claim to the Mackenzie Country. In the 1880s, too, the boundary was of significance when the rabbit plague that crippled Otago crept north. In an effort to check the advance, Canterbury erected a rabbit-proof fence along its southern boundary. While its efficacy was dubious, Canterbury did not suffer from infestation in the same way as Otago – despite conditions which would seem to lend themselves to encouraging any rabbit population. The lake draws sporting enthusiasts all year round.

Omarama The town is renowned as a gliding centre, where each summer devotees gather to share their skills and compete with each other. Local fishing, too, is excellent. Nearby Tara Hills Research Station has significantly improved the production of the region's farmland.

Lake Pukaki The epitome of the Mackenzie's paradox of hostility and elegance, the lake has lost little of its inherent grandeur through the raising of its level to increase water storage for hydro-electric power. The lake protrudes like a tongue from a panorama of snow-draped alps which include the country's highest, Mount Cook, whose peak is occasionally reflected in the lake's waters. Access to Mount Cook National Park is along the lake's western shoreline.

Lake Tekapo Arguably the most stunning of the trio of glacial lakes, Tekapo is tinted milky-green by powdered rock, ground fine by the glaciers that feed it.

Twizel Headquarters for the Upper Waitaki River power scheme, Twizel now ranks as the second largest town in South Canterbury. Here displays serve to explain the concepts behind the scheme and to demonstrate its development. The emphasis on recreation as well as irrigation in the scheme has assubed the town a substantial and permanent role, in contrast to many of its predecessors.

LAKE MIDDLETON *Near Lake Ohau is a picturesque camping and swimming spot.*

THE RUNHOLDER'S BEST FRIEND Never was a dog more needed than in the days of the early pastoralist. Struggling against time to stock his run, firing tussock to render it palatable, desperately anxious that his flock be spared the curse of "scab" infection, frequently on the move – the runholder depended heavily on his dogs but, sadly, did not always care for them properly. Today that debt is recorded on the shores of Lake Tekapo by a memorial sculpted by a local farmer's wife. It stands on the spot once known as Dog Kennel Corner, where "boundary dogs" were tethered.

Mt Cook National Park

THE HERMITAGE *An alpine haven.*

MOUNTAIN FLOWERS Above, Ranunculus sericophyllus, *an alpine buttercup;* below, Leucogenes grandiceps, *the South Island edelweiss.* Drawings by Nancy M. Adams

MOUNT COOK *The Maori's Aorangi ("cloud piercer") soars above the Hooker Valley. In the foreground, the Mount Cook lily* (Ranunculus lyallii), *a pure white mountain buttercup, is a feature of the park in summer.*

SKIPLANES ON THE TASMAN *From here skiers can tackle a demanding 15-kilometre run.*

GLENTANNER STATION *A famous early sheep station, the gateway to the park.*

Curiously, neither Abel Tasman nor James Cook ever saw the towering peaks others named after them. Today, Mount Cook National Park embraces both in its 69,958 hectares – as it does all but five of the country's 27 peaks over 3,050 metres. A rich alpine flora and spectacular scenery render the park ideal for the walker, though even from the hotel comfort of the Hermitage, the less energetic can absorb the vivid, ever-changing colours of sunrise and sunset, when the peaks are tinted with pinks, oranges, apricots and even blood-red.

Mount Cook, at 3,764 metres the country's highest, was first climbed on Christmas Day 1894, but despite the country's distinguished climbing tradition (Sir Edmund Hillary honed his skills here), the formidable Caroline Face did not fall until 1970. There is no obvious reason why Cook should thrust some 300 metres above its neighbours. Built of the same greywacke as the other giants, its enhanced height is probably due to rapid earthquake uplift rather than to special durability of rock.

THE SUMMIT *A mountaineers' Mecca.*

SOLITUDE *A camper below Mount Sefton.*

Park activities These centre on the settlement at the Hermitage, where the Park headquarters arrange holiday programmes and where climbing and skiing equipment may be hired. An "intentions book" lists the plans of trampers and climbers and should be used by those venturing off the many well-maintained walking tracks. Information on camping facilities is also available.

MOUNT SEFTON *A blaze of apricot at dawn.*

REST AND RECREATION *Not all visitors pit their energies against the mountains.*

North and East Otago

OAMARU PUBLIC LIBRARY *Just one of many buildings in Oamaru distinctive for its use of "Oamaru stone". Here limestone columns and a forecourt sculpture add grace to modern design and function.*

SHEEP GRAZE NEAR OAMARU *The area is famed for its achievements in both breeding and meat and wool exports.*

The extraordinary landscape and exuberant history of Central Otago tend to obscure the fact that for generations the population and wealth of Otago have been concentrated along the north-eastern coastal region of the province. Although Dunedin's influence pervades North Otago, its focal point is Oamaru, a town of white stone buildings unusual in a nation where wood and concrete prevail. The local granular limestone, which hardens on exposure to the elements, has been used in major public buildings throughout the country, but here it dominates to give the illusion of a more substantial population.

Surrounding the town is a highly productive zone of mixed farming, but to the south the land becomes increasingly hilly and less productive. The coastline, however, grows more interesting, and the hills take on the names of passengers who, in Maori legend, were shipwrecked on Shag Point. The curious conical boulders on Moeraki Beach are similarly explained as kumara (sweet potatoes) and gourds from the sunken canoe.

WAIKOUAITI POSTBOX *An Edwardian curiosity in Otago's earliest settlement.*

KARITANE HARBOUR A view looking towards the Huriawa Peninsula and pa site. The father of the Plunket Society, Sir Truby King (1858–1938), lived here and popularised the locality's name by applying it to the child-care and nursing establishment which he founded.

Duntroon A farming centre at the confluence of the Maerewhenua and Waitaki Rivers. Limestone bluffs in the area show traces left by itinerant moa hunters. The most spectacular is the Takiroa shelter, with rock drawings of unknown age in charcoal and red ochre.

Karitane A pretty summer-holiday spot close to Dunedin, Karitane has a name ("men digging") which may refer to the extensive earthworks on its Huriawa Peninsula. The scene of an epic siege, the locality was later a mission station and shore whaling station, though it is best known as the home of Sir Truby King, whose homestead and beloved gardens still flourish.

Kurow The farming township by the Waitaki River is a natural centre for freshwater fishermen, both in the nearby rivers and in the hydro lakes. In winter there is some easy skiing behind the town.

Moeraki A picturesque fishing village with a tiny port that was once seen as a possible rival to Dunedin's Port Chalmers, Moeraki has a beach strewn with extraordinary conical boulders. Although they appear to have been washed ashore, more lie buried in the banks, awaiting discovery by the surging sea. Farther south, Katiki Beach has a similar array of septarian boulders as well as good swimming.

Oamaru The principal town of North Otago, Oamaru presides over a rich and varied farming region. Of the many white stone buildings that lend the town such charm, those of particular interest include the Courthouse (1883), the New and Old Post Offices (1884 and 1864), the classically styled National Bank (1870) and Bank of New South Wales (1884) (*all in Thames Street*) and just off Thames Street the Gaol Stables. In Arun Street grows the Scott Oak, so named because it was from the post office here that news of the death of the Antarctic explorer was first signalled to Britain.

Palmerston A servicing and distribution centre for a predominantly sheep-farming district, Palmerston was once of such importance that it forced the city of Palmerston North to qualify its own name.

OAMARU GAOL STABLES (1869) *"The handsomest building in the colony devoted to the punishment of crime."*

BY RAIL TO SEA It was from the Totara estate near Oamaru that the country's meat trade with Britain began in 1882, when a trial consignment of frozen lamb was sent to Dunedin's Port Chalmers for shipment. Today, containerisation has streamlined transport and seen meat exports grow.

Pigroot This unlikely name is given to Highway 85 which links the coastal route to the Maniototo Plains. The appellation probably stems from an incident in which a huge boar, totally unafraid, actually rubbed noses with a surveyor's horse. It was an important and sheltered passage through to the goldfields on which the town of Palmerston began as a campsite.

Waikouaiti The very first European settlement in Otago, Waikouaiti was founded in 1840 by the remarkable Johnny Jones, a colourful, free-wheeling entrepreneur who claimed to have purchased a vast area of land in 1839 for little more than ten dozen shirts. Firmly established by the time the first Dunedin settlers arrived, Jones was well-equipped to profit from supplying their needs, and for a time he so dominated the Dunedin scene that he had £20,000 in private banknotes in circulation. Jones' homestead and outbuildings (dating from 1846) are preserved by the Historic Places Trust at Matanaka. A local museum displays interesting relics.

MOERAKI BOULDERS *These peculiar rock formations on Moeraki Beach have been formed by the gradual attraction of lime salts to a small central core* (inset).

PILLION TO SPARE *The ideal transport.*

The sheep industry

Prophetically, it was Captain Cook who, over 200 years ago, introduced the first two sheep to New Zealand. Less auspicious was the pair's death within a matter of days. Today, however, approximately 65 million sheep graze pastures which have in some cases been won from dense bush, or in others are the product of drainage schemes or the replacement of native tussock with exotic grasses.

The earliest pioneers at first had little interest in sheep, busying themselves instead with the task of survival, but in the 1840s the first pastoralists began to emerge in Southland and in the Wairarapa. The early flocks were imported from Australia, where recurring droughts ensured a plentiful supply at knock-down prices, and it was not long before many of the Australian squatters themselves grew tired of the fickle rainfall there and opted to bring their entire flocks with them across the Tasman. The sheep were almost invariably Merino, a Spanish breed noted for its superfine fleece. These were augmented by British varieties, and today the most successful breeds are the New Zealand Romney (50 per cent of the total stock), the Perendale (15 per cent) and the New Zealand Halfbred, a cross between Merino and either Lincoln, Leicester or Romney. Another important breed, the Corriedale, was developed in North Otago by crossing Lincoln and Leicester rams with Merino ewes and is now famous internationally, despite the relatively small numbers in its country of origin. There are about 5 million Corriedale, principally in the light rainfall areas of Canterbury, Otago and Marlborough. A good producer of intermediate-grade wool, the Corriedale lamb can also grade as a prime export carcass.

Today, New Zealand ranks as the third-largest wool producer in the world, with sheep accounting for about one-third of the national income.

Initially, the sheep farmer was almost wholly dependent on wool, but the advent of refrigeration and the development of a massive trade in frozen mutton with Britain completely transformed the industry. Since then a three-plane system of production has emerged. In the high country, the mountain regions of the South Island where pasture is only sufficient to sustain sheep with a slow-growing carcass, the Merino is most at home and the emphasis is on fine wool. The hill areas of both islands are for breeding, producing breeding ewes and lambs for sale to the farms on easier lowland country (the third stage), where they are fattened and dispatched to freezing works. The hill farmers augment their income with wool and cattle.

The pastures, so much a feature of the countryside, almost wholly comprise exotic grasses, and the apparent lushness of much of the land disguises the regular application of carefully selected fertilisers and a highly scientific approach to pasture management which allows year-round grazing. New Zealand may be "God's Own Country", but in rendering it so close to the Garden of Eden, humans, too, have played a major and continuing part.

Merino (Spain)

New Zealand Halfbred (New Zealand)

Romney (New Zealand)

Suffolk (U.K.)

Southdown (U.K.)

Drysdale (New Zealand)

Coopworth (New Zealand)

Corriedale (New Zealand)

Perendale (New Zealand)

Central Otago

VIEW FROM TUCKER HILL *A sweeping panorama of Alexandra, the Clutha, dredge tailings, orchards and the distant Remarkables.*

BENDIGO HOTEL, ALEXANDRA
Here miners dressed a goat as a Chinese digger and hoaxed police and doctors into a postmortem.

STONE AND COB *Viewed from Highway 8.*

In Central Otago, past and future collide. For more than a century the region has basked in the glory of gold and its aftermath, and to many the lure of departed gold towns and deserted workings has proved irresistible. Today, the rivers that once deluged the region with fortune-seekers, and temporarily rendered Dunedin the country's economic capital, threaten to drown substantial areas in perpetuity as plans to harness the Clutha River are put into effect. But with the losses come some gains: the essential qualities of "Central" – barren mountains of sparkling schist, blazing summers, biting winters and a smell of history – will linger on, and the long-term construction works and new possibilities for irrigation are some compensation for the disruption.

Alexandra A town of trees, Alexandra is girt with orchards and vast, lifeless heaps of tailings – the legacy of times when huge gold dredges worked the Clutha around the turn of the century. The seasons here are marked with a clarity rare in New Zealand: the snow in winter, the riot of spring, the green of summer and the tones of autumn. An appealing place, Alexandra affords a comfortable base from which to explore the surrounding countryside and its several "ghost towns".

LAWRENCE IN WINTER *The town where the gold rushes began has a mellow, substantial feel about it today.*

GALLOWAY HOMESTEAD (1865) *Runholders preceded the diggers, selling them meat for a high price – disruption.*

CONTRASTING LANDSCAPES *The pictures above were taken on the same day and within a few kilometres of each other. A desert-like prospect near St Bathans rubs shoulders with alps and green-gold turnip fields* (right).

Old gold centres Tumbledown stone buildings and derelict cob cottages are all that remain of many of Central Otago's once flourishing gold towns. Many more have vanished almost without trace. Only the occasional fruit tree still blooms while mine shafts or contorted landscapes tell of herculean efforts made to extract the earth's wealth.

Among the more substantial of the colourful old towns still in existence are Lawrence (a Victorian gem which owes its existence to the spectacular discoveries made in Gabriel's Gully in 1861), St Bathans (whose quaint buildings overlook the remarkable Blue Lake that now fills a vast excavation), Clyde (on the banks of the Kawerau River, with old stone buildings and a layout moulded by the "tent sections" allotted to early arrivals) and Naseby (where century-old wooden buildings resemble a film set rather than reality). Roxburgh also dates from goldmining days, but today the prize is a summer feast of peaches, nectarines and a whole range of stone fruits.

The largest apart from Alexandra, Cromwell, is experiencing a renaissance as the centre for the Clutha hydro-electric power project which will radically change the face of Central. But the waters of the Clutha offer a range of recreational facilities which soften the searing heat of a Central Otago summer. Foremost among the river's attractions are the breathtaking jet-boat trips which occasionally venture through the rapids to reach the confluence with the Kawerau. Water skiing, fishing and a host of riverside picnic spots are enticing alternatives.

CHINESE RELICS *Above*, artefacts in the Alexandra Museum once belonged to Chinese gold diggers; *above right*, the Clutha in full flow, as it was when Chinese miners toiled there for gold. Discrimination against the Chinese was blatant: aloof, frugal and capable of profiting from claims the Europeans had rejected as unpayable, they were viewed by wildly prejudiced diggers with a suspicion and hatred that occasionally erupted into violence and added to the already considerable hardship of squatting in shantytowns built of packing cases, sacking and old iron. Most came to earn enough to assure them a comfortable life on their return home; some *(right)* did not live to do so. But others remained to form the nexus of today's well integrated Chinese communities.

ST BATHANS *A hamlet heavy with the nostalgia of a golden past.*

SPRING IN ALEXANDRA *A season of kaleidoscopic orchards and a celebrated blossom festival.*

Dunedin

DOWNTOWN DUNEDIN *George Street meets the Octagon. The Octagon is enclosed by a larger octagon, the eight segments of Moray Place.*

More than any other New Zealand city, Dunedin wears its origins on its sleeve. Given the ancient name for Edinburgh by its pioneer settlers, drawn from Scotland to a site as far from their homeland as could be imagined, Dunedin relishes its past: Presbyterianism holds fast, Robbie Burns presides over the Octagon in the city's heart, there is a lively trade in kilts and the country's only whisky is distilled here. The setting for this exercise in nostalgia could not be surpassed – the city rests on the upper reaches of slender Otago Harbour, its hills rising steeply and its streets imposed somewhat arbitrarily on an unyielding topography. Essentially Dunedin is a Victorian city, its celebrated architecture reflecting the glories of the gold era and relatively unscathed by the bursts of renewal that have in recent times stripped other cities of much of their original character.

ROBBIE BURNS *His nephew led the pioneers.*

A city of poets Dunedin is redolent with the memory of its two bards, the one borrowed, the other home-grown. *Above*, the immortal son of Scotland, Robert Burns, depicted in Dunedin's Octagon and a poet perhaps more honoured than read. *Below*, Thomas Bracken (1842–98) lies on a city hillside viewing the Bay from Dunedin rather than "Dunedin from the Bay" as described in his well-remembered poem. His are the words to "God Defend New Zealand", written in 1875 as the country's national anthem but which attained official recognition only in 1940, and then as the nation's national hymn. "God Save the Queen" remains the national anthem. In recent years "God Defend New Zealand" has been played more frequently, in place of the anthem, reflecting an increasing national confidence and self-assertion which has finally recoiled at hearing the British anthem played at the Olympic Games to acknowledge New Zealand gold medallists. Bracken's best-known poem is "Not Understood", a fore-runner, perhaps, of the "Man Alone" theme that has long dominated New Zealand's literature.

FLAMBOYANCE *Dunedin's railway station.*

CARVING *An Otago Museum exhibit.*

OLD KILN *Lime was produced for cement.*

BRACKEN *At rest on the hills he loved.*

VICTORIA CROSS CORNER *Winners of the wartime award for gallantry are listed here.*

POLICE STATION (1895) *Its design was influenced by that of London's Scotland Yard.*

BLUESTONE *A Port Chalmers hotel.*

Best laid plans Ignoring the general advice of his uncle, Robert Burns, that "The best laid plans 'o mice and men/ Gang aft agley", the Rev. Thomas Burns enthusiastically embraced the scheme for a Scottish settlement to establish a "New Edinburgh" in the Southern Seas. Religious turmoil had gripped Scotland, and the Free Church of Scotland had been formed by those Presbyterians who wished a say in the choice of their ministers. Unemployment was rife, with about a quarter of the population out of work. Those lucky enough to be employed were grinding a 16-hour day to survive.

Burns joined forces with William Cargill and, aided by the New Zealand Company, the first migrant ships set sail for Port Chalmers in 1847. Although it was not long before later arrivals ensured that the Scots were outnumbered, those from north of the border had firmly placed their stamp on the character of the settlement, so much so that a Gaelic flavour persists to the present day.

As elsewhere, the plan for orderly settlement was undermined by absentee land speculation and those who did venture out here spent several grim years. First the "woolly empires", the great sheep runs of Central, were developed and then in 1861 came the first of the fabulous gold strikes in Central Otago that within a short time established Dunedin as the country's commercial capital. Gold by the millions of pounds flowed out through Port Chalmers, and many more secure fortunes were made by entrepreneurs who supplied the goldfields rather than took their chance with the diggers. The traditional Scottish skills of engineering and banking found a happy marriage in the enterprise.

The gold boom had generated rapid growth, and Dunedin was the first city in the country to become highly industrialised.

By the time the gold dwindled, Dunedin had assumed the look of substance it still wears today, and many of the older large houses reflect the aspirations of the well-to-do miner retired to town. Today Dunedin is the most architecturally interesting of the country's cities, with numerous fine Victorian buildings. These are enclosed by a town belt, provided for in the original plan for the city. Today it provides both a green backdrop to the city and many spectacular vantage points.

OTAGO UNIVERSITY Education was a priority with the new settlers and they were quick to establish the country's first university, the University of Otago. The buildings that today serve as its focal point date from 1878. The proliferation of modern buildings around it evidence the growth of recent years.

MACANDREW BAY *A school picnic beach outing on the Otago Peninsula.*

HIGH GOTHIC AND HIGH RISE *Cargill monument.*

PETER PAN AND WENDY *The statue in the Botanic Gardens echoes the one in London, but what appears as an Anglocentric exception in a Scottish environment is explained by Barrie's Edinburgh birthplace.*

ROYAL ALBATROSS CHICK *The colony at Taiaroa Head is the closest in the world to human habitation.*

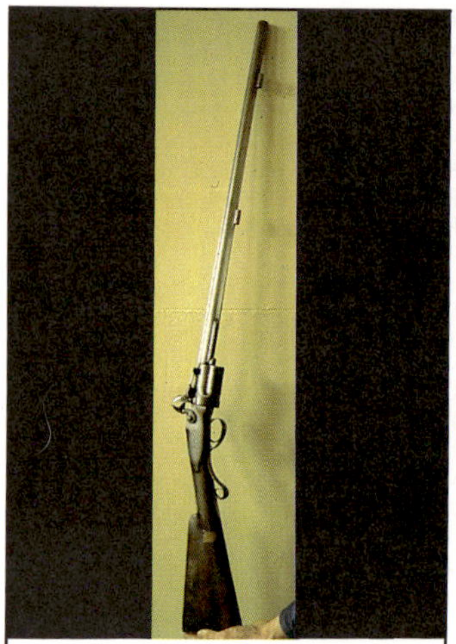

CHIEFLY RELIC Displayed in the Otago Museum is a Collier flintlock rifle, reputed to have belonged to Tuhawaiki, the renowned "Bloody Jack", who sold land for the infant settlement. He relished uniforms and signed the Treaty of Waitangi dressed as a British aide-de-camp.

SCOTT MEMORIAL The country has several memorials to Robert Falcon Scott, but Port Chalmers has perhaps the greatest claim to him, as it was his last port of call en route to the South Pole. In 1928, on Quarantine Island, a new dog biscuit was developed to save most of the explorer Byrd's dogs from a mysterious illness.

SHIPBUILDING *Dunedin has long links with the sea.* Above, *a new 20-metre tourist boat is launched for use on Milford Sound.* Right, *cheerful shipbuilders looking on.*

Otago Province The province, occupying the southernmost third of the South Island, was established in 1848 before the hinterland had been properly explored, with the Waitaki River as its boundary with Canterbury. When pastoralists opened up the grassy plains and downlands of North Otago, the settlers here found themselves in a lengthy and keenly contested boundary dispute with its neighbour as no thought had been given as to which of the Waitaki's tributaries was the border's westward extension. The question would be academic today, but in times of provincial government large areas of land (and so of money) were at stake.

Before long pastoralists had established themselves throughout the province (except, of course, in the wilds of the Fiordland forests), but this had scarcely taken place before the solitude of Central Otago was shattered by a massive influx of gold diggers – a flood of people which ebbed to and fro as one phenomenal find was followed by another.

Experiments with sheep made in the province, too, were of national importance. Long-woolled sheep were crossed with Merino to produce the distinctive Corriedale breed. It was from Dunedin's Port Chalmers that the first shipment of frozen meat was made, marking the advent of a trade with Britain that came as a godsend to a colony lamenting the decline of the gold and desperate for a sound economic base.

A large segment of the population can trace their families' arrival back to those who arrived in the first two decades of settlement, and as a linguistic legacy of their origins there survives even today a faint burr to the "r", giving Otago one of the very few regional variations in speech to be found in New Zealand.

Dunedin city The city centres on the Octagon, an eight-sided garden area presided over by a statue of Robert Burns "with his back to the kirk and his face to the pub" – the Anglican Cathedral (1915) rises behind the bard but the Oban Hotel has long since disappeared. A block away rises the city's most illustrious building, First Church (1868–73), a "psalm in stone", built as a monument to Presbyterianism in the Antipodes. Knox Church (1876) (*George Street*), by the same architect, is also notable if not as striking. Early Anglican churches include All Saints' (1865–75) (*Cumberland Street*) and St Matthew's (1874) (*cnr Stafford and Hope Streets*).

The Otago Museum (*Great King Street*) houses, in a particularly fine building, collections of the ancient civilisations, including classical Greek, Roman and Middle Eastern art and sculpture. The displays of Maori material illustrate the generally more frugal lifestyle and harsher existence of the Maoris of Murihiku ("the tail end of the land", the southern part of the South Island). The museum incorporates the Hocken Library, one of the major New Zealand research libraries. The Early Settlers Association Museum and Portrait Gallery (*Lower High Street*) affords glimpses into the city's past, and Olveston (*42 Royal Terrace*) an insight into the life of a prosperous local merchant at the turn of the century. The Dunedin Public Art Gallery (*Logan Park*) has a display of minor masters, interesting furniture and, of special note, a collection of the works of Frances Hodgkins. At St Kilda and St Clair, the pick of the city's beaches, a working steam-railway museum operates at weekends.

SHAGS ON THE OTAGO PENINSULA *A variety of sea birds may be seen. Disliked by fishermen, shags in fact do no damage to marine or estuary fishing.*

LARNACH'S CASTLE (1871) Left, *a symbol of the extravagant lengths to which pioneers would go to recreate the old world in the new.* Above, *the castle's stairwell, a Georgian hanging staircase that relies for support on a complex series of curves.*

Otago Peninsula The green undulating peninsula, slanting north-eastwards to enclose the narrow inlet of Otago Harbour, holds endless possibilities for the visitor, from lazy picnic places and solitary beaches to tours of Larnach's Castle and birdwatching at the Royal Albatross sanctuary at Taiaroa Head. The main points of interest can be taken in in a single day, though the peninsula lends itself to more leisurely exploration. The Glenfalloch Woodland Gardens are an early stop, attractive the year round but a riot of colour in early spring. By contrast, the Portobello Marine Laboratory and Aquarium a little farther on affords glimpses of nature at work under water. At Otakou, the quaint Maori church appears to be carved from wood: closer inspection reveals it to be of sculptured cement! (There are very few carved meeting houses in the South Island.) On the ocean shoreline are the blowhole at Cape Saunders and the Chasm and Lovers' Leap, fearfully precipitous drops on a wild stretch of coastline. The cliffs revealed how the penisula was gradually built up with lava flows and ash showers. At Penguin Place the rare yellow-eyed penguins may be seen in their greatest numbers between June and August, when they come ashore to their nests.

PROUD PEACOCK *Glenfalloch Gardens.*

PORTOBELLO The Marine Laboratory and Aquarium at Portobello on the Otago Peninsula. Exhibiting a wide variety of sea life in constantly changing displays, it is open to visitors daily. All the specimens, from more familiar fish to colourful sponges and octopi, come from New Zealand waters. The laboratory is maintained by the University of Otago for the purposes of research.

AN EARLY TRAMCAR *One of a variety of transport exhibits in the Early Settlers' Museum.*

"RED SAILS" by Frances Hodgkins (1870–1947), born in Dunedin and one of the finest painters the country has produced. The Dunedin Art Gallery holds a large collection of her work. Not "discovered" by art dealers until over 60, she had spent a lifetime associating with the leading European artists of her day.

PANORAMA FROM THE PENINSULA *Dunedin city and harbour viewed from the Otago Peninsula.*

Brighton Its name indicating that the Scots did not have everything their own way, Brighton is a seaside centre which saw its heyday in the early days of the motorcar, being a comfortable day's outing from Dunedin.

Lake Mahinerangi An artificial lake about 60 kilometres south-west of Dunedin, Mahinerangi feeds Dunedin's own electricity-generating complex which for years gave the city independence from the state grid and a supply of power at much lower prices than elsewhere. There is swimming and fishing in the lake in season.

Mosgiel A level town on the broad Taieri Plain, Mosgiel contrasts with the hills of Dunedin but competes with a proliferation of churches. Its woollen mills for many years enjoyed a high reputation. The town was named for a farm once owned by Robert Burns, as it was developed on farmland owned by Burns' nephew. Ironically, the Rev. Burns' homestead still stands here but it is now a Catholic seminary, something that would have enraged Burns, who despised Anglican and Catholic alike.

Port Chalmers Port Chalmers, the centre of shipping on the Otago Harbour, is very much a harbour town, filled as it is with shipping offices and warehouses. In the harbour lie a number of rotting hulks, many with colourful pasts (one is said to have been an old slave trader). Major container facilities emphasise the port's natural advantages and assure the town a continuing role in the South Island's economy.

TYPICAL OLD HOMES *Ranging from the stately* (below) *to those of Stuart Street* (above) *before shop conversion.*

"OLVESTON" *A Jacobean-styled home (1904), filled with antiques and open to the public.*

Manufacturing industries

The manufacturing sector of the country's economy is very much the junior partner to agriculture, and is dominated by activities which either add value to agricultural goods (as in food processing and the manufacture of wood products) or which meet the specific needs of farmers (as in the assembling and servicing of vehicles).

From the outset New Zealand was cast in the role of supplier to Britain of "colonial products" – food, wool and raw materials – while remaining reliant on her for manufactured goods, investment and shipping. Before the age of steam, shipping costs afforded a high degree of protection for would-be manufacturers, whose ventures began as, for example, boot-making factories to supply the needs of gold miners or woollen mills to eliminate the need to import back from Britain yarn spun from New Zealand wool.

The importance of farming, too, fostered the early development of engineering skills, the blacksmith soon becoming a maker of ploughs and harrows and, eventually, of the sophisticated farm machinery which has led local technology to be in high demand around the world. The processing of farm products was also important after the introduction of refrigeration, when meat works and butter and cheese factories sprung up all around the country. Protective tariffs helped protect the home market for clothing and textiles, and they geographically sheltered others such as brickworks, breweries and the makers of bulky furniture and perishable goods.

The shortages induced by two world wars provided further stimulus for home production when huge quantities of goods were produced for the Armed Forces. Since then, and encouraged by a blend of tariffs, import licensing and export incentives, manufacturing has grown, both to substitute home products for imports and to process raw materials. Periodic collapses in world prices for grassland products, too, have heightened awareness of the country's narrow economic base and of its vulnerability in the face of unpredictable pricing trends. This has been further squeezed by Britain's entry into the EEC and New Zealand's subsequent denial to the very markets which brought its economy into existence. To make matters worse, markets carefully cultivated elsewhere have been upset by the EEC's dumping of surplus produce there. Also significant in fostering New Zealand manufacturing have been an increasingly urbanised population and a closer economic relationship with Australia.

The pressure is on New Zealand's manufacturers to perform as never before. In this they are handicapped by a small home market, where comparatively short production runs result in an expensive final product. However, the country does have a cheap labour force compared with other market economies: OECD figures in 1981 showed the per capita GNP as less than that of the United Kingdom, two-thirds that of Australia and just over half that of the United States.

NEW ZEALAND STEEL *The Glenbrook Steel Mill in South Auckland draws on Wa ironsand deposits for the production of a wide range of steel products. Projected expa of the works aims to see output raised to 770,000 tonnes a year from 1984.*

ALLIANCE FREEZING WORKS *The mutton chain at Southland's giant meat works* (i right).

JET BOAT MANUFACTURE *A New Zealand "first" for Canterbury engineer-farmer late Sir William Hamilton, led to exciting developments in the engineering field. The Ham jet unit is renowned the world over, with production based in Christchurch* (inset far rig

Balclutha, Gore and environs

NUGGET POINT *At rest after chasing smaller fry, these fishing boats work waters where whalers once thrilled to cries of "Thar she blows".*

Evergreen from a dependable rainfall, the lush landscape of East Otago-Southland is flecked with the fleeces of well-rounded sheep, testimony to the region's richness as a foremost producer of fat lambs, incongruously marketed in Britain as "Canterbury". On the lowlands, mainly Romney breeding ewes mate with Southdown rams to produce the country's highest lambing percentages and more than double stock numbers each spring. Dairying, however, is not neglected, and the area doubles as the South Island's most important.

Lowland contrasts with the hill country which, too steep to plough, is more often clothed in bush or native grasses. Local cropping, unlike that to the north, tends to ignore cash crops in favour of turnips, rape, oats and swedes, grown as winter feed for the area's huge herds of stock, and lending, in early summer, a kaleidoscopic touch to the scene. In the hills of East Otago is testimony in charred logs and bulldozed stumps to the struggle, won elsewhere, to bring land into production.

PURAKANUI FALLS *Pictured in heavy flood.*

Balclutha The prosperous hub of a wealthy sheep-farming district, the town bears a Gaelic name, meaing "town of the Clyde". Unlike its Scottish counterpart, it is a little inland, but here the mighty Clutha flows swiftly by, with a force that hints of potential for electricity generation upsteam – and the threatened demise of towns and farmlands on its banks. The river, too, is Scottish in the sense that "Clutha" is the ancient name for the river Clyde, and is the country's largest in volume if not in length. Below the town the river separates to enter the sea at two different points.

The Balclutha-Invercargill coast road Recommended for those with time to spend idling along a coastline of great and varied beauty, the road passes through native bush and raw farmland which still bears scars of the effort it took to bring it into production. Features on the way include curious Curio Bay, where the sea washes a fossilised forest floor, and a rich variety of marine wildlife.

FIVE ARCHES *The bridge at Balclutha spans the swiftly flowing Clutha River.*

CURIO BAY *The rock terrace which, some 160 million years ago, was the floor of a forest* (see also p. 199). *The beach, one of the most southern in New Zealand, is accessible from neighbouring Porpoise Bay.*

A SATELLITE'S VIEW *The Hokonui Hills are prominent to the north-west. Dunedin is just off the picture's north-eastern corner.*

HOKONUI HOOCH For as long as governments have sought to tax alcohol, the enterprising have made their own. The Scottish pioneers of Otago-Southland were no exception and, naturally, distilled their own whisky. This cottage industry blossomed into a considerable undertaking in the Hokonui Hills near Gore, where underground pipes carried for lengthy distances the tell-tale smoke fumes from the fires which heated the stills. The practice persisted up until World War II, with even aircraft being used by disconsolate excise men, but they have now passed into the region's folklore. Tales abound of the freedom-loving rascals who ran all manner of risks (often exaggerated) to produce their own product, whose virtues have grown with time and distance.

MILTON POTTERY On display at the Tokomairiro Historical Society Museum, the pottery with its characteristic brown and cream glazes was fired at a time when it was hoped that Milton would become the centre of a considerable ceramics industry.

MISS AMY BOCK *Masquerading as "Percy Redwood", this legendary confidence trickster, whose audacity has earned her a place in local history, came to the Nuggets in 1908. She was not arrested till after her marriage to the daughter of a boarding house proprietor.* Alexander Turnbull Library, Wellington.

Edendale A dairying township from which the first butter to be carried to England by a refrigerated ship (the *Dunedin*, in 1882) was probably produced.

Gore The solid centre of a hugely prosperous farming region, Gore shares with Balclutha the distinction of enjoying the highest level of per capita retail sales of any area of the South Island. Both plains and downland are dominated by the intensive farming of fat lambs.

Hokonui Hills Here sheep breeding is the most significant farming activity, but the area's past is resonant with echoes of excise men who stalked sly-groggers and illicit whisky stills.

Kaitangata This former coal town stands by large reserves of lignite and some sub-bituminous coal, which hold potential for the township's revival as a supplier of liquid fuel.

Mataura Another town with sizeable reserves of lignite, as well as an historic paper mill (heir to the country's first) and neighbouring bagmaking factory. Nearby Tuturau witnessed the last encounter of the tribal wars, when Southland Maoris defeated invaders from the north.

Owaka The hub of the Catlins district, where settlement is sparse and holdings large as farmland is clawed back from the forest.

SLOPE POINT *An unpretentious point marks the southernmost tip of the South Island.*

Nelson

MAITAI VALLEY FROM OBSERVATION POINT *An attractive setting for picnics and for camping, and an especially pretty area in autumn.*

Nelson rests on a sundrenched site overlooking a placid, sparkling sea and golden beaches which each summer succumb to an influx of holidaymakers in search of warmth, both in and out of the water. The city is also noted for its enterprising artistic community who produce work in every medium, especially pottery made from versatile local clays. Substantial though the artists' contribution is, the city can claim an earlier landmark in the nation's culture, for it was here that the country's first game of rugby football was played.

Nelson came close to becoming New Zealand's capital when, in 1865, the site was shifted from Auckland. Mercifully it was spared, or today's prolific gardens and orchards would have yielded to urban sprawl. Near at hand are the coastal attractions of Abel Tasman National Park and the alpine appeal of Nelson Lakes National Park.

PIED OYSTERCATCHERS AT TAHUNANUI *Easily distinguished by their long red bills and black and white plumage, these wading birds breed only in the South Island, winter over in Northland, and have a taste for shellfish.*

CIVIC PRIDE *Nelson city crest in ceramics.*

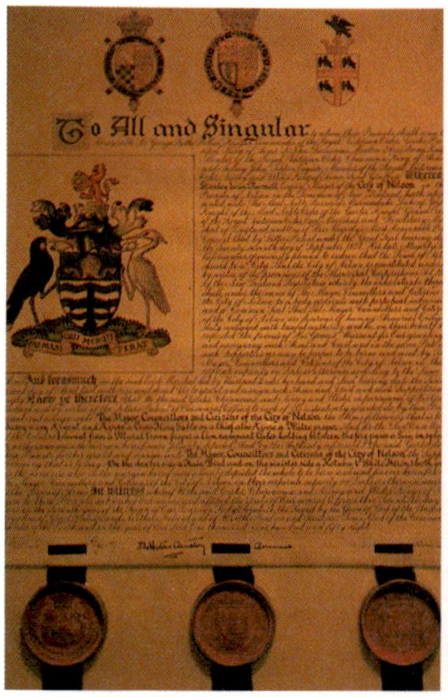

LETTERS PATENT *A township deemed city.*

NELSON CATHEDRAL *A Trafalgar Street view.*

NELSON HAVEN *A long slender bank of boulders washed down from a bluff by the sea acts as a natural shelter for the waters of Nelson Haven.*

Nelson today A city of some 33,000, it is one to visit in any season. In winter, snow-draped mountains rise from a broad blue sea; in spring, the blossom of great areas of orchard holds promise of a summer which will draw visitors from all parts of the country and which will mature into an autumn busy with fruit picking. Its climate, too, is surprisingly benign as the region is spared many of the storms that can characterise other areas near Cook Strait. This equable climate melds with fertile flats and advanced technology to render Nelson a highly successful horticultural region. Glasshouses crowd into the city itself, and nearby are the irrigated tobacco fields of Motueka and the hop gardens of Riwaka. The area also produces large quantities of berryfruits, stone fruits, peas, beans, tomatoes and other market-garden produce. Also significant are forestry, with the vast Golden Downs State Forest on the Spooner Range, and commercial fishing.

Minerals also hold tantalising promise: copper was once mined on Dun Mountain, and on walks close to the city one can still see traces of the railway, arguably the country's first, that once trucked out the deposits. Hopes of spectacular finds have been unfulfilled, but the city is developing a sound industrial base, with its pleasant environment and settled workforce affording compensations for distance from major markets.

BOTANICAL RESERVE *Scene of New Zealand's first rugby match (1870).*

WHITE HERON *In legend, the seldom-seen white heron personified rarity, grace and beauty.*

PERIOD ARCHITECTURE *A feature of the city is its many splendid early colonial buildings. Pictured left is part of Isel House, set among magnificent gardens at Stoke. At right, more humble wooden dwellings lend a special charm to the city's retail centre.*

TEAL VALLEY POTTERY *In a country known for the excellence of its pottery, Nelson's potters stand high. Local clays are particularly good, and the city's strong artistic tradition ensures that its potters should rank with the very best.*

Nelson's beginnings Today's city rests so comfortably as to wear a planned and organised air. In part this is deserved, for it began as the second (after Wellington) "Wakefield" settlement – an attempt to transplant into the New World a vertical cross-section of English society. The expedition left London in 1841, the moneyed with land already purchased but the promoters still ignorant of where the new town would be. No sooner was this sorted out than it became apparent that the concept on which the plan rested, while splendid in theory, in practice overlooked one thing – those with money might buy land in London but they included such unlikely investors as John Stuart Mill, who had not the least intention of emigrating. As a result, the founders of today's prosperous city suffered grievously through the early years, with money so scarce and hardship so acute that the venture all but collapsed.

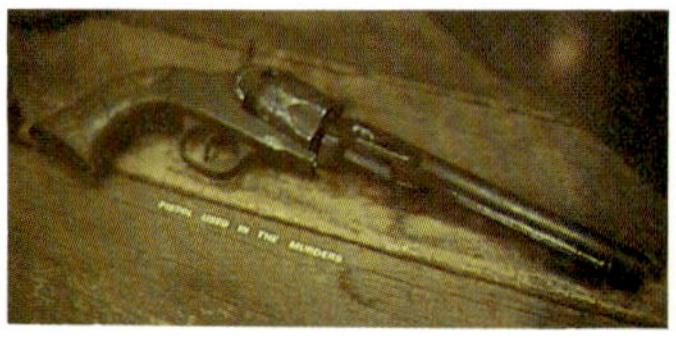

THE MAUNGATAPU MURDERS *Grisly relics of the country's most gruesome murders – the death masks of the executed convicts and a pistol used in the 1866 ambush of four unsuspecting gold miners on Maungatapu Mountain – are on display at the local museum.*

CHECKMATE *Giants have chosen the steps to Christ Church Cathedral for their game.*

A BIRD EMERGES *A local sculptor.*

NELSON APPLES *Modern processing techniques ensure the delivery of quality produce.*

APPLE WINE *New industry; new markets.*

Nelson's attractions Nearby beaches are so appealing that many visitors are happy merely to lie back and enjoy them.

OFF CENTRE? *Botanical Hill's trig plaque.*

As befits the oldest of the country's "cities" (a title bestowed accidentally in 1858 when in letters patent Nelson Diocese was created by Queen Victoria), there is much of interest from the past. The Provincial Museum, whose predecessor was actually established on board ship by the first migrants from Britain, has a variety of displays drawn from a colourful past that includes the Maungatapu murders, the epic sea rescues made by the Maori woman Huria Matenga (Julia Martin), and the forlorn and fatal attempt by local settlers to wrest lands from Maoris in neighbouring Marlborough. The museum stands in the grounds of Isel House, a venerable homestead which dates from 1848 and is occasionally open to the public. Broadgreen, modelled on a Devonshire farmhouse, dates from 1855 and is elaborately furnished in the period. More recently restored is the tiny Bishop's School (1844).

A number of drives can be made through interesting and varied countryside. The signposted local scenic drive starts in front of the cathedral and embraces many points of interest, most notably the Princes Drive lookout. Further afield lie Motueka and Kaiteriteri Beach, while the run out to the Spooner Range (en route to Nelson Lakes National Park) leads to another splendid lookout point from which to witness thousands of hectares of the Golden Downs Forest, Tasman Bay and D'Urville Island. Good walks include Flaxmoor Hill, the Maitai Valley and Dun Mountain.

TIMBER MILLING *Vast exotic forests provide a major export from Port Nelson.*

ARROW ROCK *At the entrance to Nelson Haven is the rock on which the pioneer ship* Fifeshire *foundered in 1842.*

MOTUEKA LANDSCAPE *Pasture, sea and mountain merge in an area of diverse and unspoiled beauty.*

Arable crops

Of the country's 8.5 million hectares of improved land, only about 600,000 hectares are used for growing crops, and of these over two-thirds are for livestock. For although the country's sheep and dairy farms are run as much as possible on grass, and the growth and decline of flocks and herds is locked in to its natural cycle, farmers need to grow varying quantities of crops to supplement their pasture and to carry stock through the winter and through dry summer spells.

The farmer's principal cash crops – wheat, oats, barley, maize, peas, potatoes and linseed – are usually grown in rotation, in a cycle that includes fodder crops and a period in pasture. Most of the wheat is grown on the Canterbury Plains and in North Otago; much of the barley emanates from Canterbury, and maize (needing a frost-free growing period) predominates in the Gisborne and Bay of Plenty regions. More specialised is the commercial growing of hops and tobacco, both now confined to the vicinity of Motueka.

Most of the vegetables are grown in market-gardening areas close to the major cities. Since World War II, however, great changes have taken place, both with the boom in vegetables for canning and freezing (predominantly around Hastings, Auckland, Gisborne, Nelson and Christchurch) and with the loss of large areas of land close to the cities which have expanded to house a growing population.

A small but vigorous citrus-fruit industry centres on Kerikeri, Auckland, the Bay of Plenty and Gisborne, producing a variety of oranges, lemons, mandarins and tangelos (mandarin/grapefruit hybrids). Curiously, the commercial production of other species of sub-tropical fruits concentrates on two varieties not cultivated to such a scale in their countries of origin – the tamarillo (or tree tomato), a native of Brazil and Peru, and the kiwifruit (or Chinese gooseberry), which originated in China's Yangtse Valley. Spectacular export success in the USA and Europe has boosted significant plantings in both California and Kenya. The New Zealand crop comes, in the main, from the Bay of Plenty. Avocados, feijoas and passionfruit are also grown commercially.

Apple and pear orchards are found mainly in Hawke's Bay and near Nelson, but while apples easily comprise the country's largest volume of export fruit (80,000 tonnes), the kiwifruit has soared to some 15,000 tonnes and is close to overtaking the apple in earnings. Much of the stone fruit – apricots, cherries and nectarines – comes from Central Otago, but Hawke's Bay claims the greatest volume of peaches and plums.

Vineyards for winemaking are found around Henderson and Gisborne, in Hawke's Bay and most recently outside Blenheim. Increasingly, winemakers have turned to classic grapes, and the improvement in their product has been appreciated by a more demanding public palate.

Motueka, Takaka and Golden Bay

ONE OF A PAIR *Dressed with native bush, the Kaihoka Twin Lakes appear as double oases in open farmland.*

Backed by lofty mountains and divided by Takaka Hill, Motueka and Golden Bay mark scallops in the South Island's northernmost shoulder.

To the south-east lie the rich valleys of Motueka, with fields festooned with hops and tobacco, its orchards laden with much of the nation's apple crop; to the north-west the dairylands of Golden Bay; on either hand majestic beaches, distant mountains and a congenial climate. To these must be added the grandeur of Abel Tasman National Park and the quietude of a sparse population.

It was here that Abel Tasman arrived in 1642, but his hopes to land were thwarted by Golden Bay's resolute guardians. And it was from here that Captain Cook left more than a century later, according the name of Cape Farewell to the last point of land he could see. Here, too, furious inter-tribal clashes took place as time upon time this fertile corner fell to envious invaders. Later came the frenzy of the country's first major gold rush, which provided a gilt-edged basis for abandoning Tasman's name of "Murderers' Bay", and substituting a more fitting "Golden Bay".

CHRISTMAS FLOWER *The Southern rata (*Metrosideros umbellata*) flowers profusely at Christmas time. Up to 20 metres tall and with a large, rounded canopy, the tree belongs to the same genus as the pohutukawa.*

CAVERNOUS WATERS *The Riwaka River emerges, fully grown, from a limestone cavern. The area is one of many attractive bush reserves in the region.*

Bainham The settlement from which scores of trampers embark on the four- to six-day hike along the Heaphy Track. The walk is a comparatively easy one, but those attempting it must be prepared for all weathers.

THIRSTY WORK *As well as apples, most of New Zealand's cider and apple wine comes from this area.*

Cape Farewell Seen by Tasman, yet named by Cook in 1770 as he took leave of the land he had "rediscovered". As he departed, Cook observed the inland mountains and, despite the "fogg and clowds", shrewdly concluded that "thier is a continued chain of Mountains from one end of the [South] Island to the other".

Collingwood A peaceful, rivermouth service town, cradled by the curve of Farewell Spit, with good coastal and freshwater fishing. Once the centre of hectic gold rushes, headstones in the cemetery reflect the hazards of the times, while survey pegs and traces of roads close by record plans for growth which dwindled with the gold. The Te Anaroa caves and the curious Devil's Boots, weird rock formations resembling gigantic upturned boots, are nearby.

Cobb Power Station A giddy drive, most emphatically not for the nervous, winds up the Cobb Valley through some breathtaking scenery before concluding at a small power station which, by reason of its exceptionally high head of water, is unusually productive.

Farewell Spit The slender sandbar which issues from the South Island's most northerly point arches eastwards, seeking to enclose completely the waters of Golden Bay. In its lee the bay is imperceptibly silting up, to become progressively more shallow and less extensive. Excursions run along its treacherous sands to a tall lighthouse, the construction of which began as early as 1869 to counter a growing toll of shipping.

Kaiteriteri An entrancing spot with picture-postcard appeal: steep, bushclad hills, scattered with houses, plunge to a clear, blue sea in a bay flecked with islets. Secluded Honeymoon Bay entices lovers, while the large motorcamp at the main beach throngs with people throughout the summer months.

HOP COUNTRY *The hop is a tall vine, grown on poles and wires, and cultivated for its scaly, cone-like fruit, which is dried in kilns and used in beer brewing. It is closely related to hemp, the source of marijuana.*

BLUE SKIES BECKON *Good weather is the rule at Kaiteriteri, a perfect spot for lazing, swimming and venturing off by boat to explore an infinitely fascinating coastline.*

TAKAKA HILL *Limestone caves with delicate statuary probe deep into the bowels of Takaka Hill. Some of them are believed to be among the deepest in the world.*

Motueka Visually dominated by processing plants for tobacco and hops, the town is a summer magnet for seasonal workers, who crowd in to harvest these crops, as well as fruit and raspberries. Underpinning the key industries are tobacco and hop research stations.

Onekaka A derelict wharf – and, inland, traces of plant and buildings – bear witness to a failed ironworks, founded on Puponga's coal and the area's ironsands.

Puponga Once a busy coal town, the South Island's most northerly settlement is presided over by the gnarled countenance of Old Man Rock.

Parapara Inlet The legendary home of a giant taniwha, a water monster who devoured passersby in their hundreds until five tribes united to rid the region of the scourge and render safe passage to today's travellers. The incident is portrayed in the Takaka Hotel.

Riverside community A flourishing commune, based on orchards, was established in 1940 as a Christian pacifist community, dedicated to promoting non-violence by renouncing war, private ownership and private profit. Its acceptance today contrasts sharply with the hostility and persecution which its founders first encountered; at times they were imprisoned for daring to express their beliefs. The settlement went through years of uncertainty before achieving stability.

Riwaka A centre for hop research and whose St Barnabas' Church has quaint, 1848 box pews. In an attractive bush reserve nearby, the Riwaka River issues from a cavern in a sylvan setting.

Takaka The small dairying town and its surrounding area have a special charm, enhanced in autumn by the colours of many exotic trees. Nearby are the massive Waikoropupu Springs, the hand-fed eels of the Anatoki River and such warmly inviting swimming beaches as Pohara, Tata and Patons Rock. The natural splendour of the Abel Tasman National Park contrasts starkly with the grit and grime of large cement works at Tarakohe.

MUD COTTAGE *Where wood and stone were scarce, early settlers built from cob (clay and straw), rammed earth, or cob and ricker (cob reinforced with saplings). Long neglected, some of these cottages are now being restored.*

TOBACCO Special-crop areas, marked by hop-vine trellises, hip-roofed hop kilns, tobacco-curing houses and fields of tobacco plants, give the region an individual character. At present all commercial plantings of both crops are limited to the Motueka region, whose sandy, silt-loam valleys and hot days with warm, humid nights, are particularly suited to tobacco growing.

Cultivated tobacco is an annual plant, lasting only one season and growing as tall as two metres. Once harvested, the leaves are cured to dry the sap, so producing chemical changes which improve their flavour. Some strains are air-cured (*pictured*); others require fire-curing in kilns – a process which lasts about a week.

Freshly cured tobacco has a sharp aroma and bitter taste, and most is put into storage and allowed to age before being processed. American Indians smoked tobacco long before Christopher Columbus visited them. The Maoris, too, quickly caught the taste from newly arrived settlers, who tried growing the leaf in several areas but only really succeeded here.

WAIKOROPUPU SPRINGS *An underground river surfaces abruptly to create the Waikoropupu Springs, among the largest of their kind in the world. A viewing platform stretches out over its deep, welling waters.*

BEAUTIFUL, BUT ... *The mushroom* Amanita muscaria *(or Fly Agaric) is poisonous, but rarely fatal.*

Takaka Hill Rising steeply to enjoy sweeping views over the Riwaka and Motueka valleys is this "marble mountain", littered with gaunt outcrops of grey marble and the bleached skeletons of long-dead trees. Beyond Canaan Road is the country's deepest "pothole", Harwood's Hole, a challenge to the most adventurous spelaeologist. Farther on lies the boundary of Abel Tasman National Park.

Upper Moutere Originally one of several nationalist settlements, the township was named Sarau by its German founders. Its origins are reflected in the headstone inscriptions on the quaint church, whose steeple lends a decidedly Bavarian air to the townscape.

Waikoropupu (Pupu) Springs A remarkable sight, as about 100 million litres of water an hour well silently to the surface, creating a magical river. The Maori name, meaning "bubbling waters", has been corrupted to Pupu – an improvement, if slight, on the gold miners' attempt of Bubu.

Westhaven Also known as Whanganui Inlet, the haven affords a pretty drive through bush and along causeways. There is excellent whitebaiting in season in the Patarau River.

GOLDEN BAY *A scene along the magnificent coastal highway between Waitapu and Collingwood. En route one passes several excellent bathing beaches.*

TAME EELS *Hand-fed eels in the Anatoki River are often joined by trout. Though a freshwater fish, these eels take to the ocean to breed somewhere in the vicinity of Tonga. They hibernate in winter.*

FAREWELL SPIT SAFARI *Forsaking their cars, visitors cross the tricky sands in well-equipped vehicles. The spit affords fine fishing and is also a sanctuary for wading birds.*

Abel Tasman National Park

FIRST EUROPEAN ANCHORAGE *Bush, beach and sea blend perfectly on the shores of a national park proclaimed not only for its sheer visual magnificence but also as the first anchorage of the country's earliest known European discoverer.*

This rocky, scalloped coastline, where bush meets a sea at times so tranquil that the waters mirror the headlands, was where European first met Maori – an occasion marked by bloodshed and a precursor of the violence that was to mar contact between the cultures over the next 250 years.

ON PARADE *Four seagulls drill a platoon of South Island pied oystercatchers (*Haematopus ostralegus*), wading birds who winter in Northland and whose nests are simple scrapes in shingle or sand.*

Facing northwards from Ligar or Tata Beach, and watching the sun sparkle on a friendly sea, the encounter is almost too bizarre to imagine. Two small Dutch ships in search of riches, half a world away from home and on the fringe of what was for the next century thought to be The Great Unknown Continent, were forced to abandon their mission by a single canoeload of determined warriors, who attacked a cockle-boat as it passed between the pair. Four sailors were killed in the brief clash.

Today, a grateful European population remembers the unrewarded Dutchman whose tantalising mapline led Cook to claim the country for Britain a century later.

The park itself embraces coastal and elevated bush-clad country along the shores of Tasman Bay, and includes a number of offshore islands and reefs. As a maritime park with numerous bays, coves and golden beaches, it holds unique appeal. Yet augmenting the obvious attractions of bush, sea and some limited hunting is a great diversity of plant, bird and insect life to delight botanist, ornithologist and entomologist, both professional and amateur.

Inland, on Takaka Hill, numerous sinkholes challenge the most intrepid potholer.

TORRENT BAY ANCHORAGE *A tempting destination for the walker who is prepared to spend a night out en route.*

Harwood's Hole Close to the park's boundary on Takaka Hill is a series of remarkable sinkholes, formed where underground water has dissolved limestone and caused the ground to sink. The most notable is Harwood's Hole, fully 370.5 metres deep and considered the twelfth largest in the world.

Marahau The jumping-off point for those who would explore the park from the Motueka side, and start of a three-day tramp through to Totaranui.

Tasman Memorial Just beyond the park's boundary is the country's memorial to Abel Janszoon Tasman. It overlooks the twin Tata Islands beside which he moored and where his sailors died – so close to the new-found land on which none of them was ever to set foot.

Tata Beach Close by the Tasman Memorial is beautiful, sandy Tata Beach, a popular spot for swimming and fishing, particularly for blue cod.

SOUGHT-AFTER STONE Marble hewn from Takaka Hill is of the finest quality – hard and long-lasting. Not only has it been used for many memorials and buildings of national importance – including New Zealand's Parliament at Wellington – but it has also been shipped around the world, to Kirkintilloch in Scotland. It is found at Takaka in a range of hues: pure white, soft dove-grey, and occasionally tinted a shade of pink.

MAORI AT MURDERERS' BAY *A drawing from Abel Janszoon Tasman's* Journal, *published in Amsterdam in 1898.* Alexander Turnbull Library, Wellington

SPLIT APPLE ROCK *A curiosity which adds eccentricity to an otherwise harmonious shoreline is seen on boat trips from Kaiteriteri.*

Totaranui Here a splendid beach offers a bush-girt camping site, and there is some limited cabin accommodation as well as the national park's headquarters. Walking tracks, long and short, tempt the walker, and launching facilities cater for those who would explore the fascination of the coast.

ASTROLABE ROADSTEAD *The French explorer Dumont d'Urville rested here in 1827, naming the anchorage for the ship in which he made an epic passage through French Pass only days later.*

The Heaphy Track

TOMORROW'S GIANT *Overshadowed by the mature bush, seedlings fight to perpetuate the cycle of their ecology. The forest floor may also be dense with mosses, ferns, liverworts, sedges, grasses and small flowering plants.*

WHERE BUSH MEETS SEA *After the overland crossing, the sea comes into view.*

A SENSE OF ANTICIPATION *The beginning of the track at the Karamea end seems to tempt the casual visitor at least to taste a sample of what it has to offer.*

Karamea Isolated from the rest of the West Coast, the small dairying settlement basks on a rich coastal plain as it awaits the next of the walkers from Golden Bay.

Bainham The customary departure point for those walking the Heaphy Track. The tiny farming settlement's name is a combination of those of two early families, Bain and Graham.

NOT FOR THE NERVOUS *The situation calls for care, but not alarm. Swing bridges are maintained in sound order and inspected regularly.*

To walk the Heaphy Track is to savour some of the greatest joys the outdoors can offer. The four- to six-day walk is between Karamea, on the West Coast, and Bainham, near Collingwood in Golden Bay – though starting from Golden Bay has the advantage of an overall downwards trip. The longest stretch between the huts along the route is a seven-hour hike over some 24 kilometres. On the way one walks through magnificent stands of native bush and across the red tussock of the Goulands Downs before finally descending to the coast, where nikau palms and dense ferns give the seascape a tropical island flavour.

The walk is not difficult, but its apparent ease disguises an erratic climate which can see snow in mid-summer and has on occasions claimed the lives of the ill-prepared. Sensible walkers should encounter few problems, though they should be aware that the huts along the route are often filled to overflowing. Unlike the Milford Track, the trip can only be made independently.

Curiously, Charles Heaphy (1820–81), who undertook several epic overland journeys of exploration, and for whom the track is named, never actually walked this route. He won a Victoria Cross while serving with the colonial forces for rescuing a soldier under fire. Though technically ineligible for the award because he was not serving as a member of the Imperial Army, his persistence to have it conferred was ultimately acknowledged.

NIKAU FROND *The nikau palm (*Rhopolostylis sapida*) grows to a height of ten metres, its single stem ringed by the bases of the fronds it has shed.*

Nelson Lakes National Park

LOVELY LAKE ROTOITI *Much favoured by boat owners, and with excellent swimming, it tends to be more crowded than neighbouring Lake Rotoroa. It also has fewer sandflies! Rotoroa means "long lake" and Rotoiti, the smaller of the two, "little lake".*

LAKE ROTOROA *Less developed, less peopled*

St Arnaud The park headquarters here on Lake Rotoiti has details of all that there is to see and do in the park, as well as displays of interest. In holidays times, the headquarters organises lectures and walks.

As the sluice nozzle outside the building bears witness, the area was not immune from the attentions of gold miners, who moved up into the catchment areas in search of the "mother lodes". Reasonable quantities of gold were won.

Glaciers over millions of years clawed out the long, slender beds of both Lake Rotoiti and Lake Rotoroa, lending geological credence to the Maori myth that tells of a fabled giant tearing them out of the alps with his mighty digging stick. Steep valley walls line placid shores fringed to the water's edge with beech forest – a remarkable setting for angler, sailor, hunter, tramper, climber and skier. Of the wide variety of flora, the specialised plants of the shingle slides are of particular interest, adapted as they are to survive both searing summer heat and winter snow.

THE RESTLESS BULLER *A rugged contrast to its source at serene Lake Rotoiti.*

THE TRAGEDY OF TOPHOUSE For almost a century the little cob building served as a stopping point for those driving stock on the routes between Marlborough, Nelson and Canterbury. But finally, in 1971, the quaint amenities fell foul of the requirement of the licensing laws, and what should have been in perpetuity a hostelry of old-world charm lost its licence and its livelihood. But tragedy was no stranger to Tophouse. In 1894, the licensee's brother-in-law went berserk, murdering both the postmaster and the acting licensee, and taking several women hostage before finally committing suicide, splattering the verandah ceiling with shotgun pellets as he did so.

The Tophouse route between the Wairau and Nelson had been discovered in 1842 by a youthful surveyor, John Cotterell, who a short time later went out from Nelson with a settler group bent on arresting the great chief, Te Rauparaha. As a Quaker, he refused to carry a firearm. When it became apparent that the misguided venture would lead to violence, Cotterell wanted to leave, but was persuaded that it would be safer for him to stay. No advice could have been worse, and he died in the resulting affray.

and with more plentiful brown trout . . .

BROODING UPPER BULLER *The river's Maori name of Kawatiri loosely means "river flowing swiftly through a rocky gorge".*

TOUGH BUT PENETRABLE *Tyre tracks intrude into the wilderness.*

SPORT FOR THE STRONG-HEARTED *Canoes on Rotoiti's peaceful waters prepare for more turbulent times.*

GOWAN BRIDGE STORE *An historic site at the confluence of Rotoroa's Gowan and Rotoiti's Buller.*

Walks No visit to a national park is complete without tackling at least a short walk. Here there are many to choose from, though the steep nature of the terrain renders most the domain of the energetic, except the easy tracks along the lakes' shores. The walks up Black Hill (a mound of dark, fine-grained basaltic rock that originated as a volcanic lava flow poured onto an ancient sea floor) and at least some distance up the aptly named Pinchgut Track that runs from the Mt Robert Lookout are highly rewarding, not simply in terms of views but also in the wide variety of flora seen in relatively short compass.

Birdlife A fortunate visitor may see as many as 40 of the more than 50 species of bird within the park. These include parakeet, kaka and blue duck as well as robin, tomtit, grey warbler and silver-eye. The two species of kiwi and the weka are rare, so that the predominant nocturnal bird is now the morepork. All birds here, even the rapacious kea, are protected.

MOTUPIKO RIVER VALLEY *Here glacier-sculpted walls leave an unmistakable imprint.*

Westport and district

DERELICT DENNISTON *Perched uneasily above Waimangaroa, the town's ruins are testament to an inhospitable terrain.*

Westport, the major town of the Buller region, is dwarfed by the Buller River which gave rise to its establishment as a bar harbour and natural anchorage when the gold rushes of the 1860s began. Behind the town, and extending south almost to Greymouth, rises the Paparoa Range, where many of the country's reserves of bituminous coal are found. While the future of the nation's energy needs continues to arouse debate, the importance of these reserves remains high, but much of the land in this area is deceptive in its promise, covered as it is with the notoriously difficult pakihi soil.

To the north beckons Karamea and the beginning of the Heaphy Track through to Nelson Province, of which the Buller was once a part. Indeed, until recently, the region's ties with Nelson tended to obscure its destiny as a part of the West Coast. To the east, the route across the Main Divide lies up the grand Buller Gorge and through the beech forests of the Lewis Pass. In this unlikely setting one finds the equally unlikely West Coaster, a gregarious character enshrined in the nation's folklore.

KARAMEA *Bush and sea meet at the coastal terminal of the incomparable Heaphy Track.*

The West Coast This narrow lip of land, trapped between alp and ocean, and heavily watered by rain clouds swept inland by the prevailing westerly, has attained an individualism that has largely eluded the country's other regions. This derives from a number of factors: varied landscape, isolation, exploitive industries and individualistic people, and is overlaid by echoes of the frenetic excesses of the heady gold-rush days – times of turbulence that scarred the plains and pitted the hillsides. The boom passed, yet even today the emphasis remains on industries such as coal and timber, with the land generally under-utilised and the population still in decline. A land survey has concluded that because only 8.6 per cent of the land is farmable, the area as a whole will "always be uneconomic as a farming region".

The West Coaster The West Coast is one of those rare regions which actually lives its mythology. In folklore, the West Coaster is genial, enterprising, helpful, humorous, individualistic, and very much one of a race apart. These traits, honed on the goldfields and hardened through recession and decline, remain very much in evidence, and most West Coasters still see themselves as set apart by the isolating influences of mountain barrier and Tasman Sea.

For generations their blatant rejection of liquor licensing hours added gloss to their colourful reputation. But the country has since largely fallen into line, and for all their reputation of lawlessness in this respect, and their denunciation of government from over the alps, it was often observed that theirs was the most law-abiding of the world's goldfields.

NEAR CAPE FOULWIND *Damned by Cook, the cape now boasts the country's most modern cement works.*

The Punakaiki Pancake Rocks Situated on Dolomite Point, 56 kilometres from Westport, these curious landforms (*pictured above and right*) present an astonishing sight. Here both sea and rainwater attacked the joints in a huge bed of limestone, and while the slab was being carved into a series of pillars, the softer surfaces eroded more quickly, leaving the harder layers projecting out to resemble piles of pancakes awaiting their syrup. There are blowholes, too, which when the sea is running produce at least thunder – and on occasion geyser-like spouts of water. The sense of power is awesome, and gives an indication of the force employed in shaping the rocks. Not only is there the impact of the water itself, but as the sea surges against the formations, air is trapped inside the joints and rammed with a percussive effect into any cracks in the rock.

The meaning of "punakaiki" is unclear. Some suggest that it is a combination of puna ("spring") and kaiki (a mis-spelling of kaike or kaika), meaning "to lie in a heap", a reference both to the shape of the rocks and to the blowholes. There was also a Ngai Tahu belief that "punakaiki" describes the neck and throat of a human, so that the rocks and blowholes were being likened to them. Others tell of the beach being a canoe-landing place in pre-European times. Abundant with shellfish, the beach may have been given a name which meant "place of good eating".

To the north lie Porari River and Porari Beach, good for bathing; to the south, the Punakaiki River and beach. There is also good swimming under the Punakaiki River bridge. The safety of both swimming spots is rare on this generally wild coastline.

Buller Gorge For much of its length the Buller flows through deep, steep-sided gorges. The road between Westport and Murchison follows an impressive stretch of river.

Cape Foulwind Named Rocky Point by Tasman just two days after he made landfall in 1642, the cape was rechristened by Cook. Of interest are a massive cement works, the beautiful Carters Beach and Tauranga Bay and, offshore, the solitary rock appropriately titled "Giant's Tooth".

A track leads down from near the lighthouse to a safe and sandy cove. Tauranga Bay, unsafe for bathing, is of great character and has a seal colony.

Charleston Once a roaring gold town following discoveries in 1866. Only one of over 100 hotels and dance halls remains to indicate its former bustle. Its name, The European (*pictured left*), is a survivor of times when hostelries wore their prejudices (and clientele) on their signboards. The many Chinese who flocked to the goldfields were seldom made welcome. Occasionally a hotel named All Nations showed a more liberal attitude.

Crushington A famous gold centre, named for its batteries that in the 1890s crushed vast quantities of ore. Traces of the batteries may still be seen, and there are several walks, some quite lengthy, into deserted old gold workings.

STOCKTON OPEN-CAST MINE AND ROPEWAY *Considerable ingenuity has been used to transport coal by adapting techniques originally developed on the goldfields at a time when coal was used to fuel quartz batteries.*

Coal

STRONGMAN COAL *One of the Coast's best-known mines uses dry trucking methods.*

A MINER EMERGES *At the Mt William mine the coal emerges in water chutes.*

The coalfields of the West Coast contain all the country's measured reserves of bituminous coal, used for coke by the steel industry and for thousands of coke by-products. It can also be used to produce aluminium, cement, food, paper and textiles, as well as for domestic heating. Coal is produced on the West Coast from the Buller, Reefton and Grey fields, which employ both open-cast and underground techniques. The explorer Thomas Brunner found coal well before gold was discovered, and in 1860 von Haast found the first bituminous seam near the Denniston mines high on the plateau above Waimangaroa.

The state mines are the major employers. The government was drawn into mine management in 1910 to rationalise the industry at a time when coal was still being imported.

From two-thirds of the national output in 1910, the Coast's share of national production has now fallen to less than a third, while the North Island's production has steadily grown to meet the needs of thermal power stations and the steel and pulp-and-paper industries. The uses for West Coast coal have been debated for decades: should it be extensively mined for export? Should it be more widely exploited for the local market? Should it be preserved for the energy needs of a future generation? The reserves, of around 150 million tonnes (including 116 million tonnes of the high-calorific bituminous coal), represent a major energy source that looms increasingly large in planning the nation's total requirements. Although, as noted, the West Coast has long ceased to dominate the country's supply of coal, the two continue to be strongly associated in the public mind.

COAL COUNTRY *The traveller frequently sees seams of coal in roadside cuttings.*

MARUIA FALLS *Product of the 1929 Murchison earthquake which diverted the Maruia River over an upthrust wrought by earlier earth movement. In a populous region, the earthquake would have been a major disaster; as it was, the town and its environs were transformed for ever.*

CRADLE OF POWER The country is heavily dependent on hydro-electric power, and it is testimony to Reefton's early importance as a gold centre – with even its own stock exchange – that it should be the first town to be lit in this way. Only six years after the first of New York's streets acquired electric public lighting, and only seven years after Thomas Edison invented the incandescent bulb, the turbine placed here in this hole began, in 1887, to supply electric power.

Inangahua A tiny junction settlement temporarily evacuated in 1968 after a disastrous earthquake. Slumping caused by tremors can be seen in parts of Buller. The Inangahua River is named for its whitebait (*inanga* in Maori).

Granity A coal town, like neighbouring Waimangaroa, but more salubrious than those such as Stockton, Darlington and Denniston now deserted. A focal point for the industry, the town is named for the granite found in the vicinity.

Reefton So prolific were the quartz reefs in this area, the town is named for them. Millions of pounds' worth of gold were won locally, rendering the town for a time the focal point of national attention. Gold has given way to coal, augmented by farming and some timber milling, but the coal production, like the gold before it, has dwindled.

Seddonville The smaller of two townships named for the West Coast's "King Dick", Premier Richard John Seddon.

Stockton Once a mining centre served with bituminous coal by an aerial ropeway. For over 75 years underground deposits nearby have been smouldering, their smoke billowing most spectacularly after rainfall.

Westport A port on the West Coast, Westport yet derives its name from Eire. The port handles cement from Cape Foulwind, coal and timber, while the town serves as Buller's principal retail and commercial centre.

MITCHELLS GULLY GOLD MINE *Sixteen kilometres of tunnels.*

THE PRIZE *Gold from Mitchells Gully gold mine. Fortunes were won and lost on the West Coast during the 1860s, but today the needs of an energy-hungry nation have taken precedence. Thanks to coal, however, commercial gold mining is a more sophisticated affair than it was in the days of pan and shovel.*

Greymouth, Hokitika and environs

THE WILD WEST COAST *Prevailing winds from across the Tasman Sea sweep wave after wave of rollers against the rocks and bring rain-bearing clouds towards the Southern Alps.*

Trapped between giant alps and the wild Tasman Sea, inundated by a prodigious rainfall, dissected by turbulent rivers and hindered by poor soils, the West Coast not only has a physical character of its own but has also developed the tough, insular West Coaster – a rugged individualist whose penchant for beer and distaste for such irksome restrictions as licensing laws has become very much a part of the nation's folklore.

AT ANCHOR *Greymouth's fishing fleet is witness to fantastic sunsets reflected on the alps.*

STRONG MEN *Shift change at Strongman.*

KOKATAHI BAND *This colourful and well-known group, which boasts an extraordinary collection of instruments, traces its origins back to the goldfields.*

SOUTHERN RATA *The southern rata (*Metrosideros umbellata*) has several features which distinguish it from its taller northern relative. Instead of beginning life as an epiphyte, it grows like most trees from the ground. In exposed situations it develops a distinctive, gnarled trunk and its red summer flowers are more brilliant in colour.*

OVER THE GREY RIVER *The bridges are Greymouth's hallmark and carry a rail link to the coal faces of the Paparoa Ranges and the coastal road to Westport.*

Arahura There was a large pa near here, which was often raided in pre-European times by tribes visiting the area in search of greenstone. The stone was so highly prized that, although it was found in significant quantities only in this area, the whole of the South Island was known as Te Wai Pounamu – "the water of greenstone".

Arahura River A large river, like most Westland rivers, it is also short, being only some 56 kilometres in length. Like its neighbours, it was glaciated during the Pleistocene Age so that moraines and glacial landforms extend down to the coastal lowlands. It is fabled as a source of greenstone, some of which is retrieved by helicopters from inaccessible slopes.

Greymouth The chief commercial centre on the West Coast stands by the shore near a gap torn through limestone hills by the Grey River. More than water flows through the opening, as anyone who has felt the keen edge of "the Barber", Greymouth's cutting, down-river wind, can testify. The town itself stands on an old pa site and much of it is still in Maori ownership. Originating in the days of the gold rushes, the town was maintained by coal, and today it also benefits from a timber industry, both of which surpass in importance the other major activities of dairy and sheep farming. Its port, like that of Westport, has a breakwater to direct the forces of river current and tide against the river bar, so reducing the amount of dredging needed to keep the channel free. Close by are Shantytown, Lake Brunner and, about ten kilometres upriver, a memorial to Thomas Brunner, who found the coal deposits named after him. For many years the most productive in the country, the Brunner mine is now the feature of an historic reserve. In 1896, 67 miners were killed in an explosion there.

WORKING THE GOLD *A bush-shirted West Coaster adjusts the nozzle of his sluice-gun, used to simulate the natural forces of erosion. Recent rises in the world price of gold have excited renewed interest in gold workings.*

LAKE BRUNNER *A quiet spot, not far from Greymouth, with good swimming, fishing and picnicking. It is named for an early explorer, Thomas Brunner, who in 1848 was the lake's first European visitor.*

NEW ZEALAND JADE Greenstone has long been prized by Maoris throughout the country. In days past they hazarded mountain crossings, an inhospitable coast and hostile local tribes in order to obtain precious supplies for making axes, chisels and ornaments such as the *hei-tiki*.

Found only in the Arahura–Taramakau and Milford regions, New Zealand jade has for many years been a prohibited export in its unworked state. Though used and sold by jewellers in many parts of the country, there is special significance for pieces used here, where both the stone and the craft have their origins, and where visitors to Hokitika's factories can see them being shaped.

SLUICING AT THE BLUE SPUR MINE *Gold miners would pipe water from afar to feed their sluice-guns.*

GOLD DREDGING *Environmentally destructive, a gold dredge lifts gold-bearing gravel from stream beds. The model pictured is in the Ross Museum.*

Techniques Alluvial deposits of gold (as opposed to vein deposits, which are mined) are won by panning, sluicing and dredging – and often in that order. The first miners, with simple pans and shovels, take the easy gold that has washed into shallow streams. Then follow teams who divert streams and, by judicious control of water, build it up to such high pressures that it plays with great force against the banks of gold-bearing gravel. The water washes the gravel into troughs (sluices) which have grooves (riffles) to trap the fine gold. The third and final phase involves costly dredges, which churn over river beds to win the most difficult and most marginal gold. Inside the dredges giant pulsators act as mechanised gold pans to separate out the precious metal.

Dredges are enormously destructive. High banks of shingle can be seen to this day, while the agriculturally valuable river flats have suffered heavily. The nature of the work renders dredges expensive to maintain, and though there is still much gold to be won, this cannot often be done economically.

Gold

The rushes to the West Coast goldfields followed those of Otago, but after some four or five years gave way to new finds on Coromandel Peninsula. In the first few months of 1865 about 16,000 miners poured in from Otago as well as from Victoria, Australia, in search of the fortunes offered by a series of fabulous strikes. Canvas towns mushroomed literally overnight, and many was the "duffer" rush, when false rumours of fresh finds flew and "new chums" risked their all in following them up. Many did indeed strike it rich, but, as elsewhere, the real money was often made in the less exciting realm of providing food and equipment for hungry men who were desperate for both and prepared to pay outrageous prices to get them.

On the West Coast there was gold to be found almost everywhere, but conditions were harsh, especially when flash floods could more readily destroy a promising find than reveal another. In time the pick, shovel and pan gave way to the sluice, and by 1890 sluicing yielded to mechanical dredging. The rotting hulks of several dredges are still to be seen on tributaries, and until quite recently a solitary dredge was still working the river near Kumara. Gold was also mined from underground at Ross and near Westport.

GOLD COLOURS *Time changes, but not method. Gold, being heavier than stone, sinks to the bottom of the pan. With a practised swirl the sand is tipped out, in the hope that much-cherished "colours" (gold dust) will be left glistening near the rim.*

THE HONOURABLE RODDY *Ross became quite unhinged when the country's largest nugget was found in 1907. This facsimile is in the town's museum: the original is now anonymous as tableware at Buckingham Palace after being given as a Coronation gift to George V.*

GRUFF, BLUFF, MATEY *Hokitika's goldminer statue captures the genial independence of the digger, whose fierce loyalty to his mate was a characteristic that contributed to early welfare reforms after Kumara's Richard Seddon became Premier.*

GLASSBLOWING *A Hokitika factory invites visitors to see glass being blown, a craft that dates back over 2,000 years. A blowpipe is dipped in molten glass, some of which sticks to its pear-shaped end. Gentle blowing creates a bulb which can be shaped, reheated, reworked and cut. When the still-hot glass has been given its final shape, it is broken from the pipe.*

Harihari An expanding farming settlement with major timber milling. It was here that the first single-engined plane to fly the Tasman Sea landed – upside-down in a swamp.

Hokitika The town, once capital of the short-lived Westland Province, has a varied and spectacular past. But tranquillity has long since descended on streets once festooned with a hundred or more hotels and thronged with itinerant fortune-seekers, and on a rivermouth harbour once crowded with the world's shipping. A Melbourne bank manager was promoted by being posted here. Sealing the town's decline was the closure of the port in 1954, a harbour which in its heyday posted the names of "vessels ashore" as well as those in port, so many were the ships that ran aground.

These heady days have left Hokitika with the feel and substance of a centre many times its actual size. Today it serves administrative and distribution roles for surrounding sheep, cattle and dairy farms, and for major timber mills. The steeple of the Catholic church dominates the townscape, even as the disproportionate number of Catholics on the Coast still reflects the essentially Irish nature of the goldfields. In this, the region contrasts sharply with the Anglican flavour of neighbouring Canterbury.

SHANTYTOWN Much is authentic in this reconstruction of an early gold town, for many vintage buildings were moved here then restored to create the character of times when the West Coast was truly wild. No visit to the Coast is complete without some hours spent savouring the atmosphere, panning for "colours" and riding the railway through old gold workings. The enterprise has been so successful as to vary the pattern of tourist traffic through the area, and is a community project that has struck its own kind of riches. A wildlife park is nearby, and both are near Greymouth.

SHEEP NEAR HARIHARI *The motorist is always likely to encounter stock being driven along the road – much to the surprise of those from overseas. The motorbike has largely replaced the horse on the farm.*

STYX RIVER *Pictured is the start of the track to Browning Pass and so via the Wilberforce River to Canterbury. The route lies up the Styx River and the upper Arahura River valley. It was much used by early prospectors, and the first sheep to be brought to Westland were actually driven in from Canterbury along this unlikely path. A formed track is still open over much of the route, which is a popular day tramp.*

KOWHITIRANGI FARMLAND *The Southern Alps preside over farmlands which, in 1941, were the scene of New Zealand's most renowned, and tragic, manhunt.*

CATTLE BROWSING *Near Lake Kaniere, cattle fulfil their vital role as animated mowing machines, preventing second growth from reclaiming newly won pasture.*

SAMUEL MITCHELL'S VICTORIA CROSS *The medal was won at Gate Pa near Tauranga in 1864, and is now on display in the Westland Museum.*

A PRECIOUS HERITAGE *Forestry (here pictured at Harihari) plays a pivotal role in the region's economy.*

NOT FOR EATING Pictured is the toadstool, *Entoloma hochstetteri.* As comparatively little is known about mushrooms and toadstools in New Zealand's native forests, prudence dictates that only those species known to be edible in Europe should be eaten. Ferdinand Hochstetter was an early geologist who took a keen interest in native botany. Many southern organisms are named after him.

WESTLAND FOREST HIGHWAY *A feature of South Westland is the dense native rain forest, the source of much beech and rimu. State forests include Wanganui, Mikonui, Totara, Ianthe, Saltwater, Okarito and Poerua, and there are private holdings as well. The exploitation of the forests has been a matter of controversy, with bans being sought by conservationists. Where milling takes place, a ribbon of roadside forest is generally retained intact.*

Hokitika River The river, with its eastern tributary, the Kokatahi, forms one of the largest and most fertile of Westland's plains. In its last five kilometres, the river passes through perhaps the richest of the alluvial goldfields of the 1860s. Its rivermouth harbour, dogged by a treacherous bar, claimed many ships during the heady years of Hokitika's heyday. Curiously, its southern tributary, the Whitcombe River, is larger than the Hokitika itself.

Lake Kaniere The lake offers fishing and water sports, but more especially it frequently reflects the mountains in an awe-inspiring light.

Kokatahi A locality with a reputation which belies its size. Its extraordinary and colourful band, the origins of which date back to the goldfields, still enjoys a unique and unorthodox standard of musicianship, although its ranks are mostly filled from Hokitika.

Ross A timber-milling, railway junction town nestled in a bush setting. The frantic times the town once knew are reflected in the local museum, where mining techniques are also explained. The country's largest nugget, over 2.7 kilograms in weight, was found here in 1907 on a claim known to have been carefully worked by Chinese – incentive, if it were needed, to fossick when one is picnicking! The precise location of the find has never been verified.

LAKE KANIERE *The glass-like lakes on the Coast frequently reflect the neighbouring alps, phenomena usually seen at their best in the early morning, while the angle of the light is low and before cloud begins to gather.*

Arthur's Pass

Three major South Island passes belong to historic figures – Haast, Lewis and Arthur's (approached from the north through the Otira Gorge, *above*). But none is more historic than Arthur's Pass, the shortest of the transalpine routes. For Arthur Dobson not only explored the region but, with his father, also laid out the road in 1865. The name was, however, accidental. Many other possible routes were considered, but the conclusion always was that "Arthur's pass is better". Yet the tale has a tragic ending. After toiling for a year to forge the road link from Christchurch to the plentiful West Coast goldfields, at times in conditions of extreme deprivation, Arthur's elder brother George fell victim to the infamous Sullivan gang, who mistook him for a gold buyer and murdered him for money he was not carrying.

The road, the most demanding of the major alpine passes, rises from the far-flung alluvial plains of Canterbury to wend its way up the Bealey River and over the very spine of the Southern Alps, before dropping down to follow the Taramakau River to the sea. As it criss-crosses rivers and writhes through gorges, the route constantly surprises with its variations between rain forest and fertile flats, making the journey memorable in any season. However, the mission behind the building of the road was never realised. The road proved so intimidating that those with gold to transport from the West Coast still chose to do so by ship, preferring the known hazards of the sea to the uncertainties of the new route. So Canterbury was denied the riches she had ventured so much to attract. In place of hurrying gold escorts, long lines of fortune-seekers straggled over the alps, interspersed with flocks of sheep which were shepherded across to the meat-starved goldfields.

Around the upper reaches of the road spreads Arthur's Pass National Park, an alpine park unique for its road and railway. The easier Lewis and Haast Passes, to north and south, combine into an interesting circular route for the sightseer, but one which leads many to miss the splendour that Arthur's has to offer.

Arthur's Pass Arthur's Pass, one of very few significant gaps in the Southern Alps, was formed when glacial ice-flows on opposite sides of the Divide created a col (gap in the ridge), which was later deepened into a trough by a "through" glacier – one which began on one side of the Divide and spilled over onto the other. Many mountain passes are formed in this way. The pass was long known to the Ngai Tahu of Canterbury, and provided one of several routes to the prized greenstone sources in Westland. A memorial stands here to Sir Arthur Dobson. The road, although an east-west passage, is here running north and south.

Arthur's Pass National Park Forests, lakes and river flats, snow-clad mountains and contrasting vegetation draw many visitors, who can quickly escape from the steady grind of the transalpine highway in search of solitude. Although parts of the park are busy with the bustle of road and rail traffic, there are still remote wilderness areas which few take the time to penetrate. The park's principal assets are its recreational facilities. Sport can be enjoyed year-round – and even out-of-season, with occasional summer skiing in Temple Basin. The park's headquarters are at Arthur's Pass township, which serves as the hub for activities. The museum, as is customary in national parks, records the early development of the park along with intriguing aspects of its geology, its rich flora and its fauna.

Lake Lyndon In winter the lake generally freezes completely and is popular for ice skating.

Mt Oates A splendid peak seen from the railway line up the Mingha Valley, its name records the country's admiration for Robert Falcon Scott and for Captain L. E. G. Oates, who died with him in Antarctica in 1912.

Otira Deep in the cleft of the Otira Gorge, the railway hamlet bears a name with alternate meanings – though "out of the sun" seems more apt than "food for a journey".

MOUNTAIN NEINEI Dracophyllum traversii *pictured near Otira.*

ARTHUR'S PASS TOWNSHIP *A natural stop-off point and site of the park headquarters.*

AN ALPINE MIRROR *Lovely Lake Pearson reflects its perfect mountain setting.*

JACK'S HUT *A roadman's hut immortalised in a best-selling book and the starting point for climbers of Mt Rolleston.*

A MOUNTAIN BONE-SHAKER *A specially sprung stage-coach which regularly ferried Prime Minister Richard Seddon over a bumpy pass to his West Coast constituency. It is displayed in the park headquarters.*

The changes witnessed by Sir Arthur Dobson (1841–1934) defy the imagination. Arriving at Christchurch on the first migrant ship, as a boy assisting with the initial surveys of Christchurch, then as a young man discovering a major mountain pass, Dobson went on to lead a long and active professional life as a civil engineer. Curiously, his wife was the daughter of Henry Lewis, discoverer of the Lewis Pass. Dobson's portrait (*pictured*) hangs in the national park headquarters.

THE WAIMAKARIRI RIVER *The river which rises in the park reaches the sea as one of the typically broad and braided rivers of the Canterbury Plains. Pictured at Cora Lynn and still contained in the spectacular valley which offered hope to the early trail-seekers, its glacier-fed waters merit the river's name, literally "cold waters". To the west, the road swings northwards, crossing the Waimakariri and probing up the valley of the Bealey River (one of its major tributaries) to reach the pass. The route was far from promising, one early report noting: "It would be simply impossible to construct a road through a ravine of this character. In many places the gorge is blocked from cliff to cliff with a tangled mass of timber and scrub."*

Otira tunnel Soon after the road had been completed, thoughts turned to the possibility of a railway. The dream was slow to be realised. It was not until 1923 that the first train made the crossing, using a tunnel over eight kilometres long – then the longest in the Southern Hemisphere and the British Commonwealth. There is, too, a significant difference in level between the two portals – 620 metres above sea level on the Canterbury side and only 483 metres above sea level in Westland. The gradient is 1:33. To overcome ventilation problems, trains are drawn through the tunnel by electric engines.

Lake Pearson A large, open lake bordered by a sheep station where plants are raised to fight erosion in the high country.

Porters Pass Higher than Arthur's Pass and a popular tobogganing spot, the pass is near the well-used Porters Heights ski fields, among the closest to Christchurch.

Mt Rolleston The alpine centrepiece of the park, Mt Rolleston rises to 2,661 metres. Its slopes cradle substantial glaciers (the park contains the South Island's most northerly ice-flows), which once reached down to the Canterbury Plains. At many points in the region the accustomed eye can note low stony ridges, the remains of lateral moraine, as well as steep, smooth valleys and basins, silent testimony to the awesome power and grandeur these glaciers once possessed.

The mountain, first conquered in 1891, is often climbed, and by routes of varying difficulty. It was named by Sir Arthur Dobson after William Rolleston, who later became Superintendent of Canterbury Province.

Taramakau River The Westland approach to Arthur's Pass is up the Taramakau Valley, from whose lower reaches much gold has been dredged.

Westland National Park

FOX GLACIER NÉVÉ *Viewed from the coastal lowlands, peaks and a panoply of rain forest render an unforgettable scene.*

A KETTLE LAKE *As the ice retreated, a slab was left behind to melt and form a small lake.*

MINEHAHA TRACK *A gentle walk through the rain forest.*

Fox Glacier Both longer than Franz Josef (13 kilometres as against 10) and with a lower terminal (245 metres above sea level as opposed to 275), Fox Glacier was named to compliment Sir William Fox, who visited the area while Premier. At least since 1930, the behaviour of Fox, both in advance and in retreat, has mirrored that of Franz Josef.

From here begins the walk to Lake Matheson (whose reflections are best seen in early morning) and the drive to Gillespies Beach (to view incredible sunsets reflected on the peaks – an experience which calls for total mental immersion rather than frenzied attempts at photography). At the beach itself are relics of the gold-mining era.

From near Fox begins the celebrated Copland track, which leads up the Copland Valley, past hot springs finally to curl over the ice and snow of the Main Divide to Canterbury.

THE PARK HEADQUARTERS *A mine of information on Westland's flora and fauna.*

MOUNT TASMAN *The 3,496-metre giant faithfully mirrored in limpid Lake Matheson.*

Much of the rugged splendour of the South Island landscape derives from the actions of the myriad glaciers which clawed and gouged the mountainous slopes both east and west. Nearly all of these have since retreated high into the alps, but the two most spectacular exceptions are Fox and Franz Josef – vast twin rivers of ice which ooze down from large, high-level névés where vast amounts of snow are trapped and compacted into ice. The glaciers have advanced and retreated periodically over the past century, but the general pattern is one of recession. Signs of their having extended across the coastal lowlands include the lakes that fill huge depressions created originally by the enormous weight of the glacial ice. Although now well above the bushline, from some vantage points the ice-flow appears still to penetrate right into the rain forest.

UMBRELLA FERN Gleichenia cunninghamii.

Franz Josef Glacier The best observed and recorded of all the country's many glaciers, Franz Josef lies 25 kilometres to the north of Fox and was named after the Austrian Emperor by Julius von Haast, the first European to explore the glaciers here. One should venture on to the ice-flow, and also allow time for walks to Roberts Point (*all day return*), the Callery Gorge, and perhaps the climb up Alex Knob for a fantastic view of the glacier. The park headquarters here also hold much of interest.

But come to Westland prepared for the wet weather which created and sustains the glaciers and rain forests. And be ready, too, for early-morning rises to view the peaks before mist descends, as it so frequently does, in mid-morning. Curiously, the best time to visit the region is in winter.

A WALK ON THE ICE *Children pictured on Franz Josef Glacier. Both at Fox and at Franz Josef, guided excursions are arranged, and suitable equipment may be hired. Although one can venture on to the ice unaccompanied, to make the most of the experience, and to savour fully the extraordinary colours of the ice-flow, the guided trips are recommended unreservedly. Scenic flights, too, are unforgettable, as the planes' wingtips seem to scrape the sheer valley walls.*

BELOW THE FOX *Here the valley evidences the glacier's series of advances and retreats.*

The forests

The forests, colloquially but never dismissively termed "the bush", have always played a major part in the country's life. The sub-tropical evergreen native forests to the north have an intensely luxurious growth. Rising from a floor profuse with ferns, mosses, liverworts and seedlings, the trees stand in several tiers. Uppermost tower the coniferous species, while below them are scatterings of broadleaf trees which occasionally form into closed canopies. Under these, in dense shade, grow smaller trees, shrubs and tree ferns. By contrast, the floor cover in the sub-antarctic beech forests to the south is more sparse and the canopy more regular, usually comprising only one or two species of beech in any one area.

At first inhabited solely by birds and covering about two-thirds of the country, the native forests had evolved unaffected by human interference until after the arrival of the first Polynesians, perhaps 1,000 years ago. Before people began to modify substantially the extent and structure of the forests, changes were, however, occurring as the climate varied. The eruptions of the Volcanic Plateau in the centre of the North Island also contributed to cataclysmic changes in the vegetation, both by burial under pumice and by fire.

The first Polynesians, too, burned forest areas repeatedly and apparently indiscriminately, at times using fire to drive the giant moa into swamps. The imposing kauri forests of the north largely fell victim to visiting ships, which came in to follow up Captain Cook's excellent assessment of their timber for masts and spars. But far greater were the changes wrought by the European settlers who followed. Not only did they introduce browsing animals which chewed species of native plants to the point of extinction and modified the plantlife in the forests, but they also cleared vast areas of forest for farmland. As well, millions of hectares of native timber were milled, for building and for export. The settlers also brought a bewildering variety of exotic trees which were planted in preference to slower-growing natives. These added an air of Englishness to the settlers' new homeland and served as shelter-belts for homesteads and stock. A surprising number flourished, as conditions proved more congenial to a wide range of trees than elsewhere.

The slow rate of regeneration of native forest led in the 1920s to a bold decision to plant exotics on a grand scale. This, coupled with the availability of cheap land and the unemployment of the Depression era, gave rise to the vast plantations of the central North Island, and to smaller man-made forests throughout the country. Readily renewable through natural regeneration, highly productive and capable of supporting large wood-processing units, the forests (predominantly of Californian radiata pine) today make a significant contribution to the economy, supplying local and overseas markets with wood pulp, paper products and timber.

UREWERA *Virgin forest and a giant southern rata.*

NORTHLAND *Young and adult native lancewood.*

KAINGAROA *Exotic forest of radiata pine.*

AKATARAWA *Mixed beech forest.*

WESTLAND *White pine or kahikatea.*

SOUTHLAND *Beech forest and ferns.*

MT ASPIRING NATIONAL PARK *A magnificent vista of mountain and forest.*

The Haast Pass

GATES OF HAAST *A deep ravine where, far below the road, the Haast River jousts with the huge schist boulders that contest its onward passage.*

THE APPROACH OF WINTER *Autumn tonings near Wanaka contrast both with the evergreens of Westland and the verdance of lowland pasture.*

For more than a century, a road through the Haast Pass proved an elusive dream born of visions of its serving thriving settlements on the Coast. When finally realised, the road brought a bonanza of visitors to a region in decline – not only could travellers to the South Island now follow a circular route that embraced much of the West Coast, but the wild grandeur of the Pass itself also proved a highlight in its own right.

At 565 metres above sea level and the lowest of the passes across the Main Divide, Haast is arguably the most spectacular, although its glamour is often masked by cloud. As one marvels at the ingenuity of the road builders, one should spare a thought for the Ngati Toa raiding party who, in 1835–36, clambered through the Pass (an ancient greenstone trail) after a hazardous, year-long journey down the Coast – only to be massacred by local tribes near Mataura.

The Pass was named by the geologist Sir Julius von Haast, the second European to make the traverse. He steadfastly denied the claims of Charles Cameron, a gold prospector who had preceded him.

THE HAAST RIVER *Shingle beds stand out starkly against waters of blue.*

The Haast Pass road From the tawny tussocklands of Central Otago, through hostile mountain gorges to the dense rain forests of the West Coast, the road embraces a remarkably wide variety of scenic splendour within a short compass. The road is an easy one, and the trip from Lake Wanaka to Fox or Franz Josef Glacier, or Hokitika, is well within a day's drive.

The scenery is endlessly changing and often breathtaking. The Fantail Falls, the Gates of Haast (*pictured far left*) and the Thunder Creek Falls (*pictured right*) are only three of a series of outstanding sights.

Haast River Bridge That the bridge should be single-laned comes as a surprise, but it is nonetheless the longest bridge in the country and even 20 years ago cost over $500,000 to build. Close by is Haast township, a tiny works settlement which has tenaciously clung to life long after the reason for its establishment has passed. One turns off here to make the 100-kilometre return detour to Jackson Bay.

BUSH DETAIL *The luxuriance of the native bush throughout the Haast Pass adds beauty and an air of mystery to the untouched landscape.*

Haast Pass A plaque on the Divide remembers pioneer explorers, but the route was long used by Maori greenstone parties.

THE WEKA *The inquisitive, cheeky bird for whom speed on the ground is a compensation for flightlessness.*

Jackson Bay Traces may be seen here of one of several "special settlements" of the 1870s. These failed, but only after they had eked out a full quota of human misery and despair. The bush has long reclaimed the grazing land so tortuously cleared by the pioneers, some of whom lie in the isolated graveyard. There is excellent whitebaiting in the vicinity each spring.

Bruce Bay Lying by the mouth of the Mahitahi River, the foreshore is strewn with pieces of white quartz ground smooth and round by tide and sand. A century ago this was the scene of a "duffer rush", a false alarm in which, unwittingly or not, enthusiastic fortune-seekers were led into conditions of extreme hardship in a forlorn quest for gold. More recently, traces of uranium have been found here.

Lake Paringa An idyllic spot, where lodge, brown trout and tranquillity await the angler. Whitebait is also taken here.

Lake Moeraki Perhaps even more alluring than Paringa, the lake affords a magnificent aspect of the alps from the bridge that spans its outlet. Fishing and boating facilities make this an outdoor paradise.

THUNDER CREEK FALLS *A short walk through a stand of silver beech ends at falls which plummet some 30 metres down from what was once the level of the ice when a glacier was gouging out the course that the Haast River was later to follow. As well as tempting passers-by to pause in their travels, the stretch of river also holds promise for those in search of brown trout. Despite torrential rain and looming alps, the Pass is seldom closed by the elements.*

JACKSON BAY *Successively a bay of promise, hope and despair.*

Mt Aspiring National Park and Wanaka

SUMMERTIME IN THE PARK *A number of easy walking tracks thread through the park's valleys. National parks should be savoured at leisure rather than sampled quickly.*

The youngest of the country's national parks, dissected by the Haast Pass road, is draped over a 197,000-hectare segment of the Southern Alps. Its headquarters at Wanaka are set by a glacier lake of incomparable beauty, viewed at its best when autumn colours tint the landscape. Its centrepiece is Mt Aspiring (3,033 metres), which rises sharply from the icefields of no fewer than four glaciers. The highest mountain in Otago, barely 50 kilometres from the West Coast, Aspiring can be climbed only by properly equipped mountaineers and is usually approached along the west branch of the Matukituki Valley. Viewed from the south-west it presents a classic triangular appearance that inevitably invites comparison with the Matterhorn.

PARK HEADQUARTERS *The A-frame design at Wanaka is just one of a variety of architectural styles used in national park headquarters.*

LUCERNE FOR STOCK FEED *Pasture near Luggate yields a rich harvest.*

WANAKA WILDLIFE *A flock of ducks gathers on the lake.*

Cardrona The bed of the Cardrona River yielded much gold, and its surrounds still bear scars inflicted by miners in their quest for precious metal, especially near Cardrona. Here mica schist glitters in the sunlight.

Crown Range The tortuous Crown Range route from Wanaka to Arrowtown runs up the Cardrona Valley before twisting over the Crown Range and descending into the Arrow Valley. The route, the highest main road in the country (reaching 1,120 metres), is best attempted in fine weather and is in winter closed by snow. The views en route are superb, extending to Lake Wakatipu and Queenstown.

SUNSET *The golden light of evening settles over Lake Wanaka.*

GLENDHU BAY *A superb, north-facing cove much favoured by campers.*

THE HOTEL CARDRONA Built in about 1870, the building witnessed a gold rush right on its doorstep, but was more frequently accustomed to the sight of diggers pausing here as they journeyed from Cromwell to the fabled fields on the Arrow and the Shotover.

Lake Hawea The lake, deeper than Wanaka, lacks it neighbour's sandy beaches, for it has been raised to store spring meltwaters from the alps for controlled use by the hydro-electric power stations downstream. The Hawea River feeds the Clutha.

The lake offers good fishing for rainbow trout and land-locked salmon and also helps to relieve summer-holiday pressure on Wanaka by providing boat owners with an alternative setting to explore. The route through the Haast Pass to the West Coast runs along the western shore for almost half the lake's length before crossing the Neck (where only a sliver of land divides the two lakes) to follow Lake Wanaka.

Lake Wanaka A gentle natural shoreline distinguishes the lake from Hawea and renders it among the most beautiful in the country. The best time to visit is out of the peak season when campers flock to enjoy the area's many delights.

The town stands at the southern end of the lake, sloping gently to the sun to face an exquisite tableau of mountain and water. This spectacular landscape, embodying every shade of blue , is occasionally and dramatically mirrored in the lake's placid waters. The scene is altogether different from that at nearby Wakatipu: the latter is distinguished by steeply rising mountainsides, but here the glaciers have more nearly completed their work, moulding the landscape into softer, more gentle contours. Yet if the view from Wanaka is magnificent, it is surpassed by that from Glendhu Bay, which takes in Ruby Island and includes a glimpse of Mt Aspiring.

The town has been a traditional holiday spot, but its importance and popularity soared with the opening of the Haast Pass road, which winds from Wanaka some 150 kilometres to the West Coast. There are a number of good short walks and climbs to be enjoyed in the locality: Mt Iron (527 metres), sculptured by ice into a typical *roche moutonne* shape, affords a splendid view (*1½ hours return*); Mt Roy (1,585 metres) rises much higher (*5 hours return*), but Mt Criffel (1,282 metres) offers perhaps the best view of all (*4 hours return*).

The lake's outlet marks the birthplace of the mighty Clutha River, the river with the largest catchment area in the country and one reputed to have the greatest volume of water. (The Waikato is slightly longer but has only about half the Clutha's mean annual discharge of 23,000 cusecs.) At Wanaka's trout hatchery one may see how stocks of fish are maintained. It operates during the second half of each year. Eggs are taken from female salmon and both brown and rainbow trout, are fertilised and then reared to the point where the eyes become apparent. The eggs are then distributed to various points around the country, and some are exported. Curiously, rainbow trout were originally introduced to New Zealand from California (by way of Tasmania), but because the strain has survived in its most pure form in this country, New Zealand's trout hatcheries have supplied eggs for release back in their native land.

Mount Aspiring National Park The headquarters for the park are at Wanaka and provide details of the many walks and tramps nearby as well as displays of the park's flora and fauna. The half-day drive up the Matukituki Valley leads through increasingly dramatic alpine scenery until finally an impressive view of Aspiring itself is won. Beyond 46 kilometres, the road veers up the west branch of the river, after which the possibility of being marooned by rising waters rightly deters the prudent from forging on to the road's end at Raspberry Creek, some eight kilometres on. However, from there a short walk over river terraces yields an outstanding view of the Rob Roy Glacier.

Boating apart, the park is essentially one for the climber and the tramper. It in fact extends to Lake Wakatipu where there is a ranger station at Glenorchy, as well as one at Makarora on the Haast Pass road. All stations issue permits to hunt the deer and chamois which are lightly scattered through the district.

MOUNT ASPIRING *The view from the Matukituki Valley richly merits the 92-kilometre return drive from Wanaka.*

The Routeburn Track

THE GRASSY ROUTEBURN FLATS *Three trampers approach the Harris Saddle (1,277 metres) on the boundary between two national parks.*

An appealing walk that tends to be overshadowed by its better-known neighbour, the Milford Track, the Routeburn is, however, much loved by all who know it, and those who have walked the Milford Track often return to do the shorter trip. It also offers an alternative way back to Queenstown for the walkers who, having mastered the Milford, still have the appetite for more of the same.

GEARING UP *A busload of trampers prepares for the Routeburn.*

SHINGLE RIVER BEDS *Welcome relief from the uphill grind.*

TWIN CASCADES *Waterfalls abound in a region of high rainfall.*

UNDER COVER *Here trampers wind through shade, but much of the track also passes over open country.*

The Routeburn is a gentle 39 kilometres, with a total walking time of a little over twelve hours. It has been traversed in as little as three hours, though most would prefer to devote a more leisurely three or four days to the journey.

As with the Milford Track, the walk here can be made on an organised basis, staying in privately-owned huts (with facilities superior to those afforded by the National Park Board huts, used by the independent trampers) and free from the necessity of carrying all the impediments that go with fending for oneself. As on the Milford Track, organised accommodation is limited and advance booking, through a travel agent, is essential.

The track actually winds through two adjoining national parks, Fiordland and Mount Aspiring, and runs from Routeburn (well up the Dart River from the head of Lake Wakatipu) through to Lake Fergus, on the Te Anau-Milford road. Buses from Queenstown, Te Anau and Milford are accustomed to dropping trampers off at the track's roadside terminals.

The walk is usually made between November-December and the beginning of April: none but the most experienced would tackle it in winter. Although well equipped in every way, the track is sited in the wilderness of remote back country, and no liberties should be taken. Some of those who have gone out ill-prepared have been lucky to survive, if indeed they have done so. Yet for the sensible walker, who carries appropriate clothing and plans well within his or her capabilities, the track need hold no fears.

The walk embraces stands of beech forest, tussock flats, cascading waterfalls, roaring rivers, placid lakes and rearing mountains; a variety spiced by a host of abiding views.

The route follows an old Maori greenstone trail, used later by early European prospectors and explorers. It was upgraded to form part of the route used from Queenstown to Martins Bay by the hapless groups of migrants unwillingly deposited there in the 1870s.

BUSH, RIVER AND TRACK *Passwords for the Routeburn.*

LIQUID BLUE *The view from Glenorchy en route between Queenstown and the eastern end of the track.*

Queenstown and Arrowtown

THE REMARKABLES *At sunset they flame with brilliant shades of orange and contrast with the deep blue waters of Lake Wakatipu in a spectacle that is indeed remarkable – and unforgettable.*

THE BROODING SHOTOVER RIVER *Pictured from gold-rich Arthurs Point.*

THE GOVERNMENT GARDENS *A peaceful haven in the centre of Queenstown.*

It is not surprising that Queenstown's lakes and mountains entice visitors in large numbers at every time of the year, especially as the region's captivating facade is overlain with relics from times when, a century ago, gold diggers came in their thousands to strike fabulous riches in the area's rivers and streams. Not for them the joys of the slopes in winter as they worked furiously in biting cold to capitalise on a time of year when river levels were low and gold-bearing gravel most readily accessible, then by night, in lieu of après-ski, huddling in flimsy tents close to their claims. Yet their temporary presence has left abiding marks, both in the stone huts and stores that grew as the goldfields developed substance, and in the impact the miners made with pick and sluice-gun on the landscape.

Today the gold is no longer economical to pursue – other than by visitors intent on taking a fleck or two with them – and holidaymakers themselves have replaced metal as the town's principal economic base.

If Queenstown is now crowded with hotels and other amenities expected of a major international tourist centre, nearby Arrowtown has yet managed to retain much of its old-world charm. A town on the Arrow River, where some of the fortunes were won, it lingers as a living memory of a substantial gold town, its permanence deriving not from the initial flush of riches but from a continuing and long-lived flow of gold.

Yet for all the riches of the goldfields – and their legacy hangs heavily and picturesquely over the region – the people passed on as the gold dwindled. Queenstown faded from a substantial centre to a mere village of some 190 people. Sheep-raising came to the fore, and it has only been with the rapid rise in mobility, both national and international, over the last two decades that Queenstown has been allowed to blossom again, this time as a linchpin of the country's tourist industry. From here, bus, boat and plane trips fan out to probe surrounding mountains, lakes and rivers. But while there is much to see and do that makes little physical demand on the visitor, there is also a range of walks, both short and long, through the varied country that the region has to offer.

Arrowtown Its main street lined with sentinel sycamores, Arrowtown rests gently but firmly on its past. Many of the buildings date from those times when miners were profiting handsomely as the Arrow surrendered its gold, and in recent years skilful town planning has sought to preserve this quality. The result is a living gold town, and colours are still to be won in the gold pans which are sold or hired locally.

There is an interesting gold-mining section in the Lakes District Centennial Museum. It includes old Miner's Rights, a model of a suction engine and the hefty box once carried by the gold escort. The oldest part of the museum building once housed the Bank of New Zealand banking chamber built in 1875. The Arrowtown jail was built at approximately the same date. The old stone building with its gloomy, uncomfortable cells and heavy iron doors is a reminder of days when imprisonment was a chill warning to lawbreakers.

FLYING HIGH *Gondolas ferry visitors to the restaurant and lookout atop Bob's Peak.*

Coronet Peak Named for the shape of its summit, yet felicitously echoing the nobility of Queenstown, Coronet Peak (1,619.6 metres) is renowned for its ski fields. From May to September, enthusiasts flock from many parts of the world to ski its hillocky and diversified slopes. Although the peak lacks a permanent snowfield, a lengthy season is assured by reason of its southern slopes, which present a low angle to the winter sun. Out of winter, the peak and its chairlift continue to draw visitors for the splendid panorama they afford.

Frankton The near-perfect "S" contour of Lake Wakatipu is marred only by Frankton Arm, a narrow appendage to the principal glacial sweep which, because of its comparatively shallow nature, affords much warmer summertime swimming than is available elsewhere. The settlement here has in recent times become a virtual suburb of Queenstown and boasts a reconstructed gold town.

Kingston The small township, site of an old Maori village, stands on the terminal moraine of the glacier that filled and shaped the bed of Lake Wakatipu during the last Ice Age. A glacier, as it advances, is akin to a mammoth bulldozer whose enormous weight scrapes together a huge pile of debris from the valley walls and floor. When it recedes, the debris is left behind, occasionally (as here) forming a massive natural earth dam retaining the resulting lake. The lake once drained out here, and the settlement served as a supply route to the goldfields.

Kinlock A minute lakeside settlement at the head of Lake Wakatipu, it is the jumping-off point for exploring the Dart and Rees River valleys, and for walking by the fabled Routeburn Track. The settlement is linked to Queenstown both by water and by a lengthy, if absorbing, lakeside drive.

Lake Hayes Known to the Maori as Wai-whaka-ata ("water that reflects objects"). Although famous for its trout fishing, it is for the beauty of its setting that Lake Hayes is especially famous. The green farmlands and exotic trees surrounding the lake make it a favourite scene for landscape artists.

CORONET PEAK ROAD *Often bleak and always exciting, here the landscape wears a soft face.*

QUEENSTOWN MALL *With its small shops to entice the tourist, the mall runs from Camp Street down to the waterfront. From the jetty one can admire the view across Lake Wakatipu or watch the* Earnslaw *coming and going. The most spectacular view of all is probably from Bob's Peak behind the town. Plans to build a road up here were first raised in the 1920s and were eventually carried out in the 1960s. This was followed by the successful gondola cablecar to the restaurant at the summit, the mode of transport used by most people today.*

EXHILARATION *Jet boating on the Shotover River.*

CORONET PEAK *Ski fields fit for champions. Skiers from all over the world come here to race and train for the Northern Hemisphere season.*

The Kawarau River The source of huge sums of gold, its deepest crevices remained tantalisingly out of reach for many years. A bold approach to excavation was called for – and came when a company conceived the idea of damming the river at its outlet from Lake Wakatipu. Costs soared and when, in 1926, the time came for the river to be turned off, huge crowds gathered. But as the level fell it became apparent that on some unrecorded occasion the river had fallen naturally – and had already been worked over. The commercial venture was a disaster, but it did result in today's control structure for the lake, which also serves as the road bridge at Frankton.

ARROWTOWN *Late-summer visitors stroll the main street.*

QUEENSTOWN MOTOR MUSEUM Here a remarkable collection of veteran and vintage cars is open daily to visitors. Testimony to a car-crazy nation is champion driver Bruce McLaren's first racer (*right*). McLaren, seemingly destined to follow compatriot Denny Hulme as Formula One World Champion, was killed in 1970. His cars still grace the world's motor racing circuits.

Queenstown Although there is extensive sheep farming in the district, together with cattle raising in various valleys, Queenstown is primarily a tourist centre and is smoothly geared to cater for even the most demanding of visitors and facilitate day trips to a wide variety of destinations.

As in other areas of Otago, sheep graziers were the first European visitors to arrive, only to be overtaken and overshadowed by gold prospectors and fortune-seekers who flocked to the fields they found. The legacy of the miners is to be seen in various ways and in various parts of the district, most interestingly in old stone buildings. Some (like the Packer's Arms) are still in use; others have slumped to ruin on the sites of long-departed towns whose sole signs of life today may be fruit trees descended from those planted by the diggers.

The overlay of colourful history adds glitter to a region rich in natural beauty. The marriage of mountain and lake, of dense bush and tussockland; the lure of short walks and day-long tramps; the presence of fish and game; the charming lakeside setting of Queenstown: all these would seem reason enough to linger here for days. But these outstanding natural attractions have been augmented by the additional interest afforded by such artefacts as a spectacular cableway, a motor museum, the lake steamer *Earnslaw* and a zoo.

The Remarkables To the east of the lake's southern arm, the Remarkables, snow-capped in winter, form a much-photographed barrier – from the "giant's knees" to his "toes". The range, whose west face was sculpted by the Pleistocene glacier that occupied the lake bed, rises to 2,342.5 metres at Double Cone. Three mountain basins have been developed as a commercial ski area with a variety of lifts and runs for every ability.

A PENNYWEIGHT FOR THIRTY MINUTES' WORK Gold remains in the Arrow, if not in the quantities that once brought fortune-seekers flocking to its banks. The gold pan was the most basic implement used to separate metal from gravel, though even the later huge dredges applied the same principle: that gold particles are heavier than stone and will sink. Panning requires patience and a steady hand.

THE PAST PRESERVED *A display at Arrowtown's Lakes District Centennial Museum* (above)*; an oil lamp at the Queenstown Motor Museum* (below)*.*

"THE LADY OF THE LAKE" *TSS* Earnslaw *plies Lake Wakatipu as she has done since 1912. Built to service local runholders, the* Earnslaw *now takes tourists to view the lake and Walter Peak Station.*

The Shotover River Renowned as "the richest river in the world", a chance discovery by two shepherds in 1862 sparked the largest gold rush in Otago's history. Among the lucky ones were two Maori shepherds who went to the rescue of a dog swept downriver – and who, before nightfall, had collected a full 25 kilograms of gold. More cagey was the inscrutable Chinese found on the river at what became "Tucker Beach". When asked how he was faring he despondently admitted to breaking even – making "tucker" (food), but nothing more.

Today the river is the scene of spectacular jet-boat rides through wild gorges and over threatening rapids.

A good view of the river is obtained from Edith Cavell Bridge, some 5.4 kilometres from Queenstown towards Arrowtown. The bridge acquired its name despite the efforts of officialdom. For though both a building and a monument near London's Trafalgar Square recall the heroism of the British nurse executed as a spy by the German Army in World War I, efforts by a local admirer to have the bridge renamed were rebuffed until finally his persistence in daubing her name on the then Upper Shotover Bridge eventually met with success.

Skippers The road to Skippers is surely as spectacular, as breathtaking and as positively intimidating as anyone could wish. It is so demanding on a driver's skill that rental cars are excluded and no one should attempt it in their own vehicle without either a cool nerve or a readiness to reverse for long distances along a narrow road etched high into a precipitous valley wall should they suddenly encounter a road-engulfing tourist bus! Better by far to join the bus (which does not, however, run in winter) and drink in the drama of the wild, untamed country freed of the agony of sustained concentration.

It was here, in a setting as inhospitable as any imaginable, that gold miners toiled, suffered and only occasionally prospered. They have left their mark on the landscape, carving into gravel banks with water from high-pressure sluice-guns, piling up tailings and planting trees, burying their dead and erecting buildings, some of whose traces remain.

The unusual rock formations towering above Skippers Road are very typical of this type of country. The road, which passes Lighthouse Rock, Castle Rock and Hedgehog, was first built in the 1880s as a bridle path to bring in supplies for the miners. Across the Skippers swing bridge, 90 metres above the Shotover River, is the site of the old Skippers township. In this wild and bleak spot thousands once camped as they toiled for gold. Some were never to return home and their graves can be seen in the old cemetery. A single Chinese grave is there too, left behind when others were exhumed for planned reburial in their native land. Skippers is a ghost town today, with little but the cemetery remaining.

Gold is still present in the Shotover in considerable amounts. From time to time schemes are mooted for extracting it, but the cost of such operations is usually found to be prohibitive because of the difficult access.

THE SHOTOVER RIVER *Bridges span her twisting course through Skippers Canyon.*

Te Anau and the road to Milford

LAKE TE ANAU *Autumn brings a touch of gold to shoreline foliage.*

SUMMERTIME YACHTS *Sailing is popular on Te Anau.*

From Lake Te Anau, focal point for the Fiordland National Park, one begins the famed Milford Track walk and the superb drive into Milford Sound. From here, too, one may visit majestic Manapouri and bore deep into the mountains to see the underground powerhouse and make the dizzy crossing of the Wilmot Pass to visit Deep Cove.

The lake, like Milford Sound, was chiselled out by glaciers, and the three arms of the lake (basically a reversed "E"), are named "fiords", even though the term is properly confined to glacier-cut coastal indentations.

It is worth planning some extra days here to increase the chances of a fine day for the drive to Milford, for the scenery en route rivals even that of the Sound itself. Not that the time would necessarily be idle, as Te Anau has much to offer, even without the lure of its surroundings. Swimming, water skiing and boating are summertime leisure activities; walking is an all-year-round pursuit. And for the weak-kneed, if not the faint-hearted, there are a variety of scenic trips by floatplane and boat.

Lake Te Anau drains through the Waiau River into Lake Manapouri. But while its waters once continued on down the Waiau to reach the sea at Foveaux Strait, they are now diverted through the Southern Alps at Manapouri, to meet the sea in Deep Cove.

Te Anau township, headquarters for the national park, looks across the lake to the Kepler Mountains, with the Murchison Mountains running parallel to them to the north. It was on the Murchison Range that the rare flightless bird, the takahe (*Notornis mantelli*), was rediscovered in 1948 after fifty years of apparent extinction. Rarely seen and with fears for its long-term survival still persisting, the adult has an olive-green back, indigo-blue throat, breast and thighs, and pink bill and legs.

From Te Anau, launches probe the "inland fiords" and ferry visitors across to the Te Ana-au Caves, relatively young limestone formations complete with a glow-worm grotto.

MAVORA LAKES *A fishing spot on the Mararoa, a tributary of the Waiau.*

BEYOND THE HOMER *The stunning Cleddau Valley lies beyond the Homer Tunnel.*

TE ANA-AU *In Maori, "the cave of rushing water".*

FIORDLAND BUSH *Rimu fronds and red beech leaves.*

MT TUTOKO *Fiordland's 2,755-metre alpine monarch.*

FISHING BOATS *A peaceful anchorage at Freshwater Basin.*

The road to Milford follows the barren eastern shore of Te Anau, contrasting with the rain forest of the west before swinging up the Eglinton Valley where the scenery takes on an ever-increasing grandeur. Lakes along the way perfectly mirror snowcapped peaks, and when the mountains that draw in to loom over the road are not drenched with winter snow, they are likely to be festooned with thousands of waterfalls. Eventually the Homer Tunnel is reached, and this, too, comes as a surprise – being rough-hewn from rock and sloping down in a gentle one in ten gradient. As one re-emerges, the scenery is again breathtaking, with the magnificence of the Cleddau Valley.

After such a journey, the end should come as an anti-climax. That it does not is testimony to the ability of Milford Sound to match the superlatives of the tourist pamphlets and the gloss of the posters. Here waterfalls plummet snow-fresh water into the salt of the Sound, from which Mitre Peak rises grandly if deceptively – with its secret revealed to those who join the boat trips. A lunch in keeping with the surroundings may be had at the hotel. On the return, a detour should be made down the Hollyford Valley – a tramper's and a botanist's Mecca.

MILFORD'S MITRE *The Peak, capped with snow, viewed from the Sound.*

ONE LANE ONLY *Traffic alternates direction through the narrow Homer Tunnel.*

DEER IN VELVET *A deer farm near Te Anau.*

The Milford Track

MILFORD *Above the bushline, myriad waterfalls gush down from the melting snow.*

TIME FOR A BREATHER *But remember that too long a stop can cause stiffness!*

NOT FOR THE FAINT-HEARTED *Sudden rain can swell streams to raging torrents. Swing bridges are the only way across.*

OLD MAN'S BEARD *Trees heavily festooned with creepers and moss give an eerie effect.*

"The finest walk in the world": the label threatens to become a cliché, yet it remains a truism for the many trampers – aged from nine to ninety – who journey to Te Anau each year to make the 53-kilometre traverse through to Milford Sound. The route, which winds through dramatic rain forest as well as over open country, follows the Clinton Valley, crosses Mackinnon Pass and dips down to the Arthur Valley to follow the river to the sea at Sandfly Point. A short boat trip then links to Milford and civilisation.

Because of the region's prodigious rainfall, waterfalls abound, and one of the world's most magnificent, Sutherland Falls, is seen en route. The walk is an easy one, with three nights on the way spent in simple but comfortable huts. Alternatively, one can make the trip as a "freedom walker" – free to carry everything that may be needed and free to use more primitive huts or camp in tents well away from the track (usually in rain!) Although the track is highly popular, it is not crowded, with numbers limited by the accommodation available.

THE MAIN DIVIDE *The zig-zag up to Mackinnon Pass (at 1,036 metres) marks the end of the climb and the beginning of the descent to the Arthur Valley and then the sea.*

Plan ahead Arrangements for the walk, which is done only from south to north and between the months of December and April, should be made well in advance. Accommodation both on the organised walk (book through travel agents) and in the trampers' huts (book through the Fiordland National Park headquarters) is limited. Equipment may be hired at Te Anau.

SUTHERLAND FALLS *The world's fourth highest waterfall and as spectacular as any, it plummets streamer-like from Lake Quill some 580 metres above. Donald Sutherland's early residence at Milford Sound brought with it a hermit-like existence.*

EASY WALKING *A sun-dappled pathway.*

THE END OF THE WALK *After a stop at Sandfly Point (*left*), trampers board for the short crossing to the Milford settlement. Sandflies and rain are all that can mar a memorable visit, so go prepared for both.*

Exotic animals

Except for two species of native bat, every mammal found in the country has been introduced – to the devastation of many unique features of the flora and to the transformation of much of the countryside. However, those who leap to damn this process usually overlook the self-evident fact that the most successful of the introduced animals, the millions of sheep and cattle (not to mention the exotic grasses on which they feed), have provided the nation's economic backbone.

The early Polynesian migrants brought with them only a species of dog (which became extinct with Pakeha settlement) and a rat (highly prized for food and once abundant, but now confined to outlying islands and remote corners of Fiordland). Captain James Cook left behind a number of animals on his later voyages after discovering that there were no native animals to provide meat for seafarers, and his name is still borne by a species of wild pig, the "Captain Cooker". As well as the domestic animals which today dominate the grassland economy, the European settlers brought with them a bewildering variety of creatures and a great array of birdlife. They accepted the maxim that the native bush was doomed to be replaced by English plants, and little restraint was exercised as animals were imported for commerce, for sport or simply out of sentiment. The new browsing animals attacked native plants from the ground up, and the Australian opossum (introduced to start a trade in skins) did so from the top down. The rabbit, for its part, bred so prodigiously as to bankrupt many South Island farmers and seriously to affect the pastoral economy until a massive policy of slaughter brought the situation under control after World War II. Deer, too, loomed to be a menace in the high country, destroying ground cover and accelerating erosion. Though now highly valued for farming purposes, there was for many years an official policy of extermination. Deer farming was banned and millions were shot. Curiously, the lifting of the farming ban placed such a value on live deer as to justify their recovery by helicopter, and the resulting blitz has actually brought their numbers in the wild under control for the first time.

Some other animals were introduced in a version of the old woman who swallowed a fly – the humble hedgehog to control garden pests; the weasel, the stoat and the ferret to control the rabbit. Acclimatisation societies flourished, and until the turn of the century were forbidden only from importing "any fox, venomous reptile, hawk, vulture or other bird of prey". They are active today in providing supplies of game birds and in ensuring the stocking of some of the finest trout waters to be found anywhere.

Early laxity has given way to stringent control. New Zealand is free of the diseases that plague farm animals in many parts of the world, most conspicuously foot-and-mouth disease, a condition perpetuated only by constant vigilance.

Fiordland National Park

A STORM CLEARS OVER MANAPOURI *The region's high rainfall lends an ominous air to the brooding grandeur of the terrain.*

SHINGLE RAPIDS *A view of the Eglinton River.*

SOLITUDE *A seal basks on a rock, safe at last from the designs of early European hunters who came to the Fiordland coast for oil and skins.*

New Zealand's and one of the Southern Hemisphere's largest national parks embraces a vast area of rugged, primeval wilderness in the south-west corner of the country. The terrain is so wild and the forest so forbidding that anything seems possible. The suggestion that its looming mountains and deep valleys might hide a remaining species of moa seems absurd, yet in recent years overseas camera crews have stalked moa as they might the Loch Ness monster – encouraged by the rediscovery in the park in 1948 of the takahe, a flightless bird long thought extinct. But the region is, too, a fairyland of azure lakes set in blue-misted bush.

HARVEST FROM THE SEA *Fishermen work crayfish pots on the rocky Fiordland coast.*

TWO FACES OF A LAKE The waters of Manapouri mask a gargantuan hydro-electric project. Beneath a lake of supreme elegance, a tunnel plummets water to sea level, deep beneath the Main Divide. A scheme to raise the lake for hydro development sparked one of the largest public protests in New Zealand's history, for the uniqueness of Manapouri's lushly clad shoreline defies interference.

A FOREST CATHEDRAL *Sunlight filters through Manapouri beech forest.*

The Fiordland lakes For many, these are the supreme attraction, nestled in bush-blue settings beneath giant ranges. None surpasses Manapouri, and a day spent on the cruise across the lake to visit the underground power station (accessible by bus down a cork-screw road) and Deep Cove is unforgettable. Lake Monowai evidences how Manapouri might have looked had power planners had their way with both lakes, and Lake Hauroko's Mary Island harbours the cave where, in 1967, one of the best and oldest examples of an ancient Maori "sitting burial" was found. Yet to appreciate the park one must forsake vehicle for feet. The Milford Track links Lake Te Anau to Milford Sound, and the Routeburn Track joins Fiordland to the Mt Aspiring National Park. Both can be conducted walks or done independently, and there are many other tramps besides. The park's rugged coastline also offers superb, unspoilt recreation, though its deep fiords are readily accessible only at Milford and Deep Cove.

THE TAKAHE *One of New Zealand's rarest native birds.*

MISCHIEVOUS KEA *These native parrots have an ill-deserved reputation for destroying sheep – but watch out for those valves! Olive-green plumage is spiked by bright vermilion under the wings.*

Invercargill and environs

QUEENS PARK (left and above) *Formal gardens and statuary blend with varied sporting activities in over 80 hectares of public recreation space.*

Laying claim to the title of the world's southernmost city, Invercargill lies by the Waihopai River, on an estuary by the shores of tempestuous Foveaux Strait. Its name (literally, estuary of Cargill) should place it on the mouth of a river Cargill. But there is no such river, and the name refers to that of William Cargill who, in 1867, set out from Scotland with a group of pilgrims to found a "New Edinburgh", where the newly established Free Church of Scotland might flourish in freedom.

The Scottish origins the city shares with Dunedin are reflected in streets named after Scottish rivers, the faint burr in a distinctly localised accent, and the canny way in which the sale of liquor has been turned to public benefit through a long-established licensing trust, New Zealand's first.

Deep in Foveaux Strait lie exquisite oysters, awaiting the dredges of busy Bluff Harbour. Inland spreads a prodigiously productive hinterland, where timber milling, cattle rearing, dairying and the growing of grass for seed are all overshadowed by the ubiquitous sheep. To the west lie the wild terrain and composed lakes of Fiordland National Park; to the south spread the irresistible arms of Stewart Island.

Awarua Radio A superbly sited receiving station which maintains radio links with long-distance shipping and other stations the world over, relaying messages and weather reports.

Bluff Named for the striking headland which looms above the town and which has defied all attempts to accord it an eponymous title, Bluff is among the country's busiest ports, handling vast quantities of frozen meat and wool from a wealthy hinterland. There is also a large freezing works. Here is based the fabled oyster fleet, whose annual harvest of the Foveaux Strait beds is accorded the same anticipation as the running of the Melbourne Cup. Across the water lies the aluminium smelter at Tiwai Point.

Chaslands A tiny settlement which takes its name from nearby Chaslands Mistake. The errors of sailors are occasionally perpetuated in place names, but precisely what the error said to have been made by an expert local whaler more than a century ago was, will forever remain a matter for speculation.

Curio Bay Here may be seen a part of the Jurassic "fossil forest floor" – at first glance simply an anonymous, sea-washed rock shelf, but one which on close examination suddenly focuses into a truly remarkable scene.

Dog Island Seen from Bluff, the island is distinguished by its tall, zebra-striped lighthouse, which serves as a visual aid to daytime shipping.

Fortrose The site of an early whaling station, where eleven whales were once taken in less than three weeks. Whalers were particularly active around Foveaux Strait in the early eighteenth century.

Invercargill Once described as "mere bog and unfit for habitations", only the level site of Invercargill today recalls its unpromising origins. Unusual for a New Zealand city of such substance is a comparative lack of secondary industries, with service, warehousing and storage roles predominating.

The city shares its Scottish origins with Dunedin and is named after Dunedin's founder, but this commonality has spawned rivalry rather than kinship.

Invercargill's amenities owe much to its pioneering of licensing trusts, which have enabled huge profits from the sale of liquor to be channelled to the public benefit, and which other areas have since copied. Its climate, however, is envied by none – although low average temperatures and sunshine hours, and a high number of rainy days, are generously compensated for by ever-so-long summer twilight evenings.

Within the region served by the city are vast reserves of coal and shale, which promise a bright future in an era of energy shortages. An excellent museum, art gallery, parks, gardens and fine beaches contribute to an attractive environment.

Nightcaps Curious conical mountains, occasionally capped with snow,

TUDOR-STYLED BUILDINGS *A handsome setting by Queens Park for Southland Boys' High School.*

give this mining settlement its otherwise bibulous name. After yielding more than 1.5 million tonnes of coal, the local mines are now exhausted and the workers are forced to commute to neighbouring Ohai.

Ohai Much of the coal won here fuels Southland's industries. A number of the seams are suitable for both open-cast and underground mining, and lend the township a specialised air.

Orepuki A small farming settlement which has eluded its destiny. Much fine gold was won from Monkey Island Beach, a safe and pleasant spot, and more still lies in the sands, though a little below the surface. Coal and shale mining followed, but eventually failed, leaving relics for the present-day visitor and huge, untouched reserves which sooner or later will loom large in the country's future energy plans. Times of boom may yet return.

Oreti Beach A lengthy strip of sand which runs north from the Oreti river mouth and which, in season, is a popular hunting ground for the tasty toheroa. The river's estuary is much favoured for watersports.

SOUTHLAND MUSEUM *Contemporary pottery displayed.*

Otautau A farming centre to the west of Southland plains, where huge sheep sales are staged. Local cropping is so prolific that a world record was set for wheat yield per hectare.

Porpoise Bay A fine, safe beach by the entrance to Waikawa Harbour.

Riverton A seaside resort and farming town which outbids Dunedin and Invercargill as the oldest-established settlement in Otago-Southland. Its harbour lost out to Bluff in a battle for shipping after a disastrously sited jetty caused the river's scour to alter. Local folklore tells that an early foreign visitor, a violinist, was eaten by cannibals, who were then confounded by the music that issued from their bellies. The verdict of the tohunga (priest) who was summoned to the scene was that white flesh was unworthy of the honour of being eaten and should be struck from the menu. The museum includes a sledge used by Sir Edmund Hillary in Antarctica; nearby Colac Bay was once a Maori workshop where stone tools were fashioned, and the way to Riverton Rocks is dotted with many picnic spots.

Tiwai Point The aluminium smelter here is a significant Southland employer, and provides almost half of the harbour's total output. It produces about one per cent of the world's supply of aluminium, most of which is exported. As the alumina to feed the smelter is itself imported, the country's contribution to the project can be seen as the supply of relatively cheap electricity and the provision of some labour.

FOSSILS FROM CURIO BAY'S FOSSIL FOREST BEDS The "forest" stands on the sea-swept shoreline of the bay. At low tide, stumps and fallen trees dating from the Middle Jurassic period, some 160 million years ago, can be detected. Silica has completely replaced the woody structures, some of which are related to the kauri and Norfolk pine, rendering them harder than the rock shelf in which they were once completely buried. The fossil forest beds, formed after a volcanic eruption had inundated the area, were apparently quite extensive, as fossil wood has been found for several kilometres along the coastline.

ALUMINIUM The Comalco aluminium smelter near Bluff annually processes some 300,000 tonnes of alumina, to achieve a rated annual capacity of 151,000 tonnes of aluminium. The refined, energy-intensive and continuous process requires that the alumina be dissolved into cryolite at the temperature of 975°C, then separated into aluminium and oxygen by a very high current.

Raw materials, shipped from Queensland, Australia, are discharged by vacuum unloader and conveyed from the wharf some two kilometres to the plant. Comalco's arrangement with the government to provide power originally called for the raising and ruining of Fiordland's incomparable Lake Manapouri and led to nationwide protests. The agreement also proved so generous to the foreign concern that it has had to be renegotiated.

HOME IS THE SAILOR *Laden with sacks of oysters, a dredge returns to Bluff Harbour. Relished by Maori long before the settlers arrived, the oyster is a delicacy which has been prized for thousands of years.*

Foveaux cocktail

Beard 18 Stewart Island oysters. Add ½ tbsp Worcester sauce, 2 tbsp tomato sauce, 2 tbsp vinegar, 1 tbsp oyster juice, 1 tsp sugar and pepper to taste. Chill the mixture, then stir in 142 ml whipped cream just before serving. Serve in tall glasses, on a bed of shredded lettuce, and top with a squeeze of lemon juice.

Oysters The large, succulent Stewart Island oyster is found throughout New Zealand but nowhere as plentifully as over 1,000 kilometres of Foveaux Strait, from where it is dredged commercially by boats from Bluff. Fishermen are subjected to strict annual quotas, for humans are probably their greatest enemy – even more destructive than the crabs which pull them apart with tube feet, and the oyster-drill snails and whelks which use file-like teeth to bore holes in the shells and then suck out the soft contents.

Tuatapere A major timber-milling centre, Tuatapere is an important point of access to Fiordland National Park. Here, the Waiau River, once mighty, is a victim of the Manapouri power scheme. To generate electricity for the aluminium smelter, much of the water that fed this once swift-flowing river is now channelled under the alps to Doubtful Sound.

Waikawa Minute Waikawa is a prosperous small town which services the local farming community and supports a small-scale pottery industry. Perhaps because of its size, it seems certain that no child with a surname Henry will ever be born here to claim the scholarship promised many years ago by an eccentric priest to perpetuate his own memory.

Waipapa Point A sleek, lethal point marking the eastern entrance to Foveaux Strait, it was here that in 1881 the S.S. *Tararua* went down in one of the country's worst shipping disasters. Some of the 131 who died are buried here.

Winton Renowned for a celebrated "baby-farmer" (the only woman to be executed in New Zealand), and as the terminal for the folly that was the "wooden railway", Winton is a matter-of-fact farming centre which chooses to dismiss these accolades as irrelevancies.

FROM SHEEP TO MUTTON *Carcasses on the chain at Bluff's Alliance Freezing Works.*

PROVINCIAL COUNCIL CHAMBERS *Pictured in Invercargill is the long-ignored old Provincial Council Building (1864), a symbol of Southland's frustrated hopes. Erratic communications, a feeling of neglect and a pioneering urge for "do-it-yourself" led to demands for local autonomy in various outlying regions, but never with quite the consequences it had here. For within days of Southland claiming separate provincial status came the first of the spectacular finds in Central Otago, and the mad gold rushes were on. Try as it might to find similar riches within its own boundaries, Southland could only watch with envious eyes as its young men headed north for the goldfields, and as the resultant commerce was channelled, in the main, through a detested Dunedin.*

Touched by the fever, emboldened by the modest benefits which had come from proximity to the goldfields, the Provincial Council embarked on an overly ambitious railway-building programme in the hope of forging a link with Central which would tap much more of the newly found wealth. This included a conventional line from Invercargill to Bluff, and an extraordinary "wooden railway" to Winton. But all too soon Central's gold dwindled, reality dawned, and after nine heady years a prodigal, penniless Southland accepted reintegration with Otago Province.

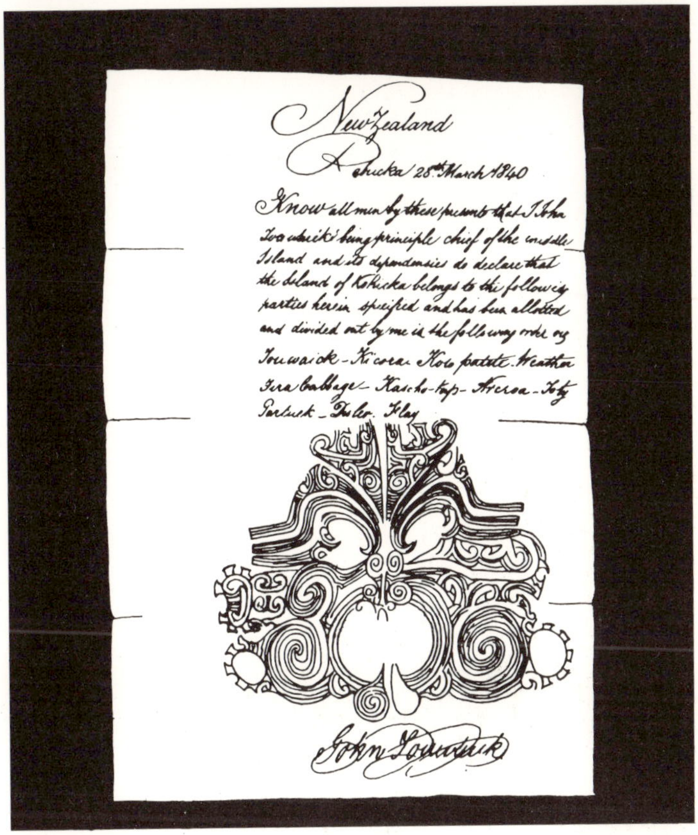

"BLOODY JACK" *Hone Tuhawaiki (c. 1805–44), was accorded his nickname by whalers and traders because of his fondness for the expletive. He also earned it in a sanguine sense, for it was he who, as paramount war chief, led South Island resistance to the ambitious Te Rauparaha, the famous warrior-chief of the north. Once, in a daring foray into Marlborough, he almost captured the Ngati Toa war chief, and in Southland he led the local forces which annihilated Te Rauparaha's southernmost raiding party.*

Converted to Christianity, Hone grew to resent his nickname and to impress deeply the Europeans who had dealings with him. Reproduced here is a deed which bears his distinctive tattoo (moko) as his signature. Tuhawaiki, who drowned when a whaleboat capsized off Timaru, used Ruapuke as his island fortress, just as his rival Te Rauparaha used Kapiti.

THE WRECK OF THE *GENERAL GRANT* The fully rigged ship *General Grant*, en route from Melbourne to London in 1866, smashed into one of the desolate Auckland Islands, 500 kilometres from Bluff, and sank with a cargo of gold insured for £165,000. Only 15 of the 83 aboard survived. Then followed an astonishing saga. The survivors had but one match between them; it was used to kindle a fire which kept burning for the next 18 months. Surviving on seal meat and dressed in sealskins, the castaways built this model boat and pushed it out to sea, praying that the appeal for help engraved on it would be heard. Miraculously, it was. The model was found some months later, on Stewart Island. Fortuitously, a Bluff whaler had by then already effected a rescue, but not before four of the castaways had in desperation set to sea in a pinnace, hoping to cross the cruellest of oceans with no navigational aids. They were never to be seen again.

The lure of the sunken gold remains, even claiming the life of one of the survivors, who returned to attempt salvage. (The model is in the Southland Museum.)

Muttonbirds The annual voyage to harvest muttonbirds remains the Rakiura Maori's most tangible link with the past. The exclusive right to take these birds was written into the 1864 Deed which ceded Stewart Island to the Crown. As an hereditary source of food, the tribe has for generations, each April and May, slaughtered the birds on some 21 islands in Foveaux Strait. Muttonbirds flock here from the Northern Hemisphere to breed each spring, flying in by the million. It is the chick, not the adult bird, which is taken, plucked, cooked and stored. Preserved in salt or sealed with fat, the birds may keep for years.

With the Rakiura tribe now so numerous and widespread, a ballot is held each year to determine who will share the 250,000 or so birds which will be trapped, at first by day in their burrows and later by torchlight at night. In early May the migratory urge swells, and the birds depart for the northern summer.

A petrel, the muttonbird (*Puffinus griseus*) is also known as the sooty shearwater (as it is sooty-coloured), and as the *titi* (for its cry). The name muttonbird may derive either from its taste, or from the woolly down of its young.

YOUNG MUTTONBIRD *A New Zealand delicacy.*

Stewart Island

DAYBREAK *A new day dawns at Halfmoon Bay, as fishing boats rest from their labours.*

"Rakiura", the island of the glowing skies, spreads invitingly, expansively, across Foveaux Strait, a stretch of water at times frenzied, at others serene. Just occasionally, the skies beyond flicker with *aurora australis*, the Southern Lights, adding further to the island's allure. Wild, well-bushed and scarcely peopled, the island's ragged 1,600 kilometres of coastline is deeply gouged by extensive inlets, probing from east and south.

To the Maori, Stewart Island was the anchor of the South Island canoe from which Maui dragged up his enormous North Island fish. The myth is lent substance by geography, not only by the outlines of all three islands but also by the shallow nature of the Strait's bed, which today ties the island to the mainland underwater, as it once did above.

For the Pakeha, flurries of tin and gold mining quickly petered out, the timber was soon milled, and farming has met with only limited success. What little activity there is to ruffle the quietude of the island centres on the township of Oban. But roads are short and cars so few that even here there is a feeling of being set apart from the bustle to the north. Access is by ferry from Bluff or by air from Invercargill. While a day trip is possible, the emphasis on walking means that such a visit affords only a sample of what may be savoured at leisure on a longer stay.

FOOD FROM THE SEA Much of the country's blue cod and crayfish comes from the Fiordland, Foveaux Strait, Stewart Island regions, and it is to commercial fishing that most of the island's population owe their living. Blue cod (*Parapercis colias*) is one of New Zealand's most esteemed fish, but supply seldom matches demand as it must be line-hooked from its rocky bottom habitat. No relation of the English cod, an average catch is about 350 grams, with 3.6 kilograms as a top weight.

Halfmoon Bay A peaceful crescent of sheltered sand (*pictured*), the bay witnessed the comings and goings of Maori, whaler, sealer, miner and timber miller before settling gently back into seclusion. Its dreamy repose is disturbed only by the thrice-weekly ferry from Bluff, and the tiny plane from Invercargill. As the periodic tide of day-trippers recedes, the bay slips back into slumber.

Horseshoe Bay Rightly named and larger than Halfmoon Bay, which it neighbours, the bay can be perfect for an evening stroll.

Mount Anglem At 979 metres the highest point on the island, the summit presents a challenge but little difficulty to the average tramper, and provides a good day's outing. Local launches can run trampers out to the foot of the peak

THE BELLBIRD *Aptly named for its clear flute-like notes, the bellbird is one of New Zealand's loveliest songsters.*

VIEW FROM OBSERVATION ROCK *The reward of a short walk from Oban, a panorama of Paterson Inlet.*

HALFMOON BAY *Approaching the island, the impression is of magnitude and of bushed shores dipping sharply to a clear sea.*

and collect them at the day's end. The superb view from the summit is across Foveaux Strait and over its sprinkled islands.

Oban Just as first-time visitors are frequently struck by the surprising size of Stewart Island, so too are they unprepared for the miniscule scale of the island's principal centre, on the shores of Halfmoon Bay. Only about 300 people live here, most of them involved with fishing.

The island's holidaying possibilities are obvious but largely unrealised, so that accommodation can be a problem. The well-organised advertise in Invercargill newspapers to rent a "crib" (as a holiday cottage is called in Otago-Southland), occasionally with neither electricity nor water-supply. Life can be as elementary and as illuminating as the surrounding bush.

The little local collection in the Rakiura Museum is startling beyond its size, for it records curious local fauna and the times of sealer, whaler, miner and castaway.

Paterson Inlet The eastern claw into the island's coastline furnishes a host of seductive coves, well sheltered from the prevailing westerly and warmed by sea currents from the Australian coast. Launch trips probe its distant corners, which may include the relics of Norwegian whaling operations.

Port Pegasus Screened by a series of islets and today visited only by determined trampers and far-flung fishermen, the lonely harbour was once the setting for mining operations, when the Tin Range yielded its ore. Somewhere on the shores may still be buried the bottle interred in 1840 which contained the original document claiming sovereignty over the island. The uninhabited spot was chosen as a precaution, for the *Herald*, the ship assigned to the task, was uncertain of the reception that awaited it at Paterson Inlet. In the event the ship's crew managed to obtain the chief's signature to the Treaty of Waitangi.

Ringaringa Beach A pretty beach, with the grave of a German missionary and visionary who, 140 years ago, toiled among the Rakiura Maori with infinite patience and dedication.

Ruapuke Island Presiding over the eastern entrance to Foveaux Strait is the low-lying island fortress of "Bloody Jack", Hone Tuhawaiki. Access is difficult, and the island is in private ownership.

Titi (Muttonbird) Islands The 21 islands, scattered by the approach to Paterson Inlet, are home to the migratory muttonbird (*titi*), and are visited annually by local Maori, who preserved the exclusive right to take the birds when Stewart Island was ceded to the Crown in 1864.

Ulva Island Bushclad and in the throat of Paterson Inlet, Ulva is a bird sanctuary and a living memorial to the life-long work of the naturalist Charles Traill, who combined the running of "the most southerly post office in the world" with the study of flora and fauna. Only an hour by launch from Oban, the island's bush and sandy beaches make it ideal for a day's trip.

Hunting Most hunters prefer to be dropped in distant coastal hunting areas by launch or by light plane. Red deer and Virginian deer are sought, as well as goats. The deer have markedly retarded the regeneration of the native forests in the wake of the timber millers.

Walks and tramps A host of walks range from very easy strolls to tramping routes several days in duration. Many tracks fan out from Oban, and for the more energetic there are strategically-placed huts in which to stay overnight – but these are mostly confined to the north of Doughboy Bay, leaving the most southerly segment as a wilderness area.

The Southern Lights *Aurora australis* occurs most frequently at times of greatest sunspot activity, taking place about 110 kilometres above the earth's surface. Like its northern equivalent, the *aurora borealis*, the curtain of light is probably caused by protons and electrons being shot from the sun to strike the earth's upper atmosphere. The earth's magnetic field directs them towards the poles, where they collide with atmospheric particles and glow like the charged particles in a fluorescent tube.

AN ELUSIVE WHITE-TAIL *The Virginian deer is hunted only here and at Lake Wakatipu. Its white tail serves to guide its young when danger threatens. The ubiquitous red deer are also on the island.*

INDEX

Numbers in bold type refer to feature coverage of subject.